MANHATTAN
COUNTRY
DOCTOR

MANHATTAN COUNTRY DOCTOR

Milton Jonathan Slocum,
M. D.

CHARLES SCRIBNER'S SONS

New York

Library of Congress Cataloging-in-Publication Data
Slocum, Milton Jonathan.
  Manhattan country doctor.
  1. Slocum, Milton Jonathan.
  2. Physicians—New York (N.Y.)—Manhattan—Biography.
  I. Title.
  R154.S5146A35 1986   610'.92'4 [B]   86-15501
  ISBN 0–684–18694–2

Published simultaneously in Canada by Collier Macmillan Canada, Inc.
Composition by Maryland Linotype, Baltimore, Maryland
Manufactured by Fairfield Graphics, Fairfield, Pennsylvania
Designed by Jack Harrison
Illustrations by Jackie Aher
First Edition

— TO —

Susan Hope Slocum Hinerfeld

CONTENTS

CONTENTS

CONTENTS

AUTHOR'S NOTE

This book has been constructed from memory of events long past. When I practiced medicine in Manhattan's Hell's Kitchen, from 1934 to 1968, I shared the joys and troubles of the men and women of the neighborhood, people who have never left my thoughts.

These adventures and misadventures are true stories. Some are remarkable. If you doubt their truth, I refer you to your family doctor, who will have a different set of remarkable stories to tell.

Here, certain names, physical descriptions, and circumstances have been changed to protect individuals' privacy. A very few characters are composite creatures. I have taken some liberty with the order of events. Not all the dialogue is verbatim, but was recreated to the best of my ability to express the spirit, personality, and style of the speaker and the gist of his or her point of view.

The past is a bottomless well of stories. I hope one day to dip into it again.

ACKNOWLEDGMENTS

My love and thanks to Bunny and Norman Perelman, Phyllis and Gene Klavan, Katherine Coker, and to Robert, Daniel and Matthew Hinerfeld, for their help and constant encouragement.

My admiration and affection to Betsy Rapoport, the most inventive and intelligent of editors.

PROLOGUE

AUGUST 1968.

I was going to practice medicine in California. Our grand-children were growing up there. We missed them.

Belle and I walked out of our office in Manhattan for the last time, and forever. Peggy stooped to place the key under the mat.

"Rappaport said it was all right to leave it for the new doctor," she said.

It wasn't necessary for her to explain. We knew she turned away to have an extra moment to compose herself. Parting was not sweet sorrow. It was a choking in the throat and a sadness that gripped the heart.

We stepped out of the lobby onto Fifty-sixth Street and stood there in the freshness of the cool, late summer evening.

Peggy and my wife Belle embraced for a long time. They were both tearful as they clung and spoke together. "You and Peggy are going to wash away," I said. They ignored me. I hoped they hadn't heard me.

Peggy turned to me and took my hand. "I figured it out this afternoon," she said. "I worked for you for thirty-three years, six months, and two days. Counting paydays." She drew me to her and kissed my cheek, and I kissed hers. She turned abruptly and walked with her firm, quick step toward Eighth Avenue. The sun, setting over the Hudson River, glistened on her silvery hair.

As she turned the corner, she stopped and waved to us. She knew we would still be standing, watching her. We couldn't just let her walk out of our lives.

Belle and I went in the opposite direction, to our car. We tried to talk of trivia, to avoid pathos. Still, there was the sense of rending, of tearing away from something precious and familiar.

As we walked I said to Belle, "There was a time when I knew all the people in these buildings. My old people are gone. I've been caring for their children and grandchildren."

"I know," Belle said softly, leaning on my arm. "But you're not abandoning them. The new doctor will be good to them."

"I hope they take to him. He certainly is well trained and friendly. But different: Lebanese."

"Of course they'll take to him. We were different and we were accepted. Peggy's being there will help."

As we passed 340 West Fifty-sixth Street, where our first office had been, Belle peered into the parlor window.

"Thirty-four years on this street," she said. "Thirty-four busy years. I'm happy we had them."

Belle laughed. "Did you hear what Peggy said when she hugged me? She said, 'It was good while it lasted.'"

NEIGHBORHOOD

THERE HAD BEEN RAIN and some freezing followed by rain and some more freezing so that there was ice wherever the sun had not been able to penetrate. The sidewalks were clear, but under the Ninth Avenue Elevated perpetual gloom had left occasional slippery sheets that would probably get worse and stay until spring.

Now, I knew Ninth Avenue and its perils, but sometimes, thinking of other things, I forgot how narrow the space was between the Elevated pillars. Whether the man in front of me stopped too suddenly or whether I was driving too fast to stop was debatable. But my brakes resented being jammed on and my tires refused to obey. I rolled over a slippery spot, lost response of the steering wheel, and crashed into a pillar. I wasn't hurt and I was glad I hadn't struck the car ahead.

If a train had been roaring overhead no one would even have noticed the crash. But there had been an interval of silence, and the smashing of glass and the crunching of steel attracted audience participation. A woman's voice from somewhere above street level, an assured voice, unexcited and assertive, called out, "It's the Doc. He's crashed his car again."

Then the rest of the chorus rose, all female and all from win-

[3]

dows above street level. "You all right, Doc?" "Nobody hurt?" "Maybe you shouldn't drive on Ninth Avenue!"

I knew those voices, and after the first loud announcement I expected them. These were my Ninth Avenue neighbor women, who spent their spare time leaning out of their living room windows. Bright-colored pillows—favored gifts at Christmas—cushioned their elbows on the sills.

A train rumbled by, obliterating all other sounds; then the voices could be heard again from both sides of the street. One, two, and three floors up, they were discussing my latest mishap. The Elevated was at the level of the second floor apartments, but almost the whole street was visible through its crossties.

There weren't many people on the street, but a crowd gathered from the small stores. One of my perennial patients staggered from a bar. His sandy hair was tousled, his face marked with so many minute veins that he looked always florid. He supported himself against a pillar and surveyed the wreckage. Finally, in a judicious voice, he said, "I seen the whole thing, Doc. What'll you give me?"

Fifty years ago the West Side of mid-Manhattan was a small town of its own. I had become part of it. Because of the Great Depression few people moved in and few moved out. There were no new buildings, but had there been, most of my patients couldn't have afforded more rent than they were paying. There was some shifting of apartments—which their inhabitants called "rooms"—but only when old people died or young ones had more children.

I decided to wait where I was for the patrolman on the beat to come around. I knew the word would spread and that he would soon show up. The men changed shifts weekly. I didn't know who the patrolman would be, but it didn't matter. I knew them all.

The streets of New York seemed filled with men in blue. The secret behind the show of force was simple. New York's police were then required to report for duty wearing their uniforms. So off-duty officers traveled through the city's boroughs in full dress.

My car, which had the habit of bouncing off the pillars of the Ninth Avenue Elevated, had started out as a brand new Plymouth. It was a handsome car to begin with.

I had determined not to buy a car until I had the cash in my hand. Why did I think that would give me an advantage in dealing with the salesman? At the end of seven months of medical practice I had the cash, seven hundred dollars, and paid a visit to the car dealership. I was pleased to have made such a good deal. I hadn't paid a penny more than the sticker on the window indicated. I drove my new car proudly out of the agency. Two blocks away it stalled. It was only a minor matter: the agency had put in just enough gas to get me out of their sight.

Two days later, the corner druggist telephoned. He was going to buy a car. Would I like to go with him? The druggist was a wiry fellow with a thin, black mustache whose customers referred to him as Mickey Mouse. We were on friendly terms, even though he practiced as much medicine as I did. His medical texts were the blurbs on the labels of his stock in trade. He still compounded drugs. But then some druggists in the neighborhood—and this in the 1930s!—sold leeches, bloodsucking worms once supposed to reduce fevers. This brought our local standards of medicine up to the most enlightened practices of the Middle Ages.

At the car agency the druggist bargained with the sales manager. I was astonished, shocked. The druggist got what he wanted, whereas the agency had gotten what I had! And now my lovely Plymouth had another dent.

When the people on the street saw that there were no injuries and would be no further excitement, they drifted off. It wasn't long before the cop on the beat, Leo Gates, came lumbering through the thinning crowd.

Leo Gates was one of my favorites. He had been a heavyweight fighter, a former sparring partner of Jack Dempsey's, and his face showed it. He had heavily scarred brows that were thickened from beating, slight bulges beneath both eyes, and flattened, elongated ears. He had taken many a pounding, but that didn't interfere with the performance of his duties. In many ways he was a meticulous officer. I had known him to check a car's distance from a fireplug with a tape measure. In fact, I had held the tape at the car while he had carried the other end back to the plug. Within six feet, a ticket. Beyond six feet, no ticket. There were not as many cars then as there are today. The police had more time.

First question from Leo: "Anybody hurt?" When he was reassured, he asked, "Your car, Doc?"

I nodded.

Leo studied the situation. "You didn't hurt the pillar none." He thought some more. "I'll call the station house and have the car towed to Hogan's garage. He takes care of my car. You call him in a few hours and he'll tell you what the damage is." He pulled out a small notebook and a stub of pencil to make out his report. He moistened the stub with his tongue. For a moment he hesitated . . . "Doc, how do you spell 'pillar'?"

Leo had married a small, slim woman of French Canadian descent, a good-natured person, vigorous and shrewd. He handed her every paycheck, and she doled him out his allowance. After all expenses had been paid, she invested the rest of the money in a number of two-story, two-family houses in upper Manhattan near their own house. She and Leo were well-to-do. They had a substantial income and looked forward to an easy retirement. They deserved it, and I expect and hope that they got it. Leo was one of the men who got me to open my office on the West Side.

The West Side was hardly prepossessing. It was the winter of 1935, and the weather was severe. So was the Depression. The common saying was that now that our shoes had worn out we were back on our feet again. Long lines formed on Columbus Circle twice a day for a cup of soup and a thick slice of bread. The people numbered in the hundreds. Almost all were men and almost all were of working age. I wondered where the women and children were, and I asked. The answer was simple. Most of the men were from out of town, and they'd left their families in Akron, Tulsa, or Dallas while they sought work in larger towns. There were bread lines in front of churches too, and some churches threw open their doors at night to house the homeless.

Broadway, once gay and bright, showed evidence of the Depression. Many of its small stores were boarded up. Landlords in their desperation had leased stores to anyone who could pay the rent. Many of these businesses were fly-by-night emporia, here today and gone far away tomorrow. Gigantic signs announced: "Going Out of Business." Those stores were in the going-out-of-business business. The tourist traffic had diminished, but hayseeds still came to the big city.

When I walked a few blocks down Broadway I would pass a believe-it-or-not freak show, a print shop that put tourists' names at the tops of fake newspaper pages, half a dozen stand-up eating counters, and a shop whose glass doors and windows were completely plastered over with old posters.

This shop intrigued me. I passed it a dozen times before I found the courage to try the door. I thought it might be abandoned, but it wasn't. The proprietor was sitting in an old upholstered chair that had sprung a decided leak. He was reading a newspaper, an unlit half-cigar propped in his mouth. He sported a week's growth of beard. I saw that his paper was The Racing Form.

I thought to apologize for interrupting the idyll. "I couldn't help coming in to see what was going on here," I told the man. He didn't answer. He wasn't antagonistic; merely uninterested.

I went on: "From the street all those posters don't give people a chance to see what you sell. What *do* you sell here?"

He looked up. "Posters," he said, and went back to his paper.

Apple vendors had become part of ordinary city life. Many men went to the freight yards and bought apples at a penny apiece. On favored corners they would make pyramids of apples on boxes, the fruit polished to a high gloss. There was no hawking. Dozens of men would stand silent and shabby, selling their apples at five cents apiece.

We were lucky. Our neighborhood was self-contained. Our working people were among those who made New York City run, and their jobs were fairly assured. The men manned the subways and streetcars, drove the cabs, collected the garbage, and raised and lowered the curtains in the theaters. Their wives worked part time in the stores and markets of the area. Without them there would have been no electricity, no gas or telephone service. The city would have shut down. And so their jobs were constant. They were indeed the hewers of wood and the drawers of water.

West of Ninth Avenue, toward the Hudson River, most buildings were four- or five-story walk-ups, built by speculators some fifty years before. A few blocks had been built before the Civil War. There was one deadly six-story walk-up, which I called the heart attack house. I avoided house calls to the sixth story whenever I could. I could run up four flights, but from there on up I felt I was a gone goose. I disliked having to stop at the top of the stairs to get my breath. It was embarrassing to have the patients open their doors to a doctor who had to hang on to the railings before he could say hello.

From Eighth to Ninth Avenue there was a scattering of ancient apartment houses in need of painting and general refurbishing. These had been built just before the turn of the century. Some had elevators, sad elevators that moaned and groaned and rattled. They resented being asked to move and often wouldn't budge at all. In European cities at that time, many elevators bore signs advising visitors to ride up if necessary but not to ride down. On the West Side the signs might have advised people not to ride at all. The landlords correctly calculated that they needn't spend money on tenants who couldn't pay more rent and had nowhere else to go.

The north side of Fifty-sixth Street between Eighth and Ninth Avenues was graced by a handsome, luxurious apartment house, the Parc Vendome. It had doormen and elevator men, and its elegance added luster to the street. The poor thing had been born before its time and had many vacancies. In one of the very large apartments on the top floor, I had a patient—female—who lived with two grand pianos and four bedrooms. She maintained three beautiful young women, never the same young women, for a week at a time. I didn't ask her her trade.

The four- and five-story tenements had no grass plots on the street. They extended to the sidewalk, as far as the law would allow. There seemed no room for anything to grow. Yet, here and there, ailanthus trees had burst through the old cement close to the houses and, by sheer fortitude, put out their few opposing leaves and one single large leaf at the top. Except for the example of courage that it set, the ailanthus was of little value. Its center was a pulpy substance, useless to man. A brave plant, originally from China, it had flourished in Malaya. There it was known as the Tree of Heaven. In Manhattan it was called the stinkweed.

The red-brick tenements were entered at sidewalk level or one step up. Our immediate neighborhood had few of the front stoops that in other parts of the city were the center of social life. Our people visited on the roofs or called from window to window or met in the shops. From the entry, a dark hallway led to the back. Some of the hallways led to a rear door that opened onto a small yard, used mainly for hanging out the wash. Facing this yard was a second tenement, usually only three stories tall but otherwise a replica of the building in front. The tenements ranged along most of the blocks. They were joined or separated (depending on your point of view) by common walls.

The quarters—or rooms—were railroad flats. From the kitchen at the rear to the living room at the front, one walked through two bedrooms past the foot of the beds. The bedrooms were perhaps ten by twelve feet, and side by side. In many flats they were like horse stalls. For some reason never clear to me—or perhaps for no reason at all—the wall between the two bedrooms was only half a wall. A person sitting up in bed in one room could see right into the other. Light and air for the bedrooms came from an air-shaft that also served the next building. The flats had no interior doors. The builders had economized on doors and walls.

It was a safe bet that somewhere in the rooms was a piece of furniture called the dresser. It was not a dressing table, nor was it a highboy. It was a wooden storage piece, waist-tall, with a mirror hung above. It belonged, logically, in a bedroom. But the small bedrooms lacked wall space or even walls themselves, so in some rooms the dresser stood in the kitchen or living room.

The dresser held worldly goods and doubled as the household budget. Each dresser had a linen runner. Some runners were embroidered; some had crocheted edges. The runners were beautifully ironed, but each lay lumpy on the dresser top. Each lump was made of money, bills and change: the butcher's money, the milkman's money, the laundry money, Victor Sinisi's ice money, wad by wad. The thickest pile was "for the landlord's birthday," an event that occurred the first of every month.

The kitchen door was the usual entrance to the rooms. By going to the front of the building, one could enter by the living room door. Few did. But the option gave the bedrooms some privacy from strangers.

Fifty years ago many of these apartments were cold water flats. There was one spigot in the kitchen sink and one in the tub. Water had to be heated on the stove. There was, of course, no central heating. Many apartments were without toilets. There were two toilet compartments in the hall.

There had to be a bathtub somewhere, even if there was no bathroom. The bathtub was in the kitchen, standing on bow-legged, wrought-iron supports and topped by a tin covering that served as ironing board, pot and pan holder, and table throughout the week. On Saturday night the top of the tub was removed and the family bathed, usually in order of their social engagements, the nubile girls first, while the rest of the family was shooed to the bedrooms and living room. Buckets of hot water were poured in, and cold water was added from the spigot. Sometimes the plug was pulled, and the water was changed between baths.

The buildings were "old law" tenements. They had been built before modern building codes were adopted and were exempt from all but the most essential requirements. Fire escapes were then added at the front. They were used for plants, infants in baskets, and general storage.

The common wall between buildings extended about two feet above the roof. Visiting was easy: up a ladder to the roof, across the roof and the two-foot parapets, and down the neighboring stairs. The roofs were covered with coal-tar pitch scattered with sand. On hot days—and nights—the residents would drag chairs, soap boxes, and mats to the roof and relax there, getting what comfort they could. It was a long trip to Coney Island.

The roofs were known as tar beach. There was one disadvantage. Tar pitch has a low melting point. Manhattan in summer is often as hot at night as in the daytime. People clambered down to their rooms spotted with tar that even Saturday night's bath wouldn't remove.

On some roofs pigeon fanciers built coops. They chased the birds daily into the air to make them exercise. Undisturbed, the lazy birds would grow fat and helpless.

On very hot nights—and there were many hot nights—literally thousands of families carried their blankets and pillows to Central Park, and spent the whole night. Our neighbors from Hell's Kitchen occupied the park's southern end. When the wealthy residents of Central Park West and Fifth Avenue complained, our mayor answered, "The parks are for the people."

Mid-Manhattan was the small town in which my wife, Belle, and I had finally opened an office for the general practice of medicine. Neither of us was a native of the area. We were not Catholic, which most of the people were, nor were we Italian, Irish, French, or German. We were a Brooklyn girl and a Virginia boy, and both of us were Jewish. Yet I knew we would be accepted. And we were.

I was making a house call on Fifty-sixth Street. As I walked along swinging my bag, I saw a beautiful Irish woman waiting to pass the time of day. She had one child in a stroller and two others tugging at her skirts. Her dark eyes sparkled and a smile lighted her face. Her shining black hair hung halfway down her back.

As I approached, she placed her hand on my arm. I could feel the warmth through my jacket. In those days we did not fear to reach out to one another. I sensed she was going to say something complimentary, and she did.

"You know, Dr. Slocum," she said, "we're glad you opened your office here. We never had any sickness on the block until you came."

DR. WILLCOX

WE HAD A DOCTOR in our town named Dr. Willcox. The town was Petersburg, Virginia. To my young mind both the doctor and the town had greatness.

Something about the town first. In 1910, when I was five years old, the Civil War (we called it the Late Unpleasantness) had been over just forty-five years. Down the street from our house, half a block down and on the opposite side, was a two-acre farm. It was owned and tended by an aged black couple who had been born into slavery. They had been manumitted, and their former owners had given them the gift of the land.

We lived on the main street, Sycamore Street. And so did the two black people. They were citizens, the same as we, although they still lacked certain rights that their descendants later gained.

The town had hardly recovered from the war. Some of our most prominent citizens, old by then of course, were officers who had fought under General Robert E. Lee.

The town was proud of its record in the Revolutionary War and the Civil War. Petersburg had housed General Lafayette on his visit to America in 1824, and people never tired of telling of it. In 1910 it was still a quiet, sedate southern town, and all unconscious of the approach of the Great War, which was to double and treble its population and destroy its serenity. When the war came Camp Lee was established a few miles to the east. Its transient population exceeded our population and overran the town.

When I was young, Dr. Willcox was my hero. When he arrived at our house, I would be waiting for him. He would throw the reins over his horse's head, and I would hold them as he clambered down from his shiny black buggy to make his call. When he and I were older he came in a shiny black car, one of the handful in our town. His wife always drove—Dr. Willcox would have none of it. The doctor handed me his bag, and I followed him with devotion.

Dr. Willcox did not come to see us often, but his arrival was to me always a great event. He did not come often because my mother was a good folk-doctor on her own.

"He's going to say, 'Take two aspirin and a hot bath and go to bed,'" she'd predict, and she was almost always right. Except for the quinine.

The doctor came most often to see my brother, a year and a half older than I. The poor chap had recurrent malaria. The quinine controlled it, and eventually the malaria disappeared. Why my brother caught malaria I can't say. Like the rest of us he slept with mosquito netting over his bed at night, and at all times he wore his tiny bag of asafetida on a string around his neck.

Of course, my mother had other remedies at hand, such as salt herring in a sock wrapped around the neck for a sore throat. There were hot or cold stupes for bruises and inflammations. (A stupe was simply a cloth or towel dipped into water—sometimes medicated water, and hot or cold, as the case indicated—and then wrung out and applied.) There was also raw potato for rubbing into warts. My grandmother, who knew more about medicine than my mother, would whisper to my brother and me that the potato wouldn't work unless we buried it by the light of the full moon. It had to be buried secretly, of course. Then it would work.

Dr. Willcox had little with which to practice except for three specifics: digitalis, morphine, and quinine. The work of Casimir Funk was just gaining recognition, and on it was based the art and science of nutrition. (In 1912 Dr. Funk actually coined the word *vitamin* to describe what he had discovered.) Insulin was still in the future, and so were most of the inoculations against disease, with the exception of smallpox vaccine. It is hardly remembered today that General Washington was the first commander to order his whole army to be inoculated against smallpox. General Cornwallis did not have the vaccine, and his troops were weakened by disease. You know what happened then.

Dr. Willcox used digitalis against failing of the heart, quinine to control the inroads of malaria and for fevers of all descriptions, and morphine for intractable pain.

Dr. Willcox was well versed in the surgical procedures of his day. He could set bones with the best of them and was expert in removing tonsils on his kitchen table while his wife administered ether through a cone.

Twenty years later, when I was beginning my practice of medicine—more than half a century ago—doctors still had little to work with. Our resources were limited, our ignorance profound. We hardly knew what we didn't know. As best we could, we managed.

Doctors and patients were closer in those days. We were the doctors for the whole patient, the whole family. The doctor in general practice delivered babies. Thus he served as obstetrician. When he turned to care for the newborn, he was a pediatrician. We took care of the grandparents, and thus were geriatricians. There were few specialists. When a visit to one was essential, the family doctor often went too, both to learn and to give the patient confidence. No non-medical personnel intervened between doctor and patient. No office helper dared inquire why you wanted to talk to the doctor.

What we had to give, like Dr. Willcox's generation before us, was our skill and our time. When we sat up nights with our patients, we became almost part of the family. To each patient the doctor gave a portion of his time and life.

Dr. Willcox carried hope and courage to the sick wherever he appeared. It is no wonder that a small boy looked on him with hero worship, particularly a small boy who knew without a doubt that he himself would someday be a doctor.

MEDICAL ETHICS

THE DAY CAME to which we'd all looked forward. The senior class, soon to graduate from New York Medical College, had been given the privilege of hearing a lecture from an ancient, retired teacher. He was to speak to us about the practice of medicine.

He was a successful practitioner, an expert on tuberculosis, a doctor who had retired from teaching the year we had entered the school. He still had one of the biggest practices in the East. He was quoted in our textbooks, and his name appeared in many footnotes. We knew him through men who'd studied under him, some of whom were our teachers. They'd told us he was a fascinating speaker. "You never know what he'll do or say next," we'd been told. "But his lecture will be one of the best of your lives."

We had two amphitheaters at our school, not counting those devoted to surgery. The larger could hold three hundred students, the smaller only one hundred. Those of us arranging the affair knew how few of our classmates were left. The faculty had been less than gentle with us. Our number had been severely reduced. We chose the smaller, more intimate amphitheater for the lecture.

The old man stood before us, leaning on the lectern, one arm swinging idly. A small, spare man, he was trim and natty, quick moving and precise. A flower bloomed in the buttonhole of his lapel. His hair was the light brown color that resists graying. He took his time scanning our faces. Then he smiled.

"A likely looking bunch of new doctors," he said.

We liked that. Not many kind words were spoken to medical students at that school and in those days. He had us. We applauded vigorously.

"I don't see any women. That will change. How many of you are there?"

"Seventy-two," someone shouted.

"How many were admitted to your class when you entered?"

The same voice shouted the answer, "One hundred and twenty-five."

"Well, you had a rough ride."

We laughed, uncertainly. It was true that we were a sadly depleted group. We'd been told at our introductory lecture four years before that many would fall by the wayside, and that was the way it turned out. We'd become accustomed to threats and intimidation. We envied the nonchalance with which students at the four other medical schools in New York completed their senior year.

"You're not here to become scientists," we'd been told over and over again. "You're here to pass your Boards and then to intern and then to get out and take care of people. The scientists will give you tools, but the only reason for your existence is the patient."

We were the only medical school from which for some years no one had failed his Boards. The statistic was comforting but also menacing. Heaven help our first graduate to fail!

"Here are my volunteers," the old doctor said. Two of our classmates panted into the theater with their arms full of books. They lined them up on the table beside the lectern.

The doctor introduced himself: "I am the author of nineteen books on the subject of medicine," he said. We were just deciding that he was a pompous old braggart when he continued, "They've often come back to haunt me. They're full of error, misconceptions, and nonsense." His audience laughed. He laughed, too.

"I began the practice of medicine in 1878. All but my last books were written before Roentgen and the Curies gave us the X-ray. How could these books not be full of nonsense? I brought them with me today to show you just how impressive nonsense can look." Now the class was with him.

"I know you've been told that the only reason for your existence is the welfare of the patient. I know because I was taught the same thing. Believe it. It's true. If you have any other idea, quit now. Anyone going into medicine to get rich is an abomination in the eyes of God and his fellow man. Oh, it can happen. A man who graduated with me had a family so gratified by his aid that they gave him an island in the St. Lawrence River! A whole island with a mansion on it. But don't look for riches.

"You will earn a good living, some of you a very good living indeed. You will have the respect and honor of your patients. No one could want more.

"Which brings us to the subject of temptations. Remember, you are all young men. Your lives are before you, to be squandered or made the most of. You will be in positions of trust. Few will have the powers granted to you. You will be privy to knowledge about your patients and their lives, you will be able to obtain medications, and intimacies of every sort will be offered you.

"There are three great temptations: alcohol, drugs, and women. Alcohol—even with the present laws of prohibition—is the most obvious. Most of you know where to find alcohol. But most of you also know when enough is enough. Too much, and you will be talked about. Your patients will lose confidence. Scandal, they say, seeks a shining mark.

"Drugs are less obvious a temptation. Sometimes, and there will be plenty such times, you will be too exhausted to sleep. But another call will come and you will want to carry on. You will know that a little injection or an inhalation will give you the necessary lift. Don't take it. One leads to another and still another. Soon you will not be able to think clearly or act quickly. Alcohol destroys the body, but drugs destroy the soul.

"Now let us get to the subject of women. Some of you will open offices on Park Avenue. Beware! It is known as the street of good dogs and bad women! Gentlemen, the world is full of beautiful women. Your women patients will look up to you as men skilled in the art of medicine. They will desire you. Those of you who yield will find you can destroy not only your good names but your families and your practices.

"Most of you will open your offices soon. We're in a Depression. People may be slow in coming, money even slower. Have patience. Wait. Do your studying and do your best.

"Remember that your fortune will be made from the misfortune of others. I knew young doctors who were struggling at the time of the influenza epidemic of 1917. None of us wanted that epidemic. But it kept many young doctors going. I remember how many repainted their houses and repaired their roofs when that time of trouble was over. But I remember, too, doctors who died.

"There will be times when you are uncertain. Your patient expects self-confidence and aplomb. Compose yourself, and it will help your patient. When you make house calls and get to the front porch breathless and weather-beaten, delay ringing the bell. Obtain equanimity. Then, as the patient expects you, so will you be found.

"Take care of your poor. They will need you. To the best of your ability, help them. Some of them will not be poor always, and they will enrich you. For your care of the others, may eternal riches be yours."

The silence in the chamber was absolute. The old doctor was the ideal parent, the most honorable practitioner, the voice of conscience rolled into one.

"Ah, yes, one more thing," he said. "A practical point. If two calls come to you at once, and one is a call to see a sick child, go see the child first. And hurry. Otherwise he or she will probably be well before you get there.

"That's all I can tell you now," he told our laughing class. "I hope some of it sinks in! Now where are my volunteers to help me to my car? I can't carry as many books as I used to!"

With a wave of his hand that was like a benediction he walked to the door and left the room, to cheers and a standing ovation.

SWEET'S

SOMEHOW I managed to graduate from medical school. The year was 1932. The country was in the midst of the worst depression in its history.

I had a few weeks to prepare for the state Boards in medicine. If I passed I would be a full-fledged physician and surgeon. If I failed I would try again. I knew that I wasn't a scholar. I hardly knew what a scholar was. My interests were too diverse to keep me on any straight and narrow path. I had worked at many things, and I had a far more varied view of life than most of the men in my class at New York Medical College. Unlike most of them, I had not gone directly from grammar school to high school to college and then to medical school.

I had spent five years, part of them while in college, working as a newspaper reporter in and around New York. I had been a reporter on the *Jersey Journal* in Jersey City and on the *Brooklyn Eagle*. On the *Brooklyn Eagle* I even had a byline, and at the age of eighteen!

It pleased me to know that when I was on the *Eagle* the paper won a Pulitzer Prize two years in a row. And why not? We had a superb staff, including Nunnally Johnson and H. V. Kaltenborn. In fact, H. V. Kaltenborn had written a letter of recommendation for me when I applied to medical school.

During those five years I even went to North Africa to free-lance as a reporter of the Riffian War. This was in 1925. I didn't get anywhere near the shooting, but there was lots of information to be gathered at the bars.

There were other techniques I never mastered. It astonished me through the four years of medical school that many of the students could pick out with accuracy the questions that would be asked on examinations. I was forced to review, to memorize, to spend hours with my books. I never knew what to study, so I studied everything. Most of the other men passed easily. I passed.

And now I was facing the state Boards. I reminded myself once again that for a number of years none of my school's graduates had failed the Boards. I didn't want to be the first. And so I studied away at my books.

It was a very welcome break when my wife, Belle, phoned to invite me to meet her for lunch. I was surfeited with information, and it was seeping out at the seams. Her message was simple: "Meet me at Sweet's at one o'clock. I want to tell you the latest."

Sweet's at 2 Fulton Street was one of New York's best seafood restaurants. It was among the six first customers for Mr. Thomas Edison's electric lights. Today it is the last remaining of this pioneer group. Established in 1842 to cater to seafaring men and those who did business with ships, it still served them. But it had been discovered over the years by the brokers and bankers of Wall Street, and it was crowded at lunch and dinner. It was difficult to get a table.

Belle was a well-liked guest. She was young and fresh and charming, and, with her brown hair and brown eyes, had a look of honey to her. She carried herself with style, and she looked smart. She looked, in fact, like a young version of the actress Tallulah Bankhead.

Belle represented an old and important part of the steamship trade. She was manager of a third-generation towboat concern that had much to do with the movement of cargo in New York Harbor. It was an unusual job for a young woman.

She ran a fleet of three tugboats and a large string of barges. One of her tugboats was among the largest and most powerful in the harbor. The craft were used to tow the barges carrying every sort of solid cargo. They towed barges to the West Indies, to ports along the eastern seaboard of North and South America, up the Hudson, through the Erie Canal, and as far west as the Great Lakes. The barges were as large as small oceangoing freighters but had no motive power of their own. The holds were tremendous.

At Sweet's I climbed the one and a half flights of rickety and slanted stairs. The staircase was dimly lit and smelled of the finest seafood cooking in the world. The manager recognized me as Belle's husband and indicated her table at the rear of the restaurant. It overlooked South Street and the piers of the Fulton Fish Market Association, which extended into the East River. From about 3:00 A.M. until the midmorning the market was busy with the day's catch. By noon all of the trucks and most of the workers had gone.

"Wait till you hear," Belle teased.

"That's what I came down for. Tell away."

"Just about the time you pass your Boards I may be out of a job."

"That's good news?"

"It's bad news for the company, of course, but it's good news for us. Both of us need a change. We have a few dollars put away. When you pass your exams let's pack up and go to Europe."

She floored me. She was the practical one. I was the one with the wild ideas. Yet she was delighted to propose something silly that I hadn't even considered.

"Tell me more. Suppose I don't pass the first time. What'll we do then?"

"You'll pass, all right." I was glad she was so sure of it.

"You know," Belle continued, "we're a hundred-year-old firm. Today a member of the firm came in with some papers from the government. They'd wanted bids on a tremendous job to deliver rock from up the Hudson to Pamlico Sound off the Carolina coast. They're constructing a breakwater.

"There's a lot of money in it. The only trouble is the government insists that the rock be there before the heavy weather sets in at Cape Hatteras. We're the only ones who could do it, and even we can't possibly do it on time. It would take at least three months. There's a stiff penalty for late delivery. Cape Hatteras waters are a graveyard of sunken ships. A towboat with barges in series can't round the cape in hurricane time or in winter.

"He had already signed the charter party without talking to me. I told him it was impossible, but he thought he knew better. I got in touch with the Army Corps of Engineers and explained the situation to the man who arranged the deal. He wouldn't withdraw it. I told him no barges could round Cape Hatteras from August until spring. He said that's what he thought. But the charter party was 'going through channels.' He couldn't stop it.

"That's how it stands." She sighed. "It was such a nice old business. Monday morning I give thirty days' notice. They won't be able to pay me long after that. When you finish your exams we can be on our way."

And so we were.

VIENNA

BELLE AND I decided to go to Vienna. We wanted to travel, to see the world before the serious business of life began. Why Vienna? Because it had long been the center of medical education in Europe. Because it was cheap. And because it was in a central location from which we could visit Rome, Budapest, Prague, and northern Italy. Our ship took eight days to reach the continent. On the way to Vienna we stopped for two weeks in Paris and Brussels.

We planned to consult the American Medical Association of Vienna for information and advice. We found it above a coffee-house. There was a small executive office and an adjoining lounge, filled with diners and drinkers. A bulletin board announced the hours and fees for classes in medicine.

We introduced ourselves to the secretary. "Delighted," he said, in unaccented American English. I suppose we looked surprised. "I was raised in Brooklyn," he explained.

"*Landsmann!*" Belle said. "We hope you can help us find a place to live in Vienna. And tell us everything about everything else."

"Are you Jewish?"

"Yes," I said.

"Well, about a quarter of the American doctors here are, and some of them are uneasy. This town is full of Nazis. Many Viennese are out of work and hope that Hitler will come. But you're Americans. To you it really doesn't matter."

"Wait here a moment," he said. He went back to his desk and returned with some pamphlets shaped like swastikas. "A small plane was over last night and dropped these."

He handed me one. On the swastika was printed in large black letters: "*Kauft nicht bei Juden*," "Don't buy from Jews." Belle said, "Bastards!"

"Oh, you needn't worry," he reassured us. "But I want you to know they're here."

In the beginning we weren't worried. Hitler, we'd decided between us on the way to Vienna, was a political hack. We were sure his party would never last. Medicine, not politics, was foremost in my thoughts. Soon enough Belle and I would witness the horrors the Nazi party brought to Vienna.

The secretary went on, "I know a very good place for you to live, not more than three blocks from here. Down Kinderspitalgasse. The people want another American doctor if they can get one. I'll call them. It's only one room, but a big one, with hot and cold running water in the room and a bathroom with a tub just outside. Room and board, and it's reasonable. Don't be finicky about the food. Remember, we import nearly all our food. The Austrian Empire was dismantled after the war." (World War I, he meant.) "They call Vienna a head without a body. We haven't enough farmland left to feed ourselves.

"You can take classes here in almost all subjects," he told us, handing me a sheaf of leaflets. "Many are given in English, and if you speak enough German, you can get into any clinic you want. We have the General Hospital and the Policlinic, where most of the American doctors go. If you study here for four months and get enough credits, you get a certificate signed by the men you study under."

I asked about the classes given by Dr. Chiari, famous for his lectures at the autopsy table in the Anatomical Institute. The secretary was well informed. "I understand that the old man is semi-retired, but they say his son is an even better teacher. He'll show you a lot of pathology. You see, this is a socialist country, and even though it's Catholic, everyone who dies at the state-run hospitals is autopsied. But here," he said, "before you go to look at the pension, let me introduce you to some of our members. . ."

We discovered that not all of the doctors who belonged to the Association were recent graduates of American medical schools in search of postgraduate study. Some of the older members were victims of the Depression who had seen their practices and their investments disappear. One doctor had had losses so great that he suffered from shock; he had decided to give up everything to come to Vienna to study and to begin all over again. He would sit alone at a table in the lounge, drinking beer and spilling the ash of his many cigarettes all over his jacket.

The apartment to which the secretary directed us was on the third floor of a gray stone building. Belle looked around our new room. "This is lovely," she said. "Large, old-fashioned, and very neat. These people have had hard times. It's needlework that's kept the bedclothes and drapes as nice as they are."

If anyone knew about needlework, Belle did. She was a modern young woman, but she cared about the traditional skills, and she was an expert needlewoman herself. She also cared about the traditional virtues. Thrift was a virtue. Here thrift had been achieved with taste and dignity. She approved.

Like the New Yorker I had become, I complained. "I don't see any fire escapes. This place could be a firetrap."

We talked it over. Belle said, "All right. Let's not have any fires while we're in Vienna."

The owner of the apartment was a large, florid woman in her fifties, overbuilt at the top, friendly, and efficient. Her English was better than my German. At breakfast, our first meal, we had soft-boiled eggs in the shell. I commented that the eggs had been stamped "Poland."

"Certainly," she said good-naturedly. "Would you rather have Polish eggs or no eggs? It's the same with meat. Would you rather have Hungarian meat or no meat? We have some of each." She laughed. "If you'd rather not eat, I save money."

The other guests roared. There were ten boarders altogether.

Besides Belle and me there were two Hindu women physicians; two Zoroastrians, or Parsees; and four American doctors, including a pleasant and cultured black doctor from Connecticut. Our pension was homelike, comforting, and tolerant. Nazi politics didn't seem to have penetrated its nineteenth-century atmosphere.

I attended classes and clinics. Belle met the wives of other doctors and socialized. She visited every handicraft shop in the city. She had been raised for the first seven years of her life in a German-Lutheran neighborhood. When anyone asked where she was born she never answered "New York," but said, "Second Avenue and Fifth Street." All her playmates spoke German. Belle hardly spoke English until she started school. Now all Vienna was hers.

I arranged to attend the younger Dr. Chiari's lecture in the autopsy room five mornings a week, from eight to eleven o'clock. It was a popular course.

The doctor would begin by having an intern read the subject's medical history and symptoms. We would discuss the diagnostic possibilities and compare our reasoning with that of the staff doctors. Then followed the autopsy, whose findings we compared with our suppositions. We found we had much to learn.

After a quick lunch I would attend lectures or clinics, depending upon what I thought was valuable. I worked under well-known men in heart and lung diseases, dermatology, and syphilology. I spent the afternoons of two weeks studying with a hypnotist. Then I attended lectures given by a student of Dr. Freud. I was unimpressed. To me Freud's real contribution was to teach us not to be afraid of words. I thought the rest of his teachings were rubbish.

Although the hospitals appeared to be secure havens, the activities of the Nazi party in Vienna became increasingly open and hostile. One day Belle went shopping in a beautiful department store in the city's Second District, a section with a large Jewish population. Men wearing brown shirts and swastika armbands dashed in. They shouted "Heil Hitler" and "Death to the Jews" as they upset counters, smashed mirrors, and set fires. Shoppers rushed for the doors. Many people were hurt, some by Nazi beatings, more from trampling by the crowd. Belle was smart. She crawled under a counter in a corner and later walked out unharmed. The incident lasted long enough for the police to gather, but they made no move to stop the marauders.

When I reached home, Belle was in our room. She listened to the details of my day. Then she asked calmly, "Did you hear about the riot?"

I hadn't heard. When she told me I was more angry than shocked. "It was to be expected," I said. "You suppose we ought to leave Vienna?" I felt torn; my medical studies were important to me, but I was concerned for our safety and horrified by the turn of events.

"Of course not," Belle said. "We'll stay until you finish the clinics you signed up for. We're not going to be frightened by a mob."

Belle may not have been afraid, but I was. I felt very proud of her. What she didn't tell me was that she'd dragged a lost child under the counter with her. Later she found the frantic mother. The mother insisted on having Belle's name and address so that she could send her a gift. I learned about the lost child afterward, when Belle unwrapped a lovely, hand-knit scarf.

A few days later I was approaching the Anatomical Institute when I heard tramping feet. A group of Nazis came from a side street, heading for the Institute. They were met by men from converging streets. They marched in step. It was obviously prearranged. I turned and walked away. The Nazis broke into the Institute to attack any Jewish students they could find there. The entrance was a great hall with a beautiful galleried staircase. Only a few students were there at the time, and the Nazis chased them up the stairs. They caught one young man, a hunchback, and threw him over the balcony to his death.

By this time, the students in the hall were joined by the other students working in the building. There were only a few Jews among them, but all the students turned on the Nazis. There was a terrific battle. The police were summoned but chose not to intervene. The next morning the bodies of some Nazis lay among the other dead on the tables at the Anatomical Institute.

I was shocked but not surprised by the brutal attack at the Institute. What shocked me was the organization of the Viennese Nazis, the Germanic thoroughness that got them to their destination in full uniform and from many directions. I was also shocked by the deliberate nonintervention of the Viennese police, subverted to the Nazi cause. Sadly, I was not surprised by the attack because I knew that a good percentage of the city's medical students were Jewish, and it was the Jews the Nazis were after.

The doctors at the American Medical Association held a meeting. They demanded that the American consul general protect them. No answer was forthcoming from him, but the British ambassador announced that he would help any foreigners who asked for protection. The next day his statement was answered in a Nazi-owned newspaper. Hitler declared that he would protect British or American citizens. Jews, he announced, had no nationality.

One day we went walking on the Graben, a delightful street despite its name. The Graben, or grave, was supposed to have been a mass burial ground during the plagues of the thirteenth and fourteenth centuries. Now it was a street of beautiful and expensive shops. We were with friends from New Jersey who were on their honeymoon, an orthopedic surgeon and his bride. Our wives saw a black-bordered sign on the door of a shop that handled luxury leather goods. They glanced at the sign, consulted together, and walked in before I could stop them.

The proprietor was delighted to see them. American customers meant dollars—and dollars were hard to come by in Vienna. The young women pointed out the things they liked. The shopkeeper hurried his salesgirls into action. He spoke excellent English. Goods were brought to the counter from the highest shelves. Our wives examined them carefully and pointed to other things. The salesgirls stacked and fetched.

An hour was spent inspecting, choosing, searching. The pile of goods on the counter rose higher and higher.

Finally, Belle said to the proprietor, "My friends and I are sorry that there's been a death in the family."

The man looked astonished. "There hasn't been a death in the family," he said. "What gave you that idea?"

Belle pointed to the black-bordered sign on the door.

"Oh, that says nothing about a death in the family," the man said. "That simply says that we don't cater to Jewish trade."

"Oh, I am sorry," Belle said. She pulled on her gloves and pushed away the boxes in front of her. "You see, we're Jewish."

We marched sedately from the store. I made sure not to be the last one out.

I didn't want to leave Vienna; it was the medical training opportunity of a lifetime. Until 1914 the city had been a great world center of medical knowledge, but after the First World War its glory waned. Austria was destitute. There was no money with which to buy the new and constantly improving equipment for diagnosis. Yet Vienna remained a good city in which to learn medicine, if only because of its autopsies. Every patient who died in the state-run General Hospital or the Policlinic was autopsied, and great teachers held forth at the autopsy table. Diagnosis is not a matter of equipment, but of the doctor's skill and experience. At the autopsy table one saw with one's own eyes the effect of disease on the human body; one saw the cause of symptoms. In New York there were only random opportunities to learn in this way.

Unfortunately, the Viennese professors, like their confreres throughout Europe, were autocrats in their departments. They hired all their help, from aspiring medical students to bottle-washers. In the surgical departments the professors also ruled over their instruments. They were known to refuse to lend these to other professors who needed them. Many of the professors were selfish and egotistical.

One professor of chest diseases under whom I studied liked me and took me under his wing. I liked him, too, and was grateful for the interest that he took in me. But like most of the Viennese professors, he was absolutely certain of his knowledge and would not be contradicted. Handicapped by the lack of X-ray equipment, he had to find another way to demonstrate the symptoms of respiratory disease. And so the professor vocalized the sounds of air passing through diseased lung tissue. It was an admirable but questionable imitation.

The professor said, "Drink all the coffee you want in Vienna but don't touch the *schlagg*." It was customary to order *kaffee mit schlagg*. *Schlagg* was a thick wad of cream spooned onto the top of the coffee. It floated there like an iceberg.

"What's the matter with *schlagg*?" I wanted to know.

"*Schlagg* is unpasteurized cream made from unpasteurized milk." He pointed to specimen bottles. "Look," he went on, "lungs. Look at the cavities. Tuberculosis. Everywhere in Austria we have tuberculosis. We call it the disappearing disease."

"Well, isn't it good that the disease is disappearing?"

He snorted. "Young man," he said, "it isn't the disease that disappears. It's the patient."

Dr. Louis I. Harris, health commissioner of New York City, was once invited to address an Austrian medical meeting. He deplored the fact that milk in Austria was unpasteurized. "That is one of the major factors in the spread of tuberculosis here," he stated, and gave statistics. But nothing could be done because of the strength of the dairymen's lobby. Vienna, he indicated, was an unsafe city in which to live. At a meeting of the American Medical Association, many of the members were furious. They said Dr. Harris was rude and certainly should apologize for insulting his hosts. I was disgusted with these high-minded and well-educated men and women who condemned a man for telling the truth.

Belle was waiting for me in one of the booths in the lounge of the American Medical Association. "I've got two letters from home," she announced. She held one out to me. A friend in the shipping business wrote that Belle's company had gone into bankruptcy. "See what I told you," Belle said. "They signed the government contract and they couldn't deliver. They even lost a barge in a storm at Hatteras. Old John Henry Smith, the captain, managed to save himself.

"I have another letter here, I think. It *should* be here," she went on with great seriousness, rummaging in her pocketbook. "I'm sure it's here. Oh, yes, here it is," and she drew out a small, official-looking envelope from the Regents of the State of New York. It had already been opened. I had passed my state Boards and was a full-fledged physician and surgeon. It was very welcome news. I walked around to Belle's side of the table and kissed her. Finally I said, "You know, honey, we've been in Vienna a long time. Don't you think we should go home?"

She smiled. "I think," she said.

So ended our four months in the city. The saying went that in Vienna it didn't rain all day, but it did rain every day. And rain it did, nearly every day that we were there. The damp was constant, the drizzle occasional. Rubbers were a must, and the walls of the buildings were always wet to the touch.

We'd made short side trips to Budapest and to the countryside, but I had been too busy to see much of Vienna; beautiful, degraded, destitute Vienna. What I had seen was cadavers, sick people, and classrooms.

Belle had done a lot of the best kind of touring; casual, interesting visits to the stores, the neighborhoods, the craftsmen's shops. She was elated by her discoveries. How had she seen so much, and I so little?

Many things had pleased us: the city's famous music, its magnificent baroque architecture, and what seemed to be the general friendliness of the people. Yet we were uncertain about the feelings of many people with whom we dealt. As the Nazi incidents mounted day by day they cast a grayness over our stay, a grayness that matched the Viennese winter itself.

On our way home we went to Rome. It was our first visit, and the first time in nearly four months that we had seen the sun.

Strange, how people think: I was very young and I thought moodily that this was the end of my greatest adventure. How could I have known that Vienna was only preparation for the greater adventures that lay ahead?

INTERNSHIP
The Ambulance

OUR SHIP PASSED Sandy Hook on the west, Sea Gate on the east, and headed upstream through the Narrows into New York Harbor. Too many idle ships swung at anchor in the bay.

Upstream, passing the piers, Belle and I could see that the structures needed painting and care. Abandoned warehouses, deserted boardinghouses where seamen once had stayed, the few drays on West Street—all told the story. The Depression had left its mark.

I was anxious to call the hospitals to find work as an intern. I had written a number of letters from Vienna inquiring about a position. The answers had invited me to come for an interview.

I'd been friendly with Saul Gordon, a young man who'd gone through medical school with me. I called him from the pier. He was interning at the old Flower Hospital at Sixty-fourth Street and the East River.

He was delighted to hear from me. "Don't go anywhere else," he shouted over the phone. "Come here. We're very short-handed. We have sixteen men and we need at least twenty-five. There's so much work we can't see straight."

That was exactly what I wanted to hear. In the meantime Belle had called her mother. She had everything figured out.

"You go to the hospital to see what the situation is," she told me. "I'll take the baggage in a cab and go to my mother's in Sea Gate. We'll stay there until we find a place of our own."

Her mother had a spacious, three-story house near the Atlantic. There were seven bedrooms. We needed only one. Belle's mother was glad to have us stay.

Sea Gate was where I had met Belle under inauspicious circumstances ten years before. She was sitting on the broad beach there when I first saw her. I thought she was beautiful. I myself was a sight to behold. I had taken a beating the night before.

University College of New York University, my alma mater, was in the Bronx. It was the home of the Hall of Fame. Each year the freshman and sophomore classes held separate banquets. The game was for one class to discover the location of the other class banquet, and to break it up. I no longer remember exactly why.

One summer I had run a skee ball game next to a freak show at Coney Island. I had many friends there. Someone tipped me off that the freshmen planned to hold their banquet at a restaurant nearby, one flight up. I led a group of sophomores up a fire escape, over a roof, and into the middle of the banquet. What happened next might be described as a skirmish. Tables were turned over, dishes were smashed, fists jabbed, and glassware went flying.

Someone called the police. In short order the hall cleared out— except for the police and me. I took a pounding. Finally a good-natured sergeant lugged me down the stairs and told me to beat it before anyone could hold me responsible for the damages. I beat it.

The question was, where to? I saw myself in a plate-glass window. My face was bloated, both eyes were partly closed, and my clothes were torn. My parents now lived in Flatbush, only a few miles away, but I couldn't go home in that condition.

I knew a man in Sea Gate, at the end of Coney Island—in fact, at the very tip of the end of New York. He told me to come out and phoned the gatehouse to have me admitted.

Sea Gate was a private residential neighborhood adjoining Coney Island but fenced off from it. Its two gates were guarded. The community had its own police and sanitation departments. A mile square, it was bordered by the ocean on the south and Gravesend Bay on the north. Its lighthouse at Norton's Point marked the gateway to New York Harbor.

My friend took one look at me and put me to bed. In the morning he handed me a bathing suit, and I went to the beach. And there was Belle.

Some of Sea Gate's more rowdy teenage boys liked to tease the policemen on the small local force. Belle looked me over.

"Were you baiting the police?" she asked me.

I assured her I wasn't, no matter how I looked. "The cops did most of the fighting."

"Well, then, you can sit here," she said, making room for me on the almost-empty beach.

Her cotton stockings were rolled around her ankles in thick coils, and her bathing suit had legs almost to the knee and arms almost to the elbow. The suit was black, which was standard for girls' bathing suits in those days. The black accentuated the honey color of her hair and of her frank and steady eyes. Occasionally she would glance up and down the beach.

"You're waiting for someone?"

"No. I'm watching for the police. Girls have to wear stockings on the beach. If you don't wear them you have to leave. Most beaches are like that. And so if I see a policeman I roll up my stockings. Then when they pass I roll them down again."

We made a date to meet later. Our interest didn't have to be encouraged. It was already there. We went to movies and shows. We met each other's friends. I had dinner at her home, possibly too often. But it was a long journey from the Bronx, at one end of New York, to Sea Gate at the extreme other end. Besides, Sea Gate—with its passing ships and the Norton's Point light—was a particularly romantic place.

Belle was fifteen. "When I'm sixteen," she said, planning ahead, "my father's giving me a car. Then we can get married." When she was sixteen her father was broke. We married when she was twenty-one. We'd waited for the stock market to crash.

"We haven't lost a thing," Belle announced cheerfully. "We didn't have a thing to lose." We did have a lot to be cheerful about. We were young and full of enthusiasm, and we were together.

Now Sea Gate would be a good place to live until we found our own apartment. Commuting would be easy. Twice a day a boat sailed round trip from the Battery on Manhattan Island to a pier in Gravesend Bay that was three blocks from the house.

*   *   *

The superintendent of Flower Hospital, a big, bulky man, led me to his office to do a selling job. It was his business to keep the hospital functioning, which meant, among other things, recruiting an adequate staff.

"Before we talk we'd better take our medicine." He got a bottle and two glasses from a cabinet. The bottle was labeled: "For Medicinal Use Only." That made it legal.

"We've got everything here," he declaimed, after pouring the drinks. "We have a fine faculty, all the latest equipment, and every sort of case. Besides that we run three ambulances for the city on the West Side. Interns handle all the ambulance cases. It gives you a chance to make decisions on your own. What you don't understand you can bring into the hospital for the teaching staff."

He paused. I could see he was getting ready for the clincher. "And at the end of your year's internship we give you—one hundred twenty-five dollars!" He smiled a benevolent smile.

I didn't need the clincher. All I needed was a place to learn and practice. I knew that Flower Hospital offered a busy internship as good as any hospital's and better than most.

I took the job. It offered a rotating service in medicine, in surgery, and in obstetrics, with pediatrics and the specialties included. The rest of the service was on the ambulance. This was just what I wanted—a general survey of the entire field of medical practice. I had always wanted to be a family doctor.

I chose the ambulance service first. The man I relieved staggered in to thank me. He said he'd been getting three or four hours sleep out of the twenty-four.

[35]

In those days all ambulances were manned by an intern and a driver. They were dispatched by Police Department calls to our emergency room. Connected to the emergency room was a small room with cots where the interns slept—if they had time to sleep —between calls. After thirty-six hours' service an intern took twenty-four hours off.

During our time off—if we could stay awake—we would go to any ward we pleased to study the charts, talk to the staff doctors, and see how they arrived at their diagnoses and treatment.

Some days we were kept out for hours, going from one call to another. Wherever we went the police who had called us would be waiting. Some of our calls were made to places that were pockets of violence, and we were pleased to see blue uniforms from the windows of the ambulance. Prohibition, that "experiment noble in motive," prohibited the manufacture, transportation, and sale of alcoholic beverages. Prohibition meant violence. Bootleggers fought for monopoly. Gang wars were rampant. As in all wars, there were profits to be made. We found bodies in the streets, in clubs, on the waterfront, in alleys and hidden apartments. Where we didn't find the dead we found the wounded. Then, siren shrieking, lights flashing, we headed for the emergency room.

To some people Prohibition was a glamorous period. Certainly it produced some larger-than-life Manhattan celebrities. Texas Guinan was one. "Hello, sucker," was her greeting to the big spenders in her nightclubs. They loved it: those two words were the basis of her fame. Another vivid character was Owney Madden, whom I thought of as the Indestructible Man. The owner of a raucous nightclub, he was shot all to pieces by his business rivals, but each time he survived. These were colorful people. It was, I admit, a colorful time. But some people enjoyed it more than others. I have no doubt that the big spenders roaring away in the clubs had fun.

If we didn't have the finest ambulance service in the city—and I think we did—we certainly had the most spectacular. The owner of a Cadillac franchise had given the hospital three brand-new Cadillac ambulances with all sorts of gadgets and the loudest sirens this side of the Pittsburgh steel mills. It was enough to gladden the heart of any ambulance driver. When calls would come in rapid sequence we would leave, one on the tail of the other, to speed crosstown on Fifty-seventh Street with the sirens shrieking. Pedestrians and motorists would watch us, stunned, wondering what sort of calamity could call out three screaming ambulances at once. There was usually no calamity. We were just hurrying to avoid one. The drivers wanted to get back in time for lunch.

We covered the West Side of Manhattan from the center of Fifth Avenue to the Hudson and from the north side of Thirty-ninth Street to the south side of Seventy-second Street. Our hospital was at the easternmost edge of Manhattan. Our bailiwick was the westernmost. Thus we were always shrieking along Fifty-seventh Street.

When we were called out on the ambulance we seldom knew what we were going to find. Mainly our calls were on sick people at their homes. Often we were dispatched to horrifying street accidents.

One morning we pulled up in front of an apartment house just west of Fifth Avenue. It was shortly after seven o'clock. The street was almost deserted, except for the cop who had summoned us and the crew of a fire truck, parked at the curb.

"Doc, there's a guy stuck in the elevator here."

"That's no hardship. Let's get the Fire Department to pry open the door."

"He's not inside the elevator. He was working underneath when it came down on him. It didn't come down all the way. He's still safe. But it could come down any time. I tried to get under to release him, but I'm too big. None of the firemen could get in either."

The fire captain joined us. "I can't let the men work on the cables," he said. "They may drop the elevator. Even a few inches is too much. That's about all he's got." We entered the building.

There was a man stuck, all right. He was very calm. His head, shoulders, and arms were projecting from under the floor of the elevator. His arms were outspread.

[37]

"Any pain?" I asked.

"Hell no, Doc," he said. "But my pants leg is caught in the cable, and I can't get an arm in to free it."

I tried to look beneath the car floor, but it was too dark to see anything. I studied the men present. The only one I could find who was rangy enough was Jack, my driver. My favorite driver. Medium tall, he had long arms and legs and I knew he was an athlete. It was not his business—unless he volunteered.

Jack saw me looking at him. He dead-panned and with his mouth hardly moving said, "Okay, Doc. Just see the firemen hold my legs." He stripped to his undershirt, got on his knees, and pushed his head and shoulders through the space beneath the elevator.

"Don't get killed," I warned him. "I'd hate driving that big cab back to the hospital."

He squirmed in a few more inches. "I've got it," he mumbled. "Somebody get me a scissors or knife." One of the firemen was quick to oblige.

We couldn't see the driver's arms, but we knew from his movements that he was working hard.

"I'm free!" shouted the repairman.

The firemen hauled both men to the floor.

"Look," said the repairman, "my pants are ruined. What'll I tell the wife?"

We all applauded Jack. He almost grinned.

By this time some of the residents had appeared. I got permission to use someone's phone.

"Come on!" I hated to hurry my driver away from a hero's glory, but I had to. "We've got another call. Seems there's a baby that wants to be born. Let's get the mother to the hospital. Then we can stop for some coffee."

Jack pulled on his shirt and his uniform jacket. He brushed himself carefully, and we were off.

We arrived at a Ninth Avenue tenement to find a woman in active labor. My examination showed that she should be delivering soon, but I wasn't sure when. It might take six hours, but then again it might take only one.

The interns disliked delivering women at home. Sometimes we would have to sit and wait for a long time. The burden of incoming calls would be heaped onto the other interns. Worse, there was a standing rule that if a woman delivered in the ambulance, the intern would have to buy a keg of bootleg beer for the rest of the staff.

I stood uncertain.

"We going to wait, Doc?" Jack asked.

"Not if I can help it," I decided. "Not after what you've been through this morning. Get her into the bus. We'll be at the hospital in ten minutes."

We started off with a lurch. Jack opened his sliding window to give us better ventilation. He hit some bumps. Hard.

I shouted, "By God, this woman's just had her baby!"

Jack slowed down and yelled back at me, "What did you expect her to have, Doc, a dogfight?" Silence for a moment. "Gee, Doc," he said, "that beer will sure taste good. Which speak you want to buy it at?"

We could have bought the beer at any of a dozen speakeasies in our area. We stopped at one on Fifty-second Street and loaded the keg in with mother and child.

❖ ❖ ❖

Riding the ambulance I got to know most of the policemen attached to the Eighteenth and Twentieth precincts. I met them at all hours and in many places. In hundreds of contacts with the police I never met an ill-tempered patrolman. They gave all possible consideration to the patients and to the doctors on the ambulances.

Jimmy Goodwin became a real friend. He had been in the Eighteenth Precinct for almost twenty years and was soon to put in for retirement, but he'd lost none of his physical prowess or quickness of movement. He was waiting for me at one call on Fifty-seventh Street.

"There's a sick woman two flights up," he told me. "I just came down to phone you, and I left the door open." He leaned against the iron handrail that led up to the main entrance. "Take it easy, Doc, so I can get a few drags on a cigarette."

I agreed to take my time and signaled my driver to bring my bag. Jack was a good-looking young fellow with an expressionless face. He seldom displayed emotion, and he spoke with hardly any movement of his mouth. As I knew from his earlier heroics, his apparent sullenness hid a generous heart. He had a real desire to help whenever possible. He carried my bag up the two flights and left it at the open door.

I knocked and entered a rectangular chamber, twenty by thirty, once the parlor of a luxury apartment. The present tenant had transformed the parlor into her bedroom by the simple expedient of moving in a bed and a wardrobe. There were few closets in these old apartments anyway. Clothes were simply kept in an armoire or a dresser.

The patient didn't greet me. She was lying in an enormous bed that had a heavy mahogany headboard. She had a fixed stare. I looked around the room. The furniture was expensive but not old enough to be antique. It was all dark and antedated the turn of the century. The patient didn't seem to be in a hurry. I wasn't either.

The woman, sallow and tall, lay in the center of the bed. Because of its width, I could only reach her by kneeling on the bed. The situation reminded me of one of my mentors, a brilliant doctor named Harlow Brooks. He was a short man and often knelt on patients' beds to do a thorough examination. His patients suffered cascades of pens and pencils and whatever else was in his vest pockets.

This patient was not forthcoming about her trouble. "What's bothering you?" I asked. She continued to stare. "I wish you would tell me if anything hurts you." At last she spoke. "I just don't feel well."

Suddenly she leapt out of bed, waving a kitchen knife. She looked as if she were engaged in some sort of ritual dance. But then she crawled across the bed in my direction, knife flashing. If this was a ritual, I was meant to be the sacrifice. I abandoned my bag and headed for the door, which I had left ajar.

As I dashed into the hall I let out the loudest yell I could muster. "Jimmee!" I shouted. I started down the stairs, the woman after me, and I was gratified to hear someone running up. Jimmy Goodwin passed me without a word and wrestled with the woman behind me. They fell, and down the stairs came Jimmy, the patient, and the kitchen knife.

I arrived at the bottom of the stairs—two flights down—at the same time as the knife. All eight inches of it clattered to the floor. I kicked it to the back of the hall as Jimmy and the patient, tangled together, hit the bottom step. By this time Jack had grabbed the seldom-used straitjacket from the ambulance. The three of us were able to hold the poor woman, pinion her arms, and strap up the jacket behind her.

She went on struggling, her long legs free. We dragged her to the ambulance through a gathering crowd.

"Anybody know this lady?" Jimmy asked, breathlessly. One woman spoke up.

"I know her. She lives across the hall from me. She peeks out the door, but I don't think she's left her room for years. We pass a few words. I order her food for her. When she came to the door this morning I could see she was sick, and I called the police."

Jimmy poised his pencil over his notebook.

"Does she have any relatives?"

"Nobody I know of," answered the neighbor.

Jack got into his seat. His expression hadn't changed in all the excitement. Jimmy said, "I'd better go with you, Doc. You going to Bellevue?" I said, "Yes," and he clambered into the rear of the ambulance and closed the doors on the crowd.

We stopped at the nearest police phone so that Jimmy could report and be released from his beat until we brought him back. Then we headed for the Psychiatric Division of Bellevue Hospital.

There was a belief among many of the interns and practicing physicians at the time that the Psychiatric Division would not accept a patient without previous consultation with a psychiatrist —unless the patient was brought across a certain line in the concrete at the entrance to the hospital. This was somehow supposed to protect the hospital from a charge of kidnapping. If an outsider took the patient across that line, the patient could be accepted on the responsibility of his deliverer. How true this belief was I never discovered. Of course, they took the poor woman right in.

On the way back Jack slid open the window behind the driver's seat. We gulped the fresh air. Jimmy said, "Doc, stop at Mc-Queen's speak and I'll buy you a beer." Jack looked back with a big smile on his face. It was always a pleasure to be treated at a speakeasy by the cop who was supposed to arrest you. "Include me in," he said.

*　　*　　*

The large ships at the piers also used our ambulance services, but only in event of a sudden, unexplained, or violent death. They had their own medical staff on board, but cases of sudden death had by law to be examined by us and then certified by the coroner. On an urgent call near the end of my internship, we arrived at the entrance to the pier where a giant vessel of the North German Lloyd Line was berthed. My driver dickered with a couple of guards and two policemen, then shoved aside his back window and said, "Doc, they want us on the ship. Is that our job?"

Above the din of loading and unloading and the grinding of machinery I shouted back at him, "If they want us, that's where we belong." He drove us down the pier to the gangway.

As we approached I saw a number of tugs with steam up, waiting to pull the mammoth ship into the stream. I also saw the Nazi flag, the crooked cross, hanging from her stern.

No visitors were being allowed near the gangway. They were herded in disgruntled groups behind hastily erected barricades. The guards let no one on board. They cleared a path for our slow progress through the crowd. My driver was careful not to brush against anyone.

A group of harassed ship's officers in uniform stood near the top of the gangplank. At their feet lay the body of a large man. He was obviously dead.

[42]

I went up first. Then came my driver and a policeman, who was good enough to carry my bag. He wanted to see the excitement, too.

The ship's ranking doctor greeted me crisply. He was covered with gold braid. "*Guten tag,*" I said, in my best singsong Viennese accent. He answered in English: "This fellow was waving good-bye to someone when he grabbed his chest and fell. Please certify him quickly so that we can move the body and sail." Stalling, I asked for a small stool so that I would not have to get on my knees to examine the body. One of the officers gave a quick order, and a subofficer started to run.

My experiences in Vienna had given me first-hand evidence of the growing power of the Nazis. I had felt there was nothing I could do over there; now I hatched a plan. On the piers, time is money; it costs to keep one's ship in the harbor, to hire the tugs to take it out of port, to pay the dockworkers and standby long-shoremen. Every minute I delayed was money out of Nazi pockets.

"As soon as I'm sure he's dead I'll notify the coroner," I told the doctor. "He has to give permission to move the body."

"Hurry then, please. It costs money to stay here."

"As soon as my stool comes," I said.

My stool came, causing a flurry of moving braid. I opened the man's shirt and listened. I insisted that his jacket be removed and rolled up his shirt sleeves before I applied my sphygmomanometer to determine the absence or presence of blood pressure. I applied the instrument to both arms. I did everything thoroughly and deliberately. And slowly. As I worked I kept thinking: Let the Nazis pay for it.

More braid came onto the deck. The Big Braid said, "Doctor, we've got to sail. We were already late when this man died. Do your work fast, please."

I continued my examination. My most important finding was that the liner was flying the Nazi flag.

There was rushing and scurrying. Big Braid said to an assistant, "Get the captain."

There was a period of expectancy. Then arrived the Biggest Braid of all. There were whispered explanations. "Doctor," the captain said to me, "if you don't hurry, I'll have to call your superior."

"You do that," I answered. "His name is Finkelstein."

Finally my examination was finished. Down the gangplank I went, leisurely, followed by my amused driver and a bemused cop.

At the foot of the gangplank the driver said, "Say, Doc, don't you think we ought to call the coroner?"

"We will," I said. "Right after we've had our lunch."

*　　　*　　　*

Jack and I stopped off at a one-armed restaurant in Columbus Circle. It was a cold night, and the wind sweeping in from the river bit into all parts of the body it could reach: the wrists and ankles, the face. We wanted hot oatmeal and some coffee before we returned to the hospital.

My taciturn young driver was late in joining me. When he came in from the ambulance he seemed troubled. He stuttered over his order, slopped his coffee carrying it from the counter, and fussed over the bowl of hot cereal resting on the expanded arm of his chair, the arm that gave the one-armed joint its name. The arm was shaped like a tennis racket or small tray, and it served as a table. There were no tables in a one-armed restaurant.

I asked Jack why he was so nervous. He paused and then said, "Doc, a fellow told me his girl is sick, and can we go see her?" He was nervous because he'd volunteered my services, and without a call to the police.

"I don't see why not," I answered. "Who's your friend?"

"I don't know his name. He spoke to me when we pulled up in the bus. She's right near here. He said he'd wait for us there."

Columbus Circle was really a circle in those days. It was surrounded by three- and four-story buildings, many boarded up except for a few decrepit stores at street level. There was one ancient theater that I remembered from long past. Its facade was crisscrossed with boards. I'd been brought to New York once on a visit and taken to see a movie there. It was a long newsreel of the action on the Eastern Front during the First World War.

I was then about nine years old, and the adults thought—correctly—that I would like such a film. The movies in those days were called flickers, and flicker they did. The armies marched with rapid movements: jerk, jerk, jerk. There were scenes of a dogfight between two biplanes, one of which fell in flames. Smoke rose in the distance where the shells of big guns had set a village afire. Men ran twitching back and forth. Bodies lay where they had fallen, and occasionally a soldier would throw his gun into the air and tumble to the ground. It was an exciting, moving film with climaxes augmented by the piano player, who joined wholeheartedly in the melee. I didn't believe I was watching men fighting and dying. It must have been one of the world's first long-run newsreels, with subtitles to explain the action. It gave me something to talk about when I got home to Virginia.

Here I was, at three o'clock on a cold morning, going back into the same theater. Only this time I was going into a side entrance, up a dusty flight of stairs, led by a strange, thin young man and followed by Jack, who carried my bag.

The young man took us down an even dustier hallway into a room with an open door. There was a mattress on the floor and a Fairy Soap soapbox to sit on. "Have you a little fairy in your home?" the soapbox asked. Lying on the mattress was a big-eyed, frightened girl, perhaps twenty years old. She extended a hand so thin it seemed nearly translucent. She shivered with cold. Jack took off his foul-weather coat and threw it over her. She looked starved.

I had heard her story in other forms many times before. "I'm from Lincoln, Nebraska," she said. "I thought I could get a job in the theater. There weren't any jobs. I tried for any sort of job. There weren't any of those either."

"When did you eat last?"

"I had some bread and milk yesterday," she told me. "Then I ran out of money. I've lived here for a couple of weeks." She pointed to the young man. "He was good enough to find me this mattress, even though we hardly knew each other."

"I thought you were his girl?"

"I told the driver that," the young man confessed. "I was afraid you wouldn't come."

"Would you like to come to the hospital with me?" I asked the girl.

"I'd hate it."

"That's a good girl. Can you walk down a flight of stairs?"

"I'll try."

We helped her into the ambulance, and I made her lie down on the stretcher. I took the young man along, too.

"I can't admit you," I told him, "but I can bum a meal for you, and here's the fare to come back on the Fifty-ninth Street car." I gave him what change I had.

At the hospital I admitted the girl with a diagnosis of pneumonia, which I knew she didn't have. That would make them keep her for at least three days. In the meantime she would have a real bed and hot meals and could recover her strength. I knew the visiting doctor in charge of the ward would be very displeased to have a bed for acutely ill patients occupied by someone who was not acutely ill. But my answer would be simple. "What the hell do I know? I'm only an intern."

Jack stood waiting for me with his newfound friend.

"Thanks, Doc," he said.

"Come on, you two. Let's go down and have a real breakfast. And after that," I told my driver, "I'm going to kill you."

*   *   *

The interns' dining room at the old Flower Hospital at Sixty-fourth Street and York Avenue was small, so small that not more than a dozen men could be seated at a time. That didn't matter because we ate irregularly and seldom used all the seats. Usually there were also a few practicing doctors who had missed their lunch or dinner because of emergency work or operations.

A number of medical men ate there regularly. I thought nothing of it until one day a sign appeared on the bulletin board stating that no staff member was allowed to eat in that dining room unless his work actually required him to be at the hospital at mealtimes.

I asked a fellow intern why such a sign was posted.

He mentioned the names of two doctors. "Hadn't you noticed? They eat practically all their meals here. They do it to save money. They also save up all their outside phone calls and make them from the doctors' room upstairs. Maybe they don't earn enough to pay their room and board."

A man specializing in urology overheard us.

"You young fellows don't feel it yet, but the Depression has hit a lot of us hard. I practiced general medicine for ten years and then quit to study urology. In six years of work I thought I'd built up a pretty good urological practice. Then came October 29, 1929. My practice just seemed to dissolve.

"Patients can't afford to go to their family doctors and then to specialists, except in the most urgent cases. If there are procedures they can postpone, they postpone them. If surgery is optional, it isn't done. Right now I'm looking at small towns on Long Island. I'm going to open a general practice. I must say it's a change from the boom of the twenties.

"Don't be too harsh in your judgment. People have had a hard time. And nobody knows how long this will last, Roosevelt or no Roosevelt."

He smiled at us, lest we think he had been too stern. "You've heard the saying that's making the rounds: 'Because of the Depression the doctors are going back to their practices, and the businessmen back to their wives.'"

*　　*　　*

Bobby Longo, the emergency room nurse, gave me a cold stare. "Don't you try to leave early," she said. "The other buses are out. We're getting a lot of sick calls. I've got two now, in the same neighborhood. They're yours."

I couldn't have left early if I'd wanted to. Bobby's great dark eyes pinned me to the wall. She was a beautiful girl to look at, with her pitch-black hair and olive skin.

It was 6:30 P.M. I had hoped to sneak out before seven. Sick calls often didn't take long. It was customary for the police dispatcher to tell us whether a call was for an accident or for some-

[47]

one who was ill. Accidents could take hours, but sick calls could be handled quickly.

Jack was waiting at the ambulance. "Where to, this time?" He really didn't care. He had had plenty of sleep.

I studied the slips Bobby had handed me. One said something about three children; the other just gave an address. I remembered the old doctor's advice from the lectern: If you have two calls and one is to a child, go to the child first, or he may be well before you get there.

I gave the driver the address of the children.

It was a brownstone in the lower Sixties, near Broadway. The apartment was three flights up, with a bonus flight from the street to the first floor. There was a large, hollow stairwell.

A man leaned over the railing and called down, "Don't hurry, Doctor. I hope I didn't get you here for nothing." He started down the stairs. "The children are better. They stopped vomiting and they've fallen asleep."

"Here I am anyhow," I said, starting up, "I might as well look in on them."

"Leave the bag there," he said. "I'll take it."

My driver was glad to be relieved of it. It was a heavy leather bag, packed for all sorts of emergencies. On a busy day it became a real burden.

As we met on the stairs the man and I stopped to talk. He introduced himself. "I'm a musician, at liberty," he said. "I don't like to ask for free service, but my play closed six weeks ago, after a two-week run." He laughed. I liked the man. We strolled upward.

"My wife thought the children were listless today. But they didn't look too bad, and she had to go to work anyway. They really got sick after she left. Retching, vomiting. It was some mess: all three sick at once."

"Sounds like food poisoning," I said. "What did they eat today?"

"Cereal for breakfast, with milk. Eggs for lunch, milk again. Crackers. Some jam."

"That doesn't sound bad. What did they have for supper?"

"None of them ate any. They were too sick."

For the moment I gave up on food poisoning. But the musician went on, "My wife worked last night, too. So I opened a can of that Argentine beef to make it easy. They all ate that, but I didn't. . ."

I heard him, but I didn't want to hear him. His story of Argentine beef, canned Argentine beef, hit me almost like a physical blow. I asked two questions at once: "Where did you get the beef? Where are the children?"

"The city gives it to the unemployed. The children are there." He pointed to an open door, and I dashed through it.

In the closest bedroom two children lay in bed. The nearest was a boy of perhaps six. His head and shoulders hung over the side of the mattress. I put him flat on the bed. "My God," I cried. "He's not asleep! He's dead!"

I ran to the other side of the bed and lifted up a three-year-old. A quick examination told me that he was beyond my help. "This child is dead, too! Where's the third one?"

The father, speechless and unbelieving, pointed to another room. I ran there.

This child, about four, was in a profuse sweat. He was cold but breathing faintly. Still alive! I covered him with a blanket from the foot of the bed, threw him over my shoulder, and ran into the next room.

The man stood there shocked and silent, the smaller dead child in his arms.

"I'm taking this child to Roosevelt Hospital," I shouted. "Come when you can!" I didn't think the child would live long enough to reach the hospital; I tried not to think at all. My brain couldn't encompass the tragedy.

I made for the stairs. The father stood in my way. He was deranged and wouldn't let me pass.

"Try to take him away and I'll kill you," he said. He pushed me back from the doorway. The arms and legs of the dead child he was carrying dangled.

I rushed at the father, struck him with my shoulder, and knocked him out of the way; then ran downstairs and into the ambulance.

"Roosevelt," I said to the driver. "Hurry! For God's sake, use the siren!"

When we reached the hospital six blocks away I rushed the

little limp body to the emergency room. Nurses and interns gathered round to help. It was too late. Gently they took the dead child from my arms.

I reported what had happened as best I could, and then I sat for a long time in a chair in the emergency room, trying to erase the tragedy from my mind. The images wouldn't go away. I felt a terrible helplessness. A nurse handed me a jigger of whiskey. "Go home," she told me. I phoned Belle. I just spoke her name. "Something terrible's happened to you," she said.

Weary, I telephoned Bobby Longo. I'd found the second of her two slips in my pocket, the one that just gave an address. "Give the call to someone else," I said. Someone waited a long time that day to see a doctor. I remembered the heavy leather bag, ready for an emergency but useless in this one. I asked Bobby to have it collected in the morning.

The authorities at Roosevelt Hospital would call the coroner and alert the Health Department. My driver dropped me off at the entrance to the subway in Times Square. I would be home in an hour.

Belle came to the door with a basin of hot, soapy water and a fresh towel. "Death may not enter the house of life," she said. I washed and dried my hands and kissed her. She had little use for orthodox customs, but she often said she felt some sense in this one, the washing of hands after a burial. Where she got the phrase about the house of life I do not know.

We went for a walk on the beach. She had many questions.

"I thought maybe they had an intestinal flu. The symptoms of botulism don't appear right away. It's twelve to twenty-four hours before they do. That's too late to pump the stomach.

"It's caused by an organism that gets into badly cooked or canned food. The organism forms a poison that attacks the nervous system. The symptoms? Sometimes there's vomiting, but not always. Double vision. And paralysis of the muscles. What people die of is respiratory failure. The muscles of the chest wall fail. More than half the victims die. The rest get well, but slowly. It depends on the quantity of poison they took in. And of course these were children; the harmful dose would be smaller."

"There are five or six different strains of the organism, and there are antidotes for strains A and B. We give them together, as soon as we can. But we only give them to prevent further paralysis. The antidote doesn't reverse the damage. In some cases the damage recedes by itself.

"What could we have done for the little one? All we could have done was to give him the antidotes, maintain his body fluids, and give him oxygen to try to ease his breathing. But it was too late."

"You told them that beef from the Argentine was probably the cause?" Belle asked.

"I reported to the hospital. They reported to the Health Department. Right away."

"You did the very best you could," she said.

"It wasn't good enough."

I saw no mention of the three deaths in the paper. There was no outbreak of botulism in the city. I never heard of the case again, but I knew that I would never be able to forget it.

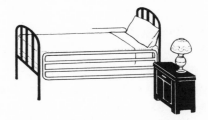

INTERNSHIP
On the Wards

FROM AMBULANCE DUTY I transferred to the wards. Service in the medical, surgical, and obstetrical wards was so busy that days ran into nights and nights into days again, with interns hardly knowing which was which. Our interest in the patients was intense, and the patients returned the interest. It was common to hear a patient ask, "Don't you ever sleep?" The only answer we could give was, "Hardly ever."

It was fascinating to see the reports of tests we had done and to watch the condition of the patients change, usually for the better. Usually, but not always. We had our disappointments and our tragedies.

It was in the surgical ward that I came across a case of a disease that was to be my guileful enemy for many years. Its name was syphilis.

Mrs. Margaret Henry was a big, blowsy, blustering blonde, good-natured and lovable, who had a dreadful infection of her right arm. It was so bad that four times the surgeons had taken her to the operating room to incise and drain the abscesses that ran from her wrist to her shoulder. Since we were undermanned, I was responsible for all the patients in the ward. I tried to review every chart to see whether anything should be done that hadn't been. I was disconcerted to see that no Wasserman test, the blood test for syphilis (known also as lues), had been done on Mrs. Henry.

I had seen enough syphilis in Vienna to believe that every patient was entitled to have that test. I ordered one, and sure enough, it came back positive. Mrs. Henry had led a varied life. There was no way to trace the origin of her disease.

The chief surgeon, when he saw the result, urged me to begin immediate treatment. In those days we didn't have penicillin. Our treatment consisted of rubbing a mercury preparation into one-eighth of the body surface daily, using a different part of the body each day; injecting an arsenic preparation into the vein once a week; and giving an injection of bismuth, usually into the buttocks, also weekly. The treatment sounds harrowing. It was.

I transferred Mrs. Henry immediately to a medical ward and started treatment. The response was rapid. Within a few days her infection had disappeared, the surgical incisions had healed well, and she was sitting up at the bedside pleased with both herself and me. Rapid healing of superficial lesions following antiluetic treatment was a marvel to behold.

"Don't let them tell you there's no such thing as gratitude, Doc," she said to me. "I was sick for months and you've cured me. I think you're wonderful and I've told everybody. If you open an office anywhere near New York, I'll be your patient."

A few days later she left the hospital. I advised her to continue her treatment for at least a year at any place convenient for her. She understood and promised to cooperate. I did open my office in New York, and before the year was out she had become my private patient.

I determined that every patient of mine except infants and children should have a Wasserman test every year. It paid off. I disclosed many cases that had been overlooked and was able to diagnose many syphilitic patients whose symptoms were baffling. Because its symptoms resemble the symptoms of many other diseases, syphilis was known as the Great Masquerader.

Syphilis is a disease caused by a spirochete, a microscopic bacterium shaped like a corkscrew. This little organism—transmitted mainly, but not always, through sexual intercourse—invades the linings of the blood vessels, particularly the smaller ones and the aorta at its origin. By occluding or damaging them, it interferes with the blood supply to many parts of the body. No system of the body is immune, and thus syphilis can cause any type of symptom. I knew a surgeon who got a primary syphilitic lesion of the finger from operating on a patient who had the disease.

The causative little beast was supposed by many to have been taken to the Old World by the men of Christopher Columbus's crew, who were infected by sexual contact with the West Indian islanders.

It may have been in Europe before. Some students of the disease believe that vestiges of pathology from syphilis have been found in Egyptian mummies.

If the Amerinds had syphilis, it existed in an endemic form to which the natives had developed an immunity. If it had been in the Old World before, the Europeans had no immunity when Columbus returned. It rapidly became epidemic. The list of historic figures who suffered and died from the disease reads like a *Who's Who.*

Treatment up to the nineteenth century consisted mainly of inunctions of mercury. The treatment of rubbing mercury into the skin lasted for years, and there were often serious side effects from the drug. The saying was: one night in the arms of Venus, ten years in the arms of Mercury.

Since the wide use of penicillin G against many infections, the spirochete has fought a losing battle. People who've had penicillin injections for other diseases retain some effect from the drug in their bodies that seems to immunize them against syphilis. Despite newspaper scareheads, new cases reported annually since the middle of the twentieth century have dropped tremendously. Today new cases are found mainly in homosexual or bisexual males. But everyone should be watched for the disease.

I continued to take Wasserman tests on every new patient, and annually on all other patients. When I lectured on physical diagnosis at the medical school I ended each talk with the admonition to take a Wasserman test on every patient.

The students asked, "Should we take a Wasserman test on a priest?" My answer was: "Yes, take it on a priest. Take it on your grandmother!" Some of my confreres laughed at my stubborn consistency. One said the reason I had such a large practice in syphilis was that I was in the theatrical district. I thought that a snide remark. There was some acid in their comments. It was probably because I had the fascinating practice everyone wanted.

✿ ✿ ✿

Obstetrics was later to become a big part of my practice. Much that I learned in that field was taught to me by the obstetrical nurses on the wards. They had seen hundreds of cases to my very few, and they were pleased to have an intern who was willing to learn. They were smart women, and I would have been silly not to listen to them. But I felt like a king once when a student nurse in the nursery ran to tell me that a newly delivered child had poor color. Did the child need oxygen? I told her to go to the ward to look at the mother. The mother was a black woman. Many black children have a purplish appearance at birth. At least I knew something one nurse didn't know.

✿ ✿ ✿

Early one morning—too early—the chief obstetrical nurse called. "Dr. Crump wants you in obstetrics."

I had just gotten into bed with my clothes on, hoping to have a few hours' sleep before the next case. I had been delivering babies since early morning, and it was early morning again. I looked at my watch. Three-thirty, it said.

Our hospital had grown haphazardly. We had taken over adjacent tenements and cut doors through where necessary. I was on the fourth floor. So was the obstetrical area, but not on the same fourth floor. I had to go down three flights to go up another three. We had no elevators in the tenements.

I stumbled into the dressing room, where Dr. Crump was waiting for me. This short, brisk man with a snowy-white goatee was

[55]

a surgeon much admired by everyone, particularly by me. "I know you've had a long day," he said, "but I especially wanted you."

I felt flattered and instantly alert. Dr. Crump handled people well.

Dr. Walter Gray Crump headed one of our three surgical staffs. He was an estimable gentleman from a New England family of responsibility, a family that owned a bell foundry. He was a man of wide reading and keen observation. He once stopped an intricate operation to ask his intern, "Why does the aspen make a rainy sound?" The intern mumbled. Dr. Crump said, "Simple. Because the leaves grow at right angles to the stem." He then proceeded with the surgery.

I assisted Dr. Crump once when he performed a tonsillectomy on an adult male. When he had finished he said, "Don't go away, Dr. Slocum. Turn the patient prone on the table. Jackknife him. I'm going to do a hemorrhoidectomy." And he did.

I was surprised that he was to do something as routine as a delivery. He was a man who had started his practice before the turn of the century. In his time he had done everything in the surgical field. He knew what could be accomplished and what couldn't be. I was delighted to work with him.

"We have a hard case," he said. "The woman's been in labor thirty-six hours. The baby's head is at the vulva, but it's too large to get through." An exhausted woman in her thirties lay on the delivery table.

Dr. Crump signaled to the anesthetist. "Put her under." He did an episiotomy. Then he said, "Now, Nurse, I am going to put these forceps on. Dr. Slocum will take me around the waist and pull me as hard as he can. You put your arms around his waist and pull him as hard as you can."

He applied the blades of the forceps to the infant's head. I should have thought anyone else was going to extremes, but not Dr. Crump. He always knew what he was doing.

He began to pull. I pulled him. The nurse pulled me. The head of the baby moved ever so slightly, then emerged suddenly. The forceps clattered to the floor. The nurse and I fell back against the wall in a heap. Dr. Crump stood there with a newborn in his arms.

As we disentangled ourselves, Dr. Crump said, "Get me a scalpel and a probe." I looked. The forceps had left a concavity in the soft bones of the baby's skull.

Still cradling the baby in his left arm, the doctor made a small incision into the skull, inserted the probe, and forced the bones of the skull back into position. He surveyed his handiwork.

"That will do it," he announced.

        ✿   ✿   ✿

The hospital had three surgical services. It was the custom for the interns to spend at least one month on each. This did not preclude them from scrubbing in, with the permission of the surgeon, on any interesting case. There were also attending doctors who practiced full time and always needed one or more assistants when they came in to operate.

I had just finished taking a medical history and doing a physical examination on a wealthy patient who lived in Baltimore but had become ill at his hotel the night before. His friends had recommended a surgeon who was as well known for his large fees as for his excellent technique.

The surgeon walked into the room.

"What do you think, Doctor?" the patient asked him.

"All I know," said the surgeon, "is that you have an abdomen that should be explored. You may not even need surgery, but if you do need it and we don't do it, you'll be in trouble. If you do need it, we can probably take care of it."

A moment of silence. "All right. What will you charge?"

"Two thousand dollars," the surgeon answered. That was an enormous fee for those days.

"Can't you charge half that?"

"Of course I can," the surgeon answered. "Then I'll do half the operation."

The patient accepted the original fee, and paid it.

Within an hour the patient was on the table prepared for the operation. It was always gratifying to watch the expertness of the nurses as they draped the patients, used cut-out sheets to expose the area slated for surgery, washed the abdomen after every particle of hair had been removed, and then applied an antiseptic solution with swabs held in hemostats. "Paint what you see," the surgeons told them.

A nurse from the floor came into the operating room. "The patient's wife is outside the hospital on her hands and knees praying," she told us. "A crowd is gathering. Shall I have someone talk to her?"

The surgeon thought for a moment. "Tell her her prayers will be answered," he ordered.

"How do you know he's going to make it?" I asked.

"How do I know what she's praying for?" he replied.

He turned to me. "Dr. Slocum, what do you think?"

"Last night I went back to the books," I admitted. "The commonest problems are ruptured peptic ulcer and acute diseases of the biliary system. But he may also have a thrombus of the blood vessels that supply the digestive tract, or even acute pancreatitis. His symptoms were pain and acute shock, which we countered with fluids. His blood pressure has stabilized. He has only a slight fever and a slight rise in his white cell count, and his serum analysis is normal. We could get those findings even after a meal. He's been comfortable since, but I couldn't overlook his history of generalized abdominal pain and rigidity. And I saw he had a tendency to draw his legs up to relieve abdominal tension."

"Now you see, that's exactly why we're going in to look," said the surgeon, palpating the abdomen. "He may have any or none of these things. If it's a surgical condition, I'll try to remedy it. If it's acute pancreatitis that seems to be subsiding, I'm merely going to turn him over to your tender mercy. Hand me the scalpel, please."

This surgeon was a fine technician. He went through the skin, subcutaneous tissue, and musculature with one stroke, exposing the peritoneum, the sac covering all the internal organs. There was a darkish color to the membrane. Palpation disclosed no stones.

"I think he didn't need the surgery," said the surgeon. "I believe he had an attack of acute pancreatitis."

The pancreas is an elongated organ that extends horizontally across the abdomen, mainly to the left of the midline. It produces insulin, which reaches the body through the walls of its blood vessels. The pancreas also produces many other fluids that are essential for digestion. Some fluids reach the intestinal tract through a duct, called the pancreatic duct. Occlusion of the duct by a gallstone, thick bile, or other substances within or outside of the pancreas can cause pancreatitis.

There are other causes of pancreatitis, alcohol being the most common, but I knew this patient belonged to a religious group that didn't imbibe. He wasn't fanatic, but his wife was. I gathered that she overpowered him.

The surgeon finished his incision into the peritoneum.

"It's acute pancreatitis," he confirmed, turning from the table and removing his gloves. "Sew him up, feed him very lightly, and take care of him."

He left the operating room and did not return at any time to see the patient. The next morning I called him on the phone. "I'm not coming to see that man," he informed me. "When a man of obvious wealth fights me about my fee I lose interest in him. He'll get well."

I took care of the patient for the next three weeks and discharged him as cured. He and his wife—particularly his wife—were lavish in their praise and promised that when he was ready to leave the hospital they would have a wonderful gift for me. I hoped it was money. Many patients, knowing that nurses got little pay and interns less, would leave gifts of cash in appreciation. In most institutions the student nurses paid to be students.

I told this patient one day that he was to be discharged the next morning. That evening the intern who relieved me was pressured to discharge him and did. My patient was gone when I returned to duty. I never saw the gift.

There is a law of retribution. Sometime after I had opened my office, both this gentleman and his wife became ill. They believed that God had sent them to me in the first place, and that there was no higher authority. So they moved from Baltimore to a magnificent suite in a New York hotel and called me. I took care of them, but this time I collected. In advance. It was the will of God.

❋   ❋   ❋

Dr. Francis Xavier Honan headed another surgical staff. He was a fine surgeon who had a practice that included many titled people from the British Isles, mainly from Ireland. He had one defect. He was good-natured. Whenever a qualified surgeon asked for admission to his staff, Dr. Honan would take him on.

This was not good for the interns. When Dr. Honan operated, three or four men already in private practice would scrub to assist. The interns had difficulty getting close to the table. When they did, the elbows of the staff men would swing back. The interns would be fortunate to escape with only bruises, not fractured ribs. With so many pushing doctors around the table it was difficult to get close enough even to see the operative field. Dr. Honan was too gentle a man to ask anyone to leave the table.

Dr. Honan always left two pairs of spectacles in the cabinet at the entrance to the operating room. When he was scheduled to operate the nurses would sterilize these along with the instruments. The good doctor would be so intent on his work that his glasses would almost invariably fall into the wound. The circulating nurse would calmly fish the glasses out and fit another pair onto his nose. But he was a careful surgeon, and his patients did well.

❋   ❋   ❋

The superintendent of the hospital came down to the wards to find me.

"Dr. Slocum," he said hesitantly, "I've come to ask you a favor."

"If I can I shall," I told him. "How much do you need?" He knew that money was the least of the things I had.

"I'm hunting for someone to help me with Dr. Batting." The superintendent was a big man who usually got his way.

"What about Dr. Batting?" I was suspicious. Dr. Batting was a neurosurgeon who brought a lot of work to the hospital and was responsible for a disproportionate amount of its operating room income.

"Well, it's this way," said the superintendent, trying to soothe me before springing the trap. "I'm having trouble getting an intern to work with him. Everyone stays a few days and then quits."

"I'm not surprised. He has the foulest temper of anyone I've ever met. I said good morning to him one day, and he looked through me as if I didn't exist."

"You know my problem." The superintendent sighed. "If I can't get him an assistant, he'll take his patients to some other hospital and we'll lose a lot of revenue. He always has a dozen patients in the hospital, and every patient is surgical. It would be a hardship to lose him."

"I know he has a big reputation," I answered. "I know how many patients he has here. He could use his own floor if you gave it to him. But what do you want of me?"

"Dr. Slocum, you're the most even-tempered man we've ever had here. I know you can handle him and his disposition." (The trap was closing.) "Besides, it will give you the opportunity to see a lot of brain surgery that you probably wouldn't otherwise see for years." (The trap had been sprung.)

Because the last sentence was true, I was in no position to refuse. Dr. Batting did as many brain operations in a day as most neurosurgeons would do in a month. I had been told that he liked his assistant to do all the preparatory and closing work and would turn the operation over to him at any time if he thought the younger man was capable.

The fly in the ointment (there's always a fly in the ointment) was that the man was working on a theory of his own that was not accepted by most other neurosurgeons.

Dr. Batting had had wide experience handling head injuries in the Great War. He had noticed that an attack resembling epilepsy could sometimes be induced by traction on adhesions that had developed between the convoluted inner surface of the skull cap and the meninges—the membrane covering the brain—or between the meninges and the brain itself. He reasoned that epilepsy could be cured by destroying the adhesions, which were like very thin cellophane strips. In order to prevent regrowth of the adhesions, he would insert a thin metal plate to take the place of the portion of the skull cap he'd removed.

Epilepsy was then, and to some extent unfortunately still is today, a socially demeaning disease, and it is often a dangerous one. In its most drastic form it causes the patient to lose consciousness and to fall. There follows a tonic spasm. The muscles become rigid, and sometimes the patient stops breathing for some seconds. The jaws clench, the limbs stiffen. This, in turn, is followed by a clonic spasm, during which the tonicity disappears. There is an alternating contraction and relaxation of the muscles. The time of the spasms varies but can usually be measured in minutes.

The different forms of epilepsy are widely diverse in severity and duration. The treatment during the harsh attacks is aimed at preventing the patient from injuring himself. This is not always possible since the coma may arrive suddenly and the patient will fall wherever he is with no chance to put out a protecting hand.

Dr. Batting had published articles about his treatment, and the articles attracted public attention. Since there was no real remedy for epilepsy, he received inquiries from everywhere, and patients came to him from all over the world.

While it may seem strange, the surgery was painless (the brain has no pain receptors) and the patient could be conscious throughout the entire procedure. Following the surgery the patient was arrayed in a prearranged turban, put to bed for twenty-four hours, and afterward was allowed to amble freely through the corridors. As far as possible all of these patients were placed on one floor, and it was common to see a group of turbaned men and women together discussing symptoms of the past and hopes for the future. What the statistics were I no longer recall, but since many epileptics have attacks at infrequent intervals—some even years apart—I doubt whether a statistical record would be of scientific value.

This treatment of Dr. Batting's was apparently not the answer to the puzzle of epilepsy. Had it been, doctors would have leaped at the chance to use it. Doctors are always on the alert for new and helpful remedies. Consider how penicillin, when it was released by the armed forces, became instantly and universally used.

The superintendent introduced me to Dr. Batting, who had already seen me dozens of times. Dr. Batting acknowledged me with a grunt and stared at me with the eyes of a dead fish. Since he didn't extend a hand, I didn't either. We met again the following morning in the operating room.

I knew the procedure exactly, having gone over it with the unhappy nurses assigned to assist him. As he watched, I had the patient's head shaved completely, inspecting it to make certain not one bristle remained. The shorn area was as smooth as an egg.

Then I had the area washed thoroughly with soap and water and rewashed with an antiseptic solution. For the preparation and the entire procedure the patient was strapped comfortably upright in a specially designed chair. The chair had been created by Dr. Donald Brace, the anesthetist, a man as big and burly as Dr. Batting was small and thin.

The anesthetist was not essential, but I was always glad to have him there in case of blood pressure or cardiac changes. I actually anesthetized the surgical area with novocaine, but Dr. Brace had relaxed the patient with oral medication. The patient never felt my needle. An incision through the coverings of the scalp with retraction of the tissues disclosed the bone. There was no arcane skill required. Any clever housewife could have done the same.

Now came a procedure like cutting through ice to fish in a frozen lake.

I would mark off a rectangular area on the skull and at each of the four corners would make a burr hole with a hand drill. I would pass a thin, flexible instrument with sharp saw teeth into one hole and out another. Then I would stand back and wait for the good doctor to finish the job.

After Dr. Batting had sawed through one side of the rectangle he would withdraw the saw, do the same thing on the other side, and then repeat the procedure through the other holes until the entire piece of bone was freed from its surroundings.

Lifting out the bone, Dr. Batting would insert his finger, break down any adhesions he could feel (we call it "lysing"), and then place a rectangular piece of light metal in the exposed area. Closure was simple: drawing the tissues covering the skull over the plate, and suturing. He covered the head with a turban of bandages to shield the postoperative area. I'd supervise the lifting of the patient onto a stretcher, and Dr. Brace would go out for a cigar.

Each time we finished an operation I'd breathe a sigh of relief. The patient was safe, and so was I.

That's the way it was, day after day for a month. I doubt that more than a dozen words passed between the old man and me during any operative procedure. He was always present during the entire preparation, ready to swoop at the slightest sign of carelessness or error, but I was careful to deny him the occasion. We never spoke in the dressing room, although we changed to operating uniforms and back into our street clothes within a few feet of each other. He never said hello or goodbye, and I certainly never did. I hoped he didn't think I was being provocative.

All good things must end. For a time I had prevented the old man from blowing off steam. Finally he had to explode. I was drawing the skin edges of the patient's scalp together after surgery when Dr. Batting suddenly took umbrage. Dr. Brace, the anesthetist, had left the room, but the two nurses were present.

"Not that way, you damn fool," he shouted. He struck me hard across the knuckles with a needle holder. Let me tell you, it hurt.

I was very deliberate. I lifted the movable instrument tray from its stand and carefully threw it in his face. There was a great clatter of stainless steel as the instruments struck the floor. The drowsing patient woke for an instant, startled, and then drowsed again. Batting was aghast. The nurses were aghast. And when the blood started to trickle down from a half dozen superficial cuts, I too was aghast. The surgeon held a towel to his face and strode from the room.

As Dr. Batting entered the dressing room Dr. Brace came dashing out of it. He sized up the situation in an instant. He said, "By God, I think I've swallowed my cigar."

Word traveled rapidly along the hospital grapevine. I expected a lot of repercussions. Except for some quiet congratulations from

[64]

staff members who had been subjected to the doctor's ill temper, there seemed to be no other effects. Surprisingly, no action was taken against me. Dr. Batting continued to operate at the hospital but with his own paid assistant. If I accomplished nothing else, I made that young man's life a little easier.

One other point. I learned a great deal training under Dr. Batting. Not one bit of it has been of any use to me in the fifty years since.

❋   ❋   ❋

The termination date of my contract with the hospital was near. I had rotated from medicine to surgery to pediatrics and obstetrics. Since interns were in short supply, I returned to the emergency room and ambulance service to finish out my time. The service was so interesting I stayed beyond my contract. Gratis. Just as Joe Louis admired to fight, so I admired to work.

One morning, returning from a late call at about two o'clock, my driver and I saw another Flower Hospital ambulance at the curb, surrounded by a swarm of police cars and policemen. Curious, we pulled over and hopped out. We were in front of a club in the east Fifties.

The club was a well-known speakeasy, frequented by businessmen, theatrical figures, and mobsters. With repeal of Prohibition, it would become a nightclub, with a fine orchestra and highly paid entertainers.

My driver and I went in to find the dimly lit hall filled with men. There were policemen of every rank, photographers, well-connected politicians, and newspaper people. There were no paying customers. No one who worked there had been allowed to leave. The orchestra was still present and still playing.

The authorities were bumping into one another in the performance of their duties. On the dance floor, scattered at random, were the bodies of three men killed in a gang fight only a short time before. Handsome Dr. Saul Gordon, from the number one ambulance, his arm around a beautiful hostess, was circling slowly to the music of a waltz.

[65]

STARTING OUT

My INTERNSHIP was over. Early in 1934, Belle and I had to decide where to open an office. Belle was even more excited than I. "We have the whole wide world to choose from," she said.

I wasn't so sure. I was seeing too much of the Great Depression: too many people without food, too many children home from school for lack of shoes. Belle had more courage than I. She was sure everything would come out all right. Economic uncertainty bothered me. I was running scared.

I decided to return to the place I considered my home. I had left Virginia at the age of twelve for Baltimore and points north, but at the slightest excuse I always went back. Tidewater Virginia life could be almighty pleasant. We'd see what the situation was down there. "Good," said Belle. "And let's drive."

We visited Petersburg, Suffolk, and Norfolk. We didn't want a town the size of Richmond. That would have been too large.

The doctors we spoke to were pleasant and helpful. The consensus was that it would be all right to open an office in any one of the towns—if I were willing to be paid in kind. In fact, most of the stores in those small towns had signs that read: "No Credit." Though we accepted in good faith what we had been told by the men practicing in the vicinity, we decided to look around on our own.

I had returned often, but the country around Petersburg had changed. The Army had taken over mile after mile to the east of town. Where woods had been was now endless lawn, studded with new, clean, trim military buildings that composed Camp Lee.

I stopped the car and stood up to survey the scene. Few soldiers were visible, but there were probably thousands within the camp.

"This isn't the way I remember it," I complained to Belle. "When I was growing up the only military around here were the Petersburg Grays, the local Guard."

I was driving a Buick convertible, a borrowed beauty. It had a rumble seat and a top we could lower by hand. That gave us a good chance to see everything around us. It was winter, but fifty years ago winters in Virginia were milder. There had been no snow. We were comfortable in our open car, but the view wasn't encouraging.

We found many roadside stores boarded up and abandoned. The country looked dried out and sterile. There was little dust, although there had been a dry summer. The shrubbery and small pine trees, though green, looked desolate.

Belle was thinking. "The country around here must always have been depressed. Too much tobacco. Too many peanuts. And the Dismal Swamp is somewhere near here. There must be malaria."

She was right. My brother had had malaria every year. We used a lot of quinine.

Belle scanned the sad landscape. "The land looks used up. I'm no farmer, but maybe it needs to lie fallow. The little towns look wretched, too. I think it's going to take a long time before things begin to prosper here. It's not a very cheerful view, is it?" She sighed. "Let's go back to New York."

I turned the car around. We headed back to the main road that would take us to Richmond and the North.

As we drove northward I was regretful. "I really did want to be a country doctor."

Belle, ever practical, resolved my problem. "People are the same everywhere," she said. "So is medicine. You can be a country doctor in Manhattan."

❖   ❖   ❖

Back at the hospital in New York I rode the ambulance to finish out my last few weeks as an intern. The cops wanted to know where I'd been. I was flattered that people had missed me. I hadn't expected them to be interested, but when they heard I might open an office in the precinct they were pleased.

Among my police friends were Jimmy Goodwin, Leo Gates, Mickey Mahoney, and many others. Jimmy Goodwin was a family man, better educated than some of the others. He had graduated from high school and had had some college training.

"That's what we need in the Eighteenth Precinct, another good doctor," Jimmy said. "I'll tell the men and we'll be on the lookout for a place for you."

It was good to know I had such backing. Most of my police friends were on foot patrol. They patrolled the same beats for months on end. That meant they knew most of the residents and the residents knew them. They could provide the best word-of-mouth advertising anyone could have.

     ❖   ❖   ❖

Belle and I pored over a map of Manhattan, studying the area from Fifth Avenue to the Hudson River and from Forty-second Street to Central Park South. My wife held a magnifying glass—for my benefit. Her eyes were sharp—she never missed a thing.

The gridiron looked attractive, but no map could convey the excitement of the city or the energy of its people. The prospect of making one's place in such a metropolis could have been daunting, but that never occurred to us. We knew the city and the area well. It already seemed like home.

"This is our section," Belle said, resting her hand on the surface of the map. "I wish us good luck."

Once we had decided on Manhattan's Eighteenth Precinct Belle went from street to street, counting pedestrians. She was a smart girl and noted also which side of the street had the most foot traffic.

"If people pass often enough and see your sign often enough, some of them eventually are bound to come in," she said.

She finally decided that a likely place would be the south side of Fifty-sixth Street between Eighth and Ninth Avenues.

After I'd told them what we'd found, the police looked at the street, too. "Great street for an office," Leo Gates said. "Doc, you open there and the boys will bring you every drunk in the neighborhood." There were a lot of drunks in the neighborhood.

There was one unfortunate thing about the chosen street: no ground floor apartment was available. I still had time to serve at the hospital, so we decided to watch for vacancies and to grab the first good prospect we could find.

One day Belle called me at the hospital. "There is a place vacant, at number 340, but it's on the second floor. When you go out in the ambulance look the building over. I spoke to the manager, and he said if we were sure we wanted the apartment he might be able to move the ground floor tenant to the second floor. I haven't seen the ground floor apartment. He said he can't let me see it yet. It sounds sort of awkward, but it may be a possibility."

I was in the emergency room when I got my wife's message. I called to the charge nurse, "Bobby, put in a call to the police dispatcher and tell him to send an ambulance to 340 West Fifty-sixth Street. Tell them it's a sick case." I wanted a ride.

Bobby Longo obliged me. While she'd been in charge of the emergency room she'd struck up a good telephone acquaintance with all the police dispatchers. They never questioned her.

I told the driver, "Use your siren. This is one case that's urgent." My driver was Jack, the brave, blank-faced boy who'd become my favorite. What was he thinking? Or was he thinking at all?

The manager was still at the building when I got there. It was an old, six-story building, with four apartments to a floor.

"I'd like to see the first floor apartment," I told him.

"Your wife wanted to see it too, but I couldn't let her."

He was a short, friendly man, with a round body and a rounder face. "You'll have to wait until I can arrange it with the tenant. I'm pretty sure she'll move upstairs. The apartment there is larger because the builder didn't have to leave room for a lobby."

I had the manager take me to the vacant apartment on the second floor. Except for its location it was perfect. I figured that the apartment below couldn't be much smaller and that it would do. I told the manager I would take it. We went back to the hospital without the siren. I turned in a report to Nurse Bobby Longo, "Sickness, treated at home," and called my wife.

We were set.

MAY

ON A CHILLY February day in 1934 the people from the ground floor moved one flight up. I stopped by in the ambulance to see how things were progressing. The manager of the building didn't live there but he'd come in to help. He was wearing a sleeveless sweater and his shirt sleeves were rolled to the shoulder. He was sweating from exertion. He and the superintendent and the movers got the furniture into the elevator for the one-flight ride. What didn't fit into the elevator was lugged up the stairs. There seemed to be a lot of beds.

I told him, "I think I ought to go up and thank the family for accommodating me."

"I wouldn't bother if I were you, Doc," he answered. "They ought to thank you for getting them to move. They're better off upstairs."

His answer gave me the idea that these must be ill-natured neighbors, or at least people who wanted to be left alone. I didn't persist in trying to see them.

This visit gave me my first chance to see my new home and office. I drew a floor plan of the place as accurately as I could and later that night showed it to Belle. "It looks small," I told her. "Do you think it will do?"

"It is small, but we'll make it do." She smiled. "I'll measure it myself. I need exact dimensions."

Space was our real problem. Each room had to do double duty. There was a twelve-by-sixteen-foot living room that looked out onto the street. It would serve as a bedroom-living room, and as a waiting room for the patients, if any came.

Belle said, "You won't mind sleeping on a sofa bed? It's the only way to turn the waiting room into a bedroom."

I assured her that I minded nothing.

Beyond the living room was a ten-by-twelve-foot room meant for a bedroom but that would be my consultation room. That room opened onto an air shaft. There was a small hall leading to a bathroom and a dead-end ten-by-twelve-foot room that would be my examining room. That room, too, was on the air shaft. We persuaded the landlord to put a sink into the examining room.

Our landlord was a Mr. Rappaport, a self-assured, slickly dressed man in his late twenties. He had a mouth full of dental work and a head full of business. He was resourceful and had good ideas. I liked him. I understood that he and his family were rich in real estate. He was to be my landlord for thirty-four years.

Belle and I speculated about our unknown neighbors and agreed that though their reticence seemed unusual, there must be some simple explanation for it. "I can think of a dozen reasons," my wife said, "and they're probably all wrong."

The next afternoon Belle and I met at the apartment. She was measuring the windows for curtains and the floor for carpeting. I was on my hands and knees scrubbing the kitchen baseboards when the doorbell rang. My wife opened the door. There was conversation. My wife closed the door. Maybe the manager, I thought.

The bell rang again; same sounds of conversation, same closing of the door. Belle rushed in beaming, full of laughter.

"I've solved the mystery," she cried. "They were running a whorehouse. Two men were here. They both asked for May. One of them gave me this card."

She handed me a business card, and we both studied it. It read simply, "May. Neckties," and gave the address and apartment number.

Through her laughter Belle managed to say, "One of them wanted to come in anyhow. He said he'd take any girl in the house. Well, there was only me. I sent him upstairs."

The mystery was a mystery no longer.

In less than a week, the place was in fair order. My wife was a demon at work, and I was what help I could be. Secondhand but very decent carpeting was put down. Curtains made by my wife were put up.

The surgical supply houses were filled with excellent used cabinets, examining tables, and files returned by doctors who had moved to smaller offices. Much of the furniture was really first rate, repossessed by the dealers from people who'd bought on credit and found they couldn't make the payments.

Almost everything was done. Belle explained the facts of life. "We'll take care not to have small objects that people can steal," she said. "And I chose as little upholstered furniture as possible; whatever can be ruined will be ruined."

On a Monday morning I was working in the kitchen-laboratory. Linoleum had to be laid, and I was laying it, not all that well. The doorbell rang.

Scalpel in hand, I opened the door.

There stood an attractive woman in her early thirties. She was about my height and slender, and her hair was yellow. Not gold. Not corn silk. Just plain yellow. Her complexion was startling; it was clear and smooth but beige, the color of bleached wood.

"I'm May," she announced.

Behind her, craning to see what there was to see, were three really delightful-looking females. And so I met my upstairs neighbor and her crew. They were harlots but they didn't look at all fierce or dangerous. In any event I was a doctor and neither a judge nor a dictator of morals. Most of the girls I met were kindly people and many of them were married.

I discovered that all of May's girls were beautiful. When I knew May better, I suggested she put over her doorway Earl Carroll's motto, "Through these portals pass the most beautiful girls in the world." May thought a long time. "They're pretty," she said. "But I don't think I ought to."

You can see why I was fond of May.

"I wonder if you'd examine my girls to see if they're all right?" she asked the first time I saw her.

"Come in and sit down in the waiting room. It will take some time to give three women physical examinations."

"I don't mean that, Doc. I just want to make sure they don't have the clap. Here's nine dollars. Examine them and send them upstairs as soon as you can." She left. The girls stayed.

I took the first girl in, got her on the examining table, threw a sheet over her from the waist down, and put a speculum into her vagina. One of the girls called from the other room, "Hey, Doc, I've never seen a girl examined. Can I come in?"

"That's up to the patient. You won't interfere with me, but the patient may be modest."

"What's modest?" said the woman on the table. It wasn't meant as a question. This was New York and she spoke New Yorkese. "Come on in, girls."

The other two jostled into the room. "Let's see what you see, Doc." As I moved my head aside, one leaned over to stare into the speculum. Then she moved aside and the other girl took a long look.

"Jesus Christ! Is that what men go crazy for? My mother told me they were fools. They really must be."

I made smears from the vaginal vault of each girl and from the opening of the uterus, stained the smears, and studied the slides under a microscope.

"No love bugs?" asked one girl.

"Men are fools," repeated the other.

"You'd better go upstairs. You're all right." I ushered them out. I certainly wasn't going to lecture about hormones.

I had earned nine dollars, the first fee in my office.

The next Monday May sent three different girls to me. This batch was as beautiful as the first. Each carried a hatbox. The boxes, I learned, contained the few clothes they would need for the week.

On Mondays beautiful girls with hatboxes could be seen all over the streets of Manhattan. If you asked one what she did for a living, she would say she was a model. They were all models!

By late Monday morning the girls vanished. Each had gone to her assigned house, not to emerge again until Sunday morning. Then the houses of prostitution were quiet. The customers were welcome all week, but never on Sunday.

I discovered later that madams expected the doctor who examined girls for houses of prostitution to treat for free any man who claimed he'd gotten gonorrhea from one of the girls. Prostitution was illegal, but highly organized. It was the mobsters, not the law, who insisted upon weekly examinations. The examination was always on Monday. The girls entertained many men each day. A man might give a girl gonorrhea on Monday and she could spread it to others before her next examination. For me it was a "thanks but no thanks" proposition. I decided that I would work only on my own terms—no man who could pay would be treated for nothing. I figured that the worst that could happen would be that the girls would be sent elsewhere.

May and the other madams who sent girls on May's recommendation were impressed with the care I gave them. I treated them as if they were "legit," they said, and so they accepted my terms.

May took the world as she found it. The only harsh words she had were for the amateurs who interfered with her regular customers: "You know, housewives from the suburbs." She often speculated as to what their husbands would say about their clandestine meetings, or if it could be their husbands who arranged customers for them.

May was fascinated by my wife and by her position as a "legitimate woman." May was pleasant, wise in her own way, quiet, and—dare I say it?—decent. We saw no reason not to open our door to her. But May felt it would impair my wife's standing to be seen with her. "Tell Mrs. Slocum never to speak to me on the street," she said. "After all, she's straight."

May would telephone to be sure that Belle was alone. Then she would peer from her doorway to see if anyone were on the stairs or at the entrance to the building. With her door ajar, she could see the whole lobby. May would come down quietly and sit with my wife in our kitchen and discuss menus and clothes and people. She hardly ever mentioned her own business. She did thank Belle for giving her the idea of moving upstairs. "It's harder for stickup men and new cops on the beat to get at me upstairs." The patrolmen on the beat usually ignored the houses of prostitution. Suppressing them was supposedly the problem of the vice squad. But new cops could be overly ambitious.

May was one of Lucky Luciano's many madams, and her pimp just happened to be Luciano's money man. It took money to run Luciano's multifarious industries, and the money had to be in cash. May's pimp was Luciano's connection to the legitimate money lenders of Wall Street. Nobody asked money where it came from.

One day I met May on the west side of Broadway, between Fifty-second and Fifty-third Streets. Hardly opening her mouth May said, "Doc, keep walking. But in a minute turn around and look back. There's Lucky." And sure enough, there was Lucky Luciano getting out of a Cadillac. Two heavily built men already stood outside the car, guarding him. The trio disappeared into a building and the chauffeur drove off.

May was afraid of her pimp. The pimp, a well-dressed, slightly flashy, slender man in his forties, kept a close check on the income of the house and made May account for every penny. The madams had a conductor's punch with which they'd punch a card for every man each girl entertained. Vice was cheaper in those days. May collected two dollars from each man (the same as I charged for my office visits!) and credited the girls with one dollar for every punch on their tickets. The money was paid to the girls early on Sunday morning.

Salesmen were admitted to the house during the week to sell costume jewelry, clothing, perfume—whatever a girl might want to buy. These things were always overpriced. The salesman had to split his profit with May's pimp, who, in turn, split his take with Lucky Luciano's boys downtown. When a girl bought from the salesmen, May would pay and deduct the sum from the money the girl would receive at the end of the week. Because they were bored, most of the girls were good customers. They stayed in the house the whole week long. Often, by demand, May turned the girl's money over to the girl's pimp instead of to the girl herself.

The girls had a simple explanation for their submission to their pimps. "When I get out of bed in the morning," the saying went, "I like to see someone lying there who's lower than me." The pimps didn't mind the joke. They got the money.

May's worries about her pimp began when she gave a delivery boy a fifty-cent tip and forgot about it. It might not have bothered her pimp at all if May could have explained where the money went. But she'd forgotten to make the subtraction when she toted up the formula: three girls times so many punches minus deductions for clothes and other expenses taken out of their pay. Now she couldn't remember where the money had gone. May was fifty cents short.

She came down to see my wife. She was embarrassed and frightened. Could my wife lend her fifty cents? Of course Belle could. May explained that if she couldn't account for every cent, her pimp would beat her up. He'd done it before; he would do it again. She got the money and was grateful. As soon as she could, she repaid it. In her attitude toward money and indeed toward life in general, May was an honest woman.

Once May came to me for a minor surgical procedure. On the way out she handed me some money.

"You don't have to do that, May. After all, we're neighbors."

"Oh no, Doc," she answered. "When I come down here I pay you. When you come upstairs you pay me."

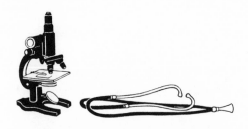

DOCTORS

SHORTLY AFTER we opened our home-and-office, Belle suggested I meet the other doctors in my immediate neighborhood. There were two on my block, one close to Ninth Avenue and the other across the street in the elegant Parc Vendome. Three other doctors had long-established practices nearby. I supposed I had much to learn from all of them.

First I called Dr. Strong, whose office was on the same side of the street as mine. I had never seen him but I knew he'd been in the neighborhood a long time. His office was on the ground floor of a brownstone building that had originally contained large apartments for the well-to-do. Now the house had become shabby. There were no more well-to-do in the area.

"Happy to see you tomorrow afternoon," he said. "I've always liked to meet the young men. They're full of new ideas."

Dr. Strong was a gentle, tall old man, stooped and bearded. He opened the door for me himself. When I told him who I was he was cordial and asked me in for a drink. I didn't refuse. He showed me into his consultation room, sat me in a comfortable old chair that today would grace someone's home as an antique, and poured an ample amount of Scotch whiskey into my glass and his.

"Hard to come by in the days of Prohibition," he said, "but I stocked up enough to see me through. I'm still drinking prohibited whiskey."

I noticed that the fabric of both his chair and mine was worn but excellent material.

He spoke of the time he had opened his office years before and how he had enjoyed the practice of medicine. "Pity the man who doesn't like his work," he said, "because that's how he spends the years of his life."

He asked what my fees were. I told him: two dollars in the office, three dollars for a house call. But more, of course, for office surgery and long-term procedures.

"That's fair enough. The neighborhood isn't well-paying the way it used to be, what with the Depression. Did it strike you that you could see ten patients at the office in the time it takes you to make one house call? You should charge more."

He had a point, but I believed my fees were all that the traffic would bear. He told me he had been in the neighborhood for some forty years. He had had to stop house calls and obstetrics because he had become too weary.

"When you stop doing obstetrics, your practice falls off. The women take their babies where the obstetrician says to go, and they stay with the obstetrician for all their pelvic problems. The men don't come, either. Irishmen and Italians don't like to visit doctors, and I don't blame them. They're shy. Their parents didn't go to doctors until they were ready to die. After all, what magic do we have to help them with?

"I suppose you notice I have no nurse. I had one nurse for thirty years, and she's my one house call now. She doesn't know it, but she'll never be able to come back."

I absorbed all he was saying. He was good-humored and very pleasant, but he seemed to have played himself out.

"From what you say, I get the impression that you don't intend to practice long. Is there anything I can do to help in the meantime?"

"Yes there is, young man. Are you a fisherman?"

"Well, I've fished."

"Then tell me. Where would you say is the best fishing in the world for a man who wants to relax?"

"That's easy," I answered. "Chesapeake Bay. I recommend a place I used to know on the Sassafras River."

The old man mused on that for a few seconds. He poured another drink for himself and for me.

"May be a good idea," he said. "I didn't tell you, but I haven't a relative or close friend left in the whole world. I was thinking of giving up practice anyhow. You're a good doctor because you've given me some good advice. You know what Osler's definition was of a good patient? Osler said, 'A good patient is a patient who goes to a doctor and stays with him until he dies.' You can think that one out."

As Dr. Strong showed me to the door, he shook hands and patted me on the shoulder. I felt very young and inexperienced with this old-timer. He exuded goodness. I felt like his grandson. I never saw him again. A few weeks later his sign had disappeared from the front of his building.

Some months afterward I received a postcard from Sassafras, Maryland. It read, "Dear Dr. Slocum, Your advice was excellent. The fishing couldn't be better, and they needed a doctor here, too." Soon after this, Belle showed me Dr. Strong's name in the obituary column of *The Journal of the American Medical Association*.

My visit to the doctor in the Parc Vendome was quite a contrast. The doctor had opened there about five years earlier to practice urology. He didn't hesitate to mix in general practice also, and I saw no reason why he shouldn't. My idea of a specialist is a man who can do many things in the practice of general medicine but who is particularly experienced in one branch of the art.

To reach his office, one entered through the lobby of the gigantic apartment house. That in itself discouraged general practice. Belle also suggested to me that people who could live in an expensive apartment usually were already taken care of elsewhere by specialists. She was right, of course.

The doctor was a morose young man who had a poor view of

life in general and a worse one of the patients who hadn't come to him. I had called and was expected. His nurse ushered me through an ornate waiting room and into the consultation room. There were mirrors and gilt everywhere. It was fancy. The doctor didn't suggest that I sit down. He sat in his chair, put his feet on his desk while I stood on the other side of it, and picked up the newspaper he'd been reading before I'd interrupted him.

I gathered from him that the neighborhood was no good, that bills were uncollectible, that he resented my being in the vicinity, and that no matter what, I couldn't expect to be able to practice there long.

I didn't stay. I recognized him as an unappetizing morsel and wondered who would want to return to him for a second visit. His sign soon disappeared. I was told by the doorman (who later became my patient) that he had given up his specialty and had moved to Brooklyn to open a general practice.

I told Belle that for the present I had had enough of doctors and would be pleased to see patients instead. Later I met a doctor from around the corner, but this was years afterward, perhaps in 1938. I was having a sandwich for lunch at a drugstore counter at Fifty-fifth Street and Ninth Avenue when a little, round man with a face flushed with red veins took the stool next to mine.

"You're Dr. Slocum, aren't you?"

I admitted that I was.

"I'm Dr. Gayly," he said. "I guess you must have seen my sign many times. I'm in the apartment house next door here."

I felt guilty for not having called on him. I explained about the reception I'd had from the doctor in the Parc Vendome.

"Oh, that's all right," Dr. Gayly said. "I'm only an old clap doctor. I long ago forgot anything else. I had a busy practice. But now, with this new sulfa drug, my practice has disappeared practically overnight.

"When I started practice thirty years ago, gonorrhea was a disease without a cure. It was common, too. A few men recovered spontaneously, but more stayed my patients for years. With these new drugs, you give the pill by mouth and after a few days there's no sign of the disease at all.

"Of course there are always some who have developed complications, mainly adhesions in the urethra, and they have to have sounds inserted every now and then." Sounds are thin, elongated instruments of varying caliber used to probe and dilate.

"What about women?"

"I never did have many women patients. First place, there's less sexual activity among young women than among young men. Then, the infection's harder to detect, by far. Many women don't know that they have the disease. Before the new pills, if you did find gonorrhea in a woman, what was there to do? Well, we could do a lot of things, but I mean what was there that was effective? When the germ got into the tubes it usually meant surgery, and if the woman got away without surgery, the tubes often wouldn't be functional." Gonorrhea was the commonest cause of sterility.

"Now that's all changing. The men get cured before they can give it to the women, and the women, if they get it, can be cured. Anyway, my practice is gone. So I might as well quit."

We shook hands on that and finished our sandwiches.

When we opened the office Belle was my office nurse. Things went well from the beginning. There were patients, interesting work, and a small but growing income. I'd soon be able to afford to hire a nurse, but we weren't in a hurry about it. I got back to the office one day to find Belle in a dither—not a dither about the office but a housekeeping dither. She was straightening instruments and moving furniture an inch or two here or there. She kept the place immaculately, but that didn't stop her from trying to perfect perfection.

"Dr. Schmahl called. He wants to come for a visit in a few minutes. Help me get things in order."

I was thrilled myself. Dr. Phillip J. R. Schmahl was my medical chief. He had been chief of medicine at New York Medical College for years and had taught me there, and later had instructed me when I was an intern. I thought it a real honor to have him come to my office.

Dr. Schmahl was a tall, slender man of German extraction whose code of ethics was of the highest. He was one of those rare individuals whose carriage and manner corresponded exactly with his attitude toward life. He was courteous but at the same time steadfast, correct, and demanding.

He already knew Belle and shook hands with her to congratulate her on the appearance of the office. He insisted on having coffee with us in the kitchen, which was also my laboratory.

"I always like to see how my young men are doing," he said. "You people are well fixed. When I was at this stage, my kitchen table was my examining table and my dining room table, and the kitchen was my consultation and examining room." He seemed pleased with our arrangement.

"This took some doing, this fitting of so much into so little space. I should say, Slocum, that your wife has done very well by you."

Belle agreed with him but was delighted that he had brought it to my attention.

Before he left, Dr. Schmahl asked if I would take over a patient he was treating, in Greenwich Village. I was glad to do so. It meant only a few minutes' ride downtown by subway from my office.

"This woman is an actress, or was before she became ill," he told us. "I don't know what she has except for a constant fever. It's gone on for more than six months. Her temperature varies from 100 to 102 degrees daily. She's flushed and irritable. Lately she talks so much that I find it hard to handle her. She may have encephalitis with an irritation of the brain that makes her talk. She stops to listen when she's spoken to, but then she starts to talk all over again. Her speech is sensible and apt, but it's almost continuous.

"The patient's husband is terribly disturbed, but he realizes that her logorrhea is the result of illness. He's eager to help. You'd be doing me a favor if you took the whole case over and saw what you could do with it."

The next day I went to visit my new patient. I was expected, and both the patient and her husband were pleased to see me. Dr. Schmahl had paved the way.

I found things as Dr. Schmahl had described them. Mrs.

Entrant moved about at will but was flushed and incredibly talkative. I could hardly get a word in edgewise. Of course I wanted to hear about her illness from its inception. She told me she had slipped and fallen on the way from the theater where she'd been performing some eight months before. She had continued working until her play closed but felt weak, nervous, and distracted, and not up to looking for another part. Then she found she had a fever, and Dr. Schmahl had ordered her to bed for two weeks. Her condition had not improved.

"I didn't mind staying in bed. I felt so weak that I didn't want to do anything else."

No, she had no pain. Her appetite had gone and she didn't want food, but ate enough to keep her strength because Dr. Schmahl and her husband thought it necessary. No, she had no vertigo or sudden weakness, no tremors, no hallucinations or delusions.

Did she know she talked more than most people? Yes, she knew that. Had she always been that way? I asked more directly.

"I always talked as much as most people, but for some reason lately I talk more and more. I don't know why."

Mr. Entrant, her husband, concurred. He was a very blond man in his early forties, with pale, watery blue eyes. He was about my size, not more than five and a half feet tall. I wondered if his lack of height held him back in his chosen profession of acting. His anxiety to help Mrs. Entrant was obvious. He did everything to make her comfortable.

After our interview we moved into the bedroom, where I examined with great care this pleasant woman. I couldn't afford to miss anything, first because she was a patient, and second, because Dr. Schmahl had sent me.

The couple's Greenwich Village apartment was a few steps down from the street. You entered through a wrought-iron gate and a small paved yard. As I sat beside the bed, I could see legs passing the window, some hurried, some idling.

Except for her fever, mild weakness, and—I later discovered—a laboratory report of a high white blood cell count, there was nothing. I was stumped.

I concentrated on the diagnosis of diseases marked by prolonged fever of undetermined origin. Many of these diseases cleared up with no diagnosis ever being established, but I knew the commonest were malignancy, tuberculosis, and a disease of the heart valves known as subacute bacterial endocarditis. I hoped it was none of these. However, the blood cell count was not indicative of any of them. There were a dozen less common diseases that could also have been considered, but they were farfetched.

I spoke frankly. "You seem to have a deep-seated infection the source of which we can't determine yet," I told Mrs. Entrant. "I know you're anxious to be well, but it's better to do nothing than to do damage. Let's wait a bit longer and have nature guide us."

They decided that, poor as it was, it was the best advice. Mr. Entrant said, "If Dr. Schmahl couldn't help, we think what you say is the only answer."

I wasn't entirely flattered. I instructed them as to diet and rest and activity. "Let her have company," I advised Mr. Entrant. "Her disease doesn't seem to be contagious, and it will help her pass the time."

I visited twice a week for four or five weeks, watching for any change that might lead to a diagnosis. The most disturbing feature in treating Mrs. Entrant was her continuous conversation. She was not to be blamed for it, but it interfered with my examination and my efforts to obtain more information. She was vivacious and chatted away about her life, her mother, the weather, and the neighbors—and added a volume about her disease as if it afflicted some stranger. I finally settled that problem by inserting a thermometer into her mouth when I entered and removing it when I left, taking it out only when I wanted her to answer a question.

One day Mr. Entrant called me. "I don't know if it means anything," he said, "but since yesterday my wife has had a red spot where the right hip bone is. It was the size of a pea, but now it's the size of a walnut. It was tender, but now it's getting painful."

I was there within the next few hours. Sure enough, there was a small raised area in the skin over the right hip bone. I rolled the protuberance between my index and third fingers. There was no question but that fluid was gathering and producing the mass. Mrs. Entrant was suffering from a hidden infection whose presence was at last making itself known.

"This will increase in size from day to day," I explained. "Nature seems to have given us the answer. This has to be incised and drained, but not too soon; otherwise another incision will be necessary. I've seen the same area incised three and four times because someone was too impatient to wait. Give the pus a chance to come to the surface. In the meantime, tomorrow morning we'll have an X-ray taken to make sure the underlying bone is intact."

I visited the next day. The X-ray showed only normal bone. I was elated. A few days later I asked Belle to include a lot of sterile bandage in my bag and a new scalpel and stylet. "I'd like you to come along. I may need you. Do you mind the sight or smell of pus?"

"It's all part of our living, isn't it?" she said, as she busied herself with packing. "By the way, what does this infection come from?"

"She probably struck her hip when she fell months ago and devitalized her tissues. Then germs began to grow there."

The lesion was ready for incision and drainage. Belle placed old newspapers beneath Mrs. Entrant in case the pus was under pressure. She handed me sterile rubber gloves, put a pair on her own hands, and washed the affected area with soap, water, and iodine. When I was ready she held a pus basin under the wound. "It shouldn't hurt," Belle told Mrs. Entrant. "What the doctor is going through is all dead tissue." (No one would have believed I had just explained the whole procedure to her on the subway.)

One incision and it was all over. We recovered half a cup of pus. I probed the wound with a stylet and felt that it didn't go to the bone. Belle stood by with iodoform gauze. I packed the wound lightly and placed a thick but loose bandage over it to permit drainage.

The next day the wound had drained itself out. Mrs. Entrant felt fine. Her fever was gone and she had an appetite for the first time in weeks. Best of all, her speech was back to normal! Within ten days the wound had closed entirely, and Mrs. Entrant notified her agent that she was available for any part in any play. She and her husband were very grateful to me for what nature had accomplished. "Thank God, Doctor," her husband said when we were out of her hearing. "By curing her you've saved my life."

Belle and I talked it over at dinner the night I discharged the patient. "It's a good lesson in how doctors' reputations are made," I said.

"Yes," Belle agreed. "You can't deny the old saying: 'The last doctor is the lucky doctor.'"

NURSE

When Belle and I moved into our apartment the rent was $62.50 a month. With the first month's rent and a last month's deposit we had to pay out exactly what I had earned as an intern. Belle was gleeful about the coincidence.

Of course the apartment was small. It was all we could afford. Belle was stuck in it, as wife and nurse. She worked hard and the hours were long. Keeping house meant cleaning an office, too. We were determined to devote ourselves to building a practice, no matter what. That meant we never left the phone unmanned and we were always ready to open the door.

It was easier in those days in Hell's Kitchen, before narcotics took the place of alcohol, not to be frightened. Besides, the cops took care of us, dropping in for a drink and dashing into our place first if there were reports of trouble in the neighborhood. The cops came in so often that we were forced to buy a particularly reasonably priced whiskey for them. We called it "the cops' bottle." Prohibition had been repealed and life was calmer. It hadn't interfered with us much. As Ring Lardner said, "Prohibition was better than no liquor at all."

So my wife was cooped up in the apartment except when I was there, which was mainly during office hours. And she was kept constantly busy during office hours. She didn't complain. But I knew she was taking a beating and should have help.

We decided it was time to advertise for a nurse.

The doorbell rang early on the day my advertisement appeared in the *New York Times*. Hoping it might be a patient, we quickly tried to make the place look like a professional office. I opened the door.

"You're the doctor that wants a nurse?" asked a neat, trim young girl with blonde hair and green eyes. "I'm a nurse who's looking for a doctor. So I've come to take the job."

That shook me up, she was so brash. I invited her into the room I used as my office and then hurried back to speak to my wife in the kitchen-laboratory.

"She's here about the job," I said. "She looks about eighteen. I don't know anything about interviewing. Will you talk to her?"

"Talk to her yourself. You know what you need," Belle said.

I marched bravely back to my office.

"By the way," I said, "I didn't get your name."

"I didn't give it. It's Margaret Voyna." She offered her hand. "Margaret, but nobody ever calls me that. It's Peggy, really."

This was a young girl, too young, I thought, to be a graduate nurse. But she had credentials and excellent references, the latest only a few days old and from a very responsible hospital in the neighborhood.

"I'm older than I look. I'm twenty-three and I graduated at twenty. You can read all about it."

She had a freshness and exuberance about her that was attractive.

"Why do you want this sort of job? It's confining."

"I'm tired of sitting up all night as a special with sick old people when there's nothing for me to do. And I'm tired of carrying bedpans and taking orders from really old nurses who don't have any training and who ought to be retired. I don't want to be one of them."

"Well, come on then. I'll show you what you have to do."

She scanned the room. "I know what I have to do. You just keep out of my way and I'll do it. Look at these instruments," she said, rearranging them with small, deft hands. "They're not lined up right to use. I can see they've been scrubbed, but most of them are old. It'll make a better display if you get shiny new ones." Peggy looked into my bag. "This needs straightening, too. Whoever set this up did a nice clean job but didn't know exactly what you need for a house call. And you can save a lot of money and time using the latest hospital files instead of business files."

I wasn't used to being talked to that way. She was young and slender and pretty, but she was very, very brash.

"You're only the first person I've interviewed. I think I ought to see some other nurses."

"You'll be wasting your time," she said. "Where can I change my uniform?"

I went to tell my wife we had a nurse. "I hope you did right," Belle said.

Peggy turned out to be all she'd claimed. She created a really professional air about the place. When she wasn't working, she went around the neighborhood meeting people and becoming part of many lives. I was astonished at the number of patients who came because Peggy managed, in her offhand way, to tell them that I would be good for what ailed them.

I was amazed, too, that she and my wife got on so well together. "You're like a couple of old crones sitting there sipping coffee and going silent when I walk in on you. What sort of secrets are you keeping from me?"

"Girl talk," my wife said.

One day, when Peggy had been with me three months, she said to me, "You've got to get that woman out of here."

"I don't see any woman. What woman?"

"Your wife. She deserves a place to live like anyone else, and you keep her cooped up in an office. Where can she entertain her friends? Where's her privacy? She has no place but the kitchen to sit in. How long do you think she can take it?"

"It hadn't occurred to me."

"Nothing occurs to you except your practice."

"Where will we move to so I won't lose my practice?"

"I'm glad you asked me, sir." The way Peggy said "sir" made me wince. "I'll tell you."

"The two girls in the rear apartment are going to jail on Monday. Not for whoring. For fencing stolen goods. They've been out on bail, but they'll be sentenced at their next hearing."

"Where do you get your information?"

"Mrs. Slocum and I have already spoken to the manager. We can have the apartment Monday. This is only the middle of the month. That gives you two weeks' rent free. The manager says he'll put a door in the examining room so you won't have to go through the hall. You can keep this to live in and use the rear apartment for the practice. It's twice as big. Then you and Mrs. Slocum can have a home. You should hear the ideas she has for decorating the place. She's gifted. She knows how to make a home."

"So that's what you two have been talking about?"

"That and a thousand other things."

"I ought to fire you."

"If you did, I wouldn't work for you anymore."

"Oh, well, then forget it."

I had been called to see the girls in the back apartment on several occasions. I knew they were prostitutes, but I never could figure out the dozens of bottles of expensive perfume or the rack of mink coats or the silverware. I just thought that whoring paid off better than I had imagined.

It didn't surprise me that there was a fencing operation in the house. We had had everything else, so why not that? The house had been used as a hideout and several times was searched from basement to attic for men who had taken it on the lam.

All manner of strange things occurred on West Fifty-sixth Street and in its environs. The area wasn't called Hell's Kitchen for nothing. We were really pleased to have the police drop in. All sorts of activity around us was of interest to the law.

The truth seems to be that Hell's Kitchen was called after a German restaurateur named Heil who in the 1880s ran a rough joint in the neighborhood. But I'm convinced that the name would never have stuck had the neighborhood not lived up to it.

Once, before Peggy arrived, I had opened the door to a tall, thin fellow who needed a shave and was dressed as if he'd just come from a laborer's job.

"Doc," he said, "I think I got a clap."

I examined him. "I think so, too," I agreed. "Where did you get my name?"

"Some of the boys were talking about you. They said you were a good doctor. How long will it take to clear this up?"

"I can't tell you that," I said, "but I'll do the best I can. The fee's the same, anyhow."

"How much?"

There was no telling how long the patient would be under care. It might be from six weeks to a year.

"One hundred thirty-five dollars."

He pulled out a wad of paper money and counted out the sum I'd mentioned. He put far more back into his pocket than he'd put on my desk. I treated him and told him to come back in two days. As he left I thought how easy it was to misjudge someone by his appearance. My "laborer" was rich! I didn't see him again for a long time.

One day two men came to see me. They told Peggy they were not patients. "These guys look like cops," she told me. "Cops look like cops the world over. These say they're Feds. They've got short haircuts, so I guess they're Feds."

The men identified themselves. One showed me pictures of my long-lost patient, front and side views with numbers underneath.

The one with the pictures said, "This man is an escaped convict. He told one of our informers you owed him money and he would come to get it. Have you seen him?"

I remembered the man—maybe because I had had his money in my pocket. "I haven't seen him for a year or so."

"You in any danger from him?"

"No. I owe him money for treatment I never finished. If he comes I'll give it to him." I thought quickly. I was neutral in this matter. "What do you expect me to do?"

"Nothing, Doctor. We just wanted to make sure this was the right place. We already have a twenty-four-hour watch on the house. If he comes we'll pick him up."

After they had gone I called Peggy in and told her all I knew. "Did they show you his picture?"

"Yes, but I never saw the man."

"You wouldn't know him. He was here once, before you were. When he comes in treat him as you would anyone else. If we're busy let him wait his turn. If we're not, show him right in."

Sure enough, shortly thereafter the man returned. "Remember me, Doc? I was here for treatment and paid you. I couldn't come back. I'd like my money, if it's all right with you."

"Where've you been?" I asked.

"Down in West Virginia, collecting sassafras root bark."

"What on earth is that for?"

"They use it to make soft drinks."

I counted out a hundred and twenty-five dollars.

"I'm taking out ten dollars for your first visit."

"That's okay, Doc. Thanks for remembering."

"Did you get yourself cured?"

"You bet," he said. "And for free." He grinned.

I didn't ask where.

He said goodbye to me and then to Peggy. She followed him to the door and closed it after him. Then she came back in and sat on my desk, swinging her legs.

"That's eight," she said.

"Eight what?" I wanted to know.

"Eight times the cops have picked up people in this house. Some place you run here, I must say."

"How do you count eight?"

"Well, there was the counterfeiting ring on the top floor, the two girls who ran the fence in the back apartment, and five raids for prostitution. That's a pretty good record."

"Does that frighten you?" I asked.

"No, I think it's real exciting. We never have any excitement in my house." She thought for a moment. "Why don't they ever bother May?"

"They can't," I explained. "There's a fellow named Joey Silver who protects her. May belongs to Lucky Luciano."

"Oh," said Peggy. She said it with the reverence due the *capo di tutti capi*. She pushed herself off my desk and returned to her duties.

My nurse was right. The two girls from the back apartment went to jail and the apartment fell vacant. We rented it, and knocked through a wall to join the old and new spaces. For a while I practiced in falling plaster and splintered wood and then in the smell of fresh paint and wallpaper glue.

My wife did a beautiful job on our old-but-new home, and Peggy spent many extra hours setting up the new office in the rear, with its own separate patients' entrance from the hall.

One day, when things were nearly in shape, I said to Peggy, "I don't know how to thank you."

She was cleaning paint from her hands and nose with turpentine. She gave me an angelic smile, but her eyes were full of mischief.

"You don't have to thank me. Put it in the pay envelope where it shows."

As time went by, Peggy and I became accustomed to working together. There was otherwise little personal business between us, although she and Belle were close. The practice grew, and we were able to hire another nurse. I called the girls "Number One Nurse" and "Number Two Nurse." The second girl understood that she was to follow all orders given by Number One, Peggy.

There were many Number Two's in the next thirty years. There was never any other Number One Nurse but Peggy.

I came in one day and found Number One chewing pensively on an eraser. She didn't say hello or good morning but just stared at me with the blankest of blank expressions. Finally she asked, "You a Jew?"

"Sure," I said, "I thought you knew."

"I'm not certain I like working for a Jew."

"Why? Something wrong?"

"That's what I'm trying to think of. The job's good. The pay's good. Your wife's a wonderful friend."

"Then what makes you think you might not like working for Jews?"

"My mother. She came from Pittsburgh to stay with me for a little while. Your wife gave me the recipe for the beet soup we had for dinner last night. My mother enjoyed it and ate all she could hold. Then she said, 'This is Jew food, isn't it?' I told her I didn't know. Then she said I must be working for Jews. She said there weren't any Jews in the part of Slovakia she came from." A pause. "My mother's a Slovak."

"So I gathered."

"My mother said she didn't think she liked Jews although she didn't know any, but she thinks maybe I shouldn't be working for Jews. She said maybe I should get another job."

"Maybe you should get another mother."

"No, thank you. The one I've got is trouble enough. That's why Dad sent her to stay with me."

Then she gave a deep sigh. "It's been very nice here. Oh, well. I think I'll give it a try for another few years."

NOTRE CHÈRE
GABRIELLE

MY OFFICE hadn't been opened long before interns from Flower Hospital began to drop in to visit and see how we'd set up shop. They would soon face the same problem I'd had to face: what to do when their contracts expired. My medical practice was showing promise after a very few weeks, and the young men came out of friendliness and out of curiosity. My wife and I were pleased to have them. They were fresh and vivacious company and they brought their girls to look us over.

When interns on ambulance service came they would telephone Bobby Longo at the hospital emergency room to inform her of their whereabouts. "I know," Bobby would say, "you're at the Slocums'. I wish I were. Have a good time." Bobby was a superb nurse: smart, efficient, and beautiful. She later married Dr. Testa, whom she met when he served his stint in her department. Their son is now an orthopedic surgeon in New York.

One night, close to midnight, an ambulance pulled up silently at our curb. The intern, Dr. Robbins, and his driver came in blowing on their hands and rubbing their ears and noses.

"If it isn't zero it ought to be," said the handsome doctor. The driver nodded in agreement. He had been one of my drivers, too. He was a man of few words.

"Boy!" continued Dr. Robbins, "I'll be glad to get back to the nice warm emergency room and into my soft bed."

"Yeah, for ten minutes," said the driver. The drivers were lucky. They worked an eight-hour shift.

"Slocum," said Robbins, "I just left a house where there's a patient for you, an old woman with a bad heart. Fine people. Put on your warmest gear and we'll take you there. You'll have to come back by yourself."

My wife insisted on gloves, a sweater, and a muffler. "I don't intend to lose the breadwinner at this stage of the game," she said. "Call me if they have a phone, so I'll have your number. I may need it." She didn't have to remind me. It was our brand-new routine procedure. She pushed me out the door into the cold.

We traveled by ambulance on Ninth Avenue from Fifty-sixth Street to Forty-eighth Street. The Elevated roared above us. We stopped at a red brick tenement between Ninth and Tenth Avenues. The streets were dark in this neighborhood of early-to-bed working people, but there were lights in the ground floor apartment.

"I'll go in with you," said Robbins. "You may need the advice of one of the world's greatest and newest cardiologists."

We walked to the rear of the entrance hall, knocked on the door, and were admitted to a spotless kitchen. We were shown forward through the two bedrooms of a standard railroad flat, and into a tidy parlor whose windows faced the street.

There in an armchair sat a plump and handsome gray-haired woman, smiling beatifically. Her face glistened with perspiration, and she struggled slightly for breath. Standing next to her, holding her hand, was a tall, statuesque young woman. The daughter wore a robe over her nightdress. Her smile was as welcoming as her mother's, but her glance was anxious. Her dark hair was the longest I have ever seen, hanging in great masses to mid-calf. There were also three tall sons and a tall blonde daughter, all of us crowded into the parlor. These were French-speaking Europeans, but far too staid, I thought, to be Parisians. They all spoke English well.

After courteous formal introductions, Dr. Robbins told me what he had found and what he had done for the patient. Mrs. Vandenborre had fainted suddenly and had recovered, but was sweating and short of breath. Dr. Robbins had diagnosed her trouble as Adams-Stokes syndrome, a disease named for two doctors who had described it independently. Another doctor named Morgagni had also described it—and at approximately the same time—but he didn't get his name onto the syndrome. He must have had poor public relations.

Mrs. Vandenborre was suffering from a malfunction in her heart, inadequacy of a cardiac node from which electric impulses originate.

We function much as electric lights do, particularly those electric lights with on and off switches. The machine readings of heart function, called electrocardiograms, and of brain action, called electroencephalograms, remind us that our systems run by electricity.

In one peculiar part of the heart there is a switch, a node that is stimulated chemically, and which distributes an electric current through the heart muscle. This synchronizes the rhythm of the heart. In Adams-Stokes syndrome an interference with the current causes a sudden change in rhythm and often an acute slowing of the heart. The interference may be caused by scar tissue or other damage to the nerves carrying the electrical impulse, or by a diminution of blood supply to the area from which the impulse emanates. There is an acute drop in the pulse rate, sometimes from seventy-two to thirty-six beats per minute. It is during this sudden change of pulse that fainting occurs. The symptoms may last only a few seconds and may occur several times a day—or they may last long enough to cause death.

Dr. Robbins had given Mrs. Vandenborre an injection of adrenaline. This seemed to help her but caused tremors. As these subsided she felt much stronger. I decided that I would give her the same treatment with a similar but weaker drug. I promised to look in on her in the morning. Within the week I saw her three times, twice on emergency calls after midnight. She was very frightened by her fainting spells and was grateful that I came so quickly.

The family was not French, but Belgian, and had been behind German lines throughout World War I. In Belgium they'd been well-to-do, but in New York they had to struggle for a bare living. All the children went out to work—all, that is, save Gabrielle, the dark-haired daughter, who stayed home to care for their mother. She had been a babies' nurse before her mother's illness.

A bystander can sometimes see clearly the pattern of a family's relationships. Many families have an angel: one individual whose care and consideration nourishes the others. Gabrielle was the Vandenborres' angel. She was devoted to her mother: in fact, she now devoted her life to her. I understood Gabrielle's attachment: Mrs. Vandenborre was a woman of great charm whose strong character had held her family together. Still, I wondered. Could Gabrielle manage to maintain her independence, or would the situation turn into a classic case of self-sacrifice?

There was no point in intervening: events will proceed in a manner appropriate to the characters involved in them. I was concerned, but I tried, as an outsider, to stay out of the business of other people. Occasionally I succeeded.

I expected Mrs. Vandenborre to grow worse; it was inevitable. A cardiac pacemaker would have saved her, but in 1934 that technology was beyond our imagining. Throughout that bitter winter I trudged back and forth the eight cold and windy blocks to the Vandenborres'. Elevated trains thundered overhead. I taught Gabrielle to inject the medication needed to bring Mrs. Vandenborre out of her syncope, her fainting.

The Vandenborres asked if I would mind if they consulted a doctor they knew from home. I leapt at the chance: perhaps he would help with the case. The old Belgian doctor was delightful. He quietly explained to the family what he thought. For emphasis he made the very Gallic gesture of closing the second and third fingers of his left hand into an O with his thumb. He suggested tincture of digitalis, ten drops in water three times a day. With this advice he withdrew. As far as I knew we hadn't used digitalis in that way for years. I tried it but it was ineffectual.

Monseigneur Roosens from the Belgian Church was a frequent visitor to the Vandenborre house and often would stay for tea or a drop of whiskey. He said to me, "You have done a wonderful job keeping Madame alive. We hope the Lord spares her. But of course to us it is more important that we have prepared her for the next world."

Any doctor will tell you he has learned from his patients. Mrs. Vandenborre was a great teacher. She had been rich and poor, well and ill, a native and a stranger in a foreign land. She had taken her experience—both good and bad—with equanimity. She had grown wise. One thing she taught me should be passed on to all young doctors—to all young people, really. She said, "Write everything down." It was invaluable advice. I hope some day to follow it.

Mrs. Vandenborre's health continued to deteriorate. Two years after our first meeting she died.

At the funeral, Gabrielle collapsed. For the next few months she was unable to walk. Of course her paralysis resulted from an emotional condition. I call it delayed shock, and I have seen it strike again and again. The devoted one is always the most vulnerable. The longer the crisis, the more damaging the shock. For two years Gabrielle had spent days and nights at her mother's side, answering every summons and watching over her. She never thought of her own exhaustion. When the end came it came suddenly. No matter how long it has been expected death is a blow to the members of a close family. Time is the only remedy.

Gabrielle was sensitive and sensible and understood her own condition. She had demonstrated patience first in her care of babies and then in her care of her mother. Now she was patient with herself. She exercised her legs while she was bedridden and got up from her bed and into a chair as soon as possible. After some weeks she was able to grope her way from one piece of furniture to another. The time came when she was able to stand and walk alone.

Gabrielle had undertaken, willingly and lovingly, great responsibility. What would happen to her now? She was young and strong. I hoped that she would make a life for herself.

To my surprise her life blended with ours, and she became Notre Chère Gabrielle—Our Dear Gabrielle.

WINTER

THE WINTER of 1935 was a bitter one, with one storm after another. The streets were piled high with snow, and the freezing temperature made it impossible to clear the streets. The snow didn't melt but froze. One layer of ice covered another. Where there was traffic, ruts were formed by the cars and trucks, converting the streets into single-lane roadways.

As the days passed the private cars became fewer. Some had been parked at the curbs and were frozen in for the season. The snowplows had covered them over. We all expected that when the snow melted the cars would be removed, but the snow didn't melt. Except in wide thoroughfares like Broadway and Fifth Avenue, the snowplows had completely stopped running. The plows could no longer function on the narrow streets, and they quit trying.

The side streets had become furrowed. Only one lane was left in the center, channeled by compressed ice. As storm followed storm, the furrows became deeper and deeper. The streets were abandoned to delivery trucks; these vehicles could hardly push through the lanes without dragging their undercarriages on the ice.

For days the temperature never rose above zero degrees Fahrenheit. School attendance dropped. Cold and poverty kept many children at home. The youngsters had little warm clothing, and many had shoes that were worn through. They couldn't venture out without fear of frozen feet. Many who got to school arrived with frozen fingers, ears, and noses. Doctors in general practice received calls daily to take care of these children. There was no question of payment. Teachers and school nurses were superb in following treatment to make sure that no permanent damage was done.

Peggy lived near the Eighth Avenue subway and arrived every day, battered a bit from sliding over the ice packs but serviceable. Few patients were able to reach the office, but I was busy enough outside it. The subway was a great help. The fare was a nickel. Often I used the subway as a shelter from the cold: I'd descend the stairs and pay the fare at Fifty-sixth Street, walk along the train platform north to Sixtieth Street, and climb back up to the street.

Few of the apartments in our neighborhood had central heating. Their heat was supplied by Victor Sinisi. Victor made his deliveries by horse-drawn wagon. All year long he climbed the stairs from floor to floor delivering ice for iceboxes. In winter he also delivered kerosene for the small stoves that could be carried from room to room.

In winter the pervasive odor was kerosene. The neighborhood smelled of it. The rooms smelled of it. People and their clothes smelled of it. In most living quarters kerosene heaters were the only way to keep warm.

Victor Sinisi was our savior. In his early twenties he'd come to New York from somewhere in southern Italy. Victor found his niche in our neighborhood. He had been there years before I arrived. A clever, even brilliant, man, Victor learned English quickly and established himself in a basement two steps down from the street. There he had his office and his storehouse.

Outside his door, Victor placed a waist-high wooden stand that he himself had built. On the stand was a large pad to which a pencil was attached by a string. Customers would stop by and write down their orders, and later Victor would appear with the requested fifty-pound block of ice in the summer or can of kerosene in the winter. To protect himself from the melting ice, Victor fashioned a heavy piece of leather that fit over his shoulder. Balancing the ice on his shoulder, he clambered up the flights of stairs. No other form of refrigeration was known in the neighborhood.

Victor was in his forties when I met him. Thirty years later, despite the invention of refrigerators, he was still carrying fifty-pound blocks of ice up the stairs. To his neighbors, Victor was always important. No one was surprised when he was the subject of a long feature article in the *New York Times*.

Late one very cold night that winter, Jimmy Goodwin, the cop on the beat, rang the bell. He looked very bulky, with two sweaters under his blue winter uniform coat. His collar was up about his ears. "Doctor, sorry to bother you, but we have a problem in the next block and we can't get an ambulance. Young girl in labor. You won't believe it until you see it, and maybe not then."

We floundered around the corner, slipping along the ice. Jimmy insisted on carrying my bag, for which I was grateful. The darkness was broken by the glow of street lamps and their reflections on the ice. We entered an old building that was set back from the sidewalk. Two steps down, and we were in a dark basement. We could see a dim light in the rear. Jimmy took a flashlight from his pocket to illuminate our way.

There was no furniture in the front room and no other light than Jimmy's torch. In the back room a small light bulb swung loosely from the ceiling and threw our shadows on the wall. A kerosene stove heated the area immediately around us, spreading its acrid odor.

Massive Leo Gates, the fighter-turned-cop, was waiting in the room. Next to him, an old woman swayed back and forth in the wreck of a rocking chair. She was asking repeatedly, "Is my granddaughter all right? Will she be all right?"

Jimmy Goodwin turned to me. "We've known her for a long time. She's blind and deaf and a little mental. She lives here with her granddaughter. They're both on charity. That's the granddaughter, there on the floor." He pointed to a young girl who lay between layers of blankets.

"I got the blankets from the neighbors," Leo explained. "It was freezing here."

The old woman swayed back and forth. "Is my granddaughter all right? Will she be all right?"

I removed my gloves, rubbed my hands to get some feeling into them, and turned to examine the girl. She was not just thin, she was skinny, a sixteen-year-old-starved-skinny. And she was in active labor.

I yelled into her grandmother's ear, "She'll be all right. You don't have to worry about her."

Leo said, "She don't hear you, Doc. You take care of the girl and I'll handle the old woman."

"I'll need all the light I can get. And hot water, if there is any. And newspaper to put under the girl."

Jimmy said, "I've already started water boiling on the stove. If this is a normal delivery, I've got everything you need. It's not my first baby," he said modestly.

The girl had a tough young body. Her delivery proceeded without incident. Soon we had a female infant with a lusty cry. Leo kept two flashlights focused. Jimmy washed the child and kept her covered. Very soon I had the afterbirth wrapped in newspaper for disposal.

To prevent gonorrhea I instilled a drop of silver nitrate into each of the baby's eyes. Later the law made it obligatory to do so at every birth.

"Everything is fine if we have no infection, and we shouldn't have any. I brought along a sterile tie for the cord."

Leo said, "We'll manage to get all three of them to the hospital as soon as it's daylight." The old woman swayed back and forth. "Is my granddaughter all right? Will she be all right?"

I was weary. As I gathered the contents of my bag together, I wondered whether anything would ever be all right for these neglected and abandoned people.

"We'll take care of everything," said Leo. "Go home, Doc, and go to bed."

Which is exactly what I did.

❖   ❖   ❖

The winters in the early 1950s were severe. The relentless weather reminded me of the bitter winters in the first years of my practice, especially when I was called on for an unexpected delivery.

After World War II there was a surge of building in Riverdale, just north of Manhattan Island. Many people who moved to Riverdale were astonished to discover they'd moved to the Bronx! Oh, the ignominy of it! I had a patient who lived in one of the new apartment buildings there. She was to be delivered soon at a midtown hospital. One bitter-cold day my patient's husband called me in a panic.

"My wife's had a couple of labor pains. What do I do?" It was their first baby, and he was panicking.

"You have plenty of time," I said. "Get her to the hospital."

"I can't. There's no way out of the street. The ice is packed six feet high. We haven't had a delivery truck through here for more than a week. There's a store two blocks down I can reach on foot. That's as far as I can go."

"Can I get a car close to you?" I thought of the difficult drive uptown and wondered if I could make it in time.

"I don't see how. The streets are completely closed off. You can't get within ten blocks of the building. After you cross the Henry Hudson Bridge you won't be able to turn off the main road."

"There's no use calling an ambulance," I said. "Wait a minute."

My nurse Peggy, who'd heard my end of the conversation, was pulling at my elbow. "Ask him if there's a doctor living in his building."

I glared at Peggy, but I asked. We were in luck.

"There is one, but he's a psychiatrist," the husband told me.

"A psychiatrist is a doctor, too. See if you can get him to call me."

I hung up the receiver and turned to face Number One. "Peggy, you're too damn smart. Some day it'll get you into trouble."

Peggy looked unrepentant. "All right, Doc. Go yourself. You'll get there in time to attend the baby's bar mitzvah."

"How do you know it's a boy?"

"You'll see," she said, smugly.

A few minutes later the phone rang. It was the psychiatrist,

Dr. Carlin. I thanked him for calling back. "How are you on babies?"

"I don't know. I haven't seen one for thirty years."

"If you can stand by, I'll be at the phone. Childbirth is a perfectly normal process." I thought I was joking with him.

"I don't think that I've seen anything normal, either, in thirty years." We agreed that he would oversee the birth and call me if anything came up he couldn't handle. Dr. Carlin did stand by. Some hours later he called again.

"The baby's here. A nice boy. What'll I use to tie off the cord?"

Enter Peggy, with some files. I put my hand over the mouthpiece and said, "It's a boy. They ought to name it after you."

"That's one you owe me," she said.

I got back to business. "Take a shoestring or any piece of mending tape or string, dip it into boiling water, and use that," I suggested. "First, press any blood in the cord into the baby. He may need it. Then use the household scissors to cut the cord. But cut it on the side near the mother."

"Look, Dr. Slocum," Dr. Carlin said, "I've forgotten almost everything but not quite everything. Hold the phone. She's having another pain. I think the placenta's coming."

I held on. In a few minutes he was back. "Everything's fine," he said. "I even remembered a pan for the placenta and Argyrol for the eyes."

"What did you two men do with the baby?" I wondered how the proud father had worked out as a delivery nurse.

"We washed it in warm water, used some olive oil, wrapped it in a receiving blanket, and gave it back to the mother. That's where it came from."

"Hooray for you," I shouted into the phone. "Tell them to call me every four hours or whenever they have questions, and say that I'll come as soon as I can reach them."

"There's no need for that," he answered proudly. "There's a doctor in the house."

JOEY SILVER

JOEY SILVER was a protectionist. Protection was his stock-in-trade. He was not a big racketeer, but he knew Lucky Luciano, the biggest, and was trusted by him. That was why he was allowed to protect a section of the West Side—my section.

Lucky Luciano was the biggest of big shots. His real name, Lucanio, had somehow been transformed into Luciano. He controlled gambling, prostitution, alcohol, and narcotics.

The places Joey protected were gambling joints, whorehouses, and, during Prohibition, clubs that served alcoholic beverages. After repeal of Prohibition, he saw to it that the clubs were stocked with beverages of Luciano's choice.

Joey did not protect these places from the police—the police weren't interested, and anyway they had their orders from the politicians. Joey protected his customers from other racketeers who tried to invade his territory. He also protected them from himself.

This is how he was paid off. Gamblers and booze sellers paid him an agreed amount. If their business improved, they paid more. They knew better than to lie to Joey, because there were always those who made a living by seeing and talking. The alternative was broken limbs, frequently not one but two.

As for the whorehouses, the madam paid ten dollars a week

for herself, ten for her maid, and ten dollars for each of the girls —usually two or three, seldom more—who worked in the house.

Joey's take was considerable, even though he had to split it with the man who had given him the territory. But, as he told me, it was nice work if you could get it.

Joey was almost forty and had no other trade. "When I was a kid," he later told me, "they gave me a machine gun and sent me to France to kill Germans. I killed a lot of them. Then I come home and look around for work. But there wasn't none for a guy who didn't know anything except how to handle a gun. Then friends suggest that I see the Big Man, Lucky Luciano. He could use a man like me. That's my whole story."

Among Joey's clients was May, our upstairs madam. May had called me once to introduce him. "Doc," she said, "there's a particular friend of mine that I want you to take care of. Name's Joey Silver. He looks out for our house and the neighborhood for Lucky. Take good care of him."

May, it turned out, did not pay Joey for his services. Her pimp was Lucky's connection with the Wall Street banks and was important to Lucky's organization. Hence May's establishment was exempt from tithe.

Joey stood five feet nine inches tall. His hair was beginning to turn iron-gray, and his small eyes were a bit closely set. Once when I examined him I commented on the strength of his back and shoulder muscles.

"Yeah, I work out."

"What does that mean?" The phrase hadn't yet entered the vocabulary of the ordinary New Yorker. I didn't know that even then it was in common use on the California beaches.

"Aw, you know, Doc. I use my muscles." There was a pause. He laughed. "I work out all right, but sometimes I work out on people."

As Joey was leaving he took out a roll of bills and handed me five dollars. "Keep the change," he said.

"You don't have to do that, Joey."

"I don't have to do a lot of things, but I like you. You're legit and you don't take no advantage. The girls say you treat them right even though they're whores. The other fellows they get treated by take advantage all the time. You don't try to overcharge or anything, and they like you. Even the cops like you."

All that seemed reason enough for him to like me. After that speech I never feared Joey. Even he had a code of ethics. I knew I had found a friend, such as he was.

Joey couldn't understand why I didn't have a car. I explained to him that I was doing all right in the general practice of medicine but that I had no intention of buying a car until I could walk into the dealer's with the money in my hand.

"That ain't right, Doc. You tell me what sort of car you want and what color. Maybe a Caddy? You name it, you'll have it. It won't cost you nothing."

I turned him down and laughed off his proposition. I didn't bother to explain too much to Joey. He wouldn't have understood.

I had found a neighborhood in which the people were glad to have another general practitioner and seemed to need one. I was delivering babies and taking care of them, treating all the infectious diseases, doing some surgery, and getting to know and like, and to be liked by, some of the population of an area that comprised about a quarter of a million people.

I was never entirely comfortable with Joey and his friends, but in the general mix of patients, most of them solid citizens, I had mobsters, whores, and madams to deal with. They were a minute, sparkling, sometimes frightening part of my practice. To balance them, many police officers came to me as patients. When the mobsters and the police met in my waiting room, relations were always cordial. Each earned his living in his own way.

Late one Saturday evening Joey asked to come to my office. When he removed his jacket I saw that he was wearing a belted holster under his right arm. From it protruded the handle of a gun.

"What's that doing there?"

"I'm left-handed."

"I mean what are you coming in here with that thing for?"

"Oh. I had a job tonight and I haven't been home yet. So it came with me."

"What was the job?" I should have known better than to ask.

"I'll tell you, Doc. Tonight's Saturday night, and that's when the money's made. My partner and I heard that one of our houses was going to be ripped off by another mob, so we thought we'd go up there, to Seventy-second Street."

I had heard about Joey's partner, but I had had the good fortune never to have met him. I knew he was an Italian, about forty-eight years old. I had been told he was a good man to avoid.

"Anyhow," continued Joey, "we drove up there about eight o'clock and saw a car parked with its lights out. We parked on the other side of the street and waited. We could see three men in the car. We waited and they waited.

"Finally, my partner says go talk to them, so I did. I crossed the street to their car and put my foot on the running board. I knew the men. They looked at me but didn't say anything. I figured it was my turn.

"'Look, you fellows,' I said, 'this is one of my houses. It's the way I earn my living. I got a wife and three kids of my own to support and four kids of my brother's, who was killed last year.'

"'Now,' I says, taking out my knife and sharpening it on the car door, 'my partner and I want you to think about it and go home.'"

Joey told me that at this point he returned to his car. He sat in his car and the other men sat in theirs. They seemed to be having a discussion. Finally, they started their car and drove off.

"You didn't say you had a knife."

"Sure I have, Doc. I always have."

He pulled a switchblade from his pants' pocket, and it opened immediately.

"Put it away. I'm convinced. But how did you know they were going to stick up one of your houses?"

"Oh, they called us up to let us know."

That was a gang technique I never figured out. I hesitated to ask more. I didn't want to know too much.

The whole underworld seemed to agree to certain conventions. If a man took it on the lam—that is, if he fled retribution—the Ben Franklin Hotel in Philadelphia provided sanctuary. The same absolute security from any gang was given lammisters at a hotel in Akron, Ohio. If there was not honor among thieves there was at least understanding.

One day Joey came to see me, and he was beaming. "Doc, I got a good thing for you. How would you like to make three hundred bucks every Monday examining girls?"

That was fifteen thousand dollars a year, and this in the middle of the Depression!

"I'd like it very much, but what's the catch?"

"No catch, Doc. Lucky says if I like you so much I can send you one hundred girls every Monday to examine for clap and the syph, and each one gives you three bucks. 'Course, you'd have to get another couple nurses and tables."

The money sounded good to a beginner, but this was not ordinary medical practice. As soon as Joey had left the office I called and asked two of my friends who were on the vice squad to drop in and see me when they could. They were good enough to come that day.

Detectives Kiley and Maher heard out my story.

Detective Kiley, a young, handsome Irishman, said, "You're a doctor. You can examine anyone you please. The catch is that Luciano wants to use you as a front. There'll be someone here who'll use your phone to assign the girls to the whorehouses. Then you're in trouble. If you want the job, tell Joey that you'll examine the girls, but that immediately after the examination they must leave. As long as no one uses your phone, you're in the clear."

I thanked them. Their advice increased my lasting regard for the Police Department.

When Joey returned for his answer, he was greatly disturbed. "Lucky ain't going to like this," he said. "He may take it out of my hide. Nobody turns Lucky down."

Later he came back with even worse news. "Lucky is madder than hell. He's out to get you. He says he can buy any doctor in New York. He says he don't intend to be insulted by a creep like you."

I took Joey's words to heart. For weeks thereafter I dodged into doorways when I heard cars approaching. Two corpses were found with my professional cards in their pockets. One was a man, one a woman. When they were identified an assistant district attorney asked me if I knew them. I had never heard of either one. Nor did I inquire into the cause of death. I didn't want to know.

I hadn't bothered to think about it before, but I learned that I liked being alive. The next patient, male or female, might have been sent to me for purposes of demolition instead of consultation. I didn't relish the idea of being blown away. I didn't feel completely safe until Luciano and his cohorts were in prison. I have always felt grateful to Thomas E. Dewey, who put them there.

Thomas E. Dewey was the special prosecutor appointed to rid New York County of organized crime. That meant all of Manhattan. Dewey persevered with the investigation and indictment of Luciano. More than five hundred witnesses appeared before the grand jury. The underworld was shaken.

One day Peggy flounced into my office. "Two of your friends are in the waiting room with two of their friends."

I knew what she meant. I was reading and didn't bother to look up. She was telling me that two girls that Dewey was using as witnesses in the case against Luciano were present, guarded by a policeman and a policewoman. Over a period of a few months we had become accustomed to their procedure. The girls were patients of mine, and they were guaranteed police protection from the Mafia until their testimony. The guarantee was in effect twenty-four hours a day—every day.

One of the girls was named Merri. I'd asked her once how her parents had chosen her name.

"That isn't the name they gave me, Doc. I thought it up myself," she answered. "In this business we choose our own names. Right now it's any name, so long as it ends in *i*. It's the fashion, see? Next year maybe I'll put an *e* on the end of it."

"I never had it so good," Merri told me. "We're always guarded in pairs, but we live all over town at the best hotels. The only trouble is, we move every few days. How do you like my coat? They bought it for me." She pointed to a fur on the hanger behind the door. By "they" I took her to mean Dewey's team.

"I never let it out of my sight," she said. "I never had such luxury."

"How many girls are working for Dewey?" I asked.

"Maybe fifty. Maybe a hundred. I hear he sent some of them to Paris. With cops, of course. It's just as cheap as staying in the good places here.

"Funny thing, Doc. The gossip is that Dewey's trying to get Luciano for the one thing he's not guilty of, prostitution." She laughed. "If he's not guilty of prostitution, I'm not guilty of prostitution."

Peggy was always in the room when I examined women, so she had heard most of the conversation. She fondled the fur coat.

"May I try it on?" she asked Merri.

"Sure. Go ahead."

Peggy practically purred. She turned back and forth in front of the mirror, stroking the coat, her little white nurse's cap perched on her head.

"This is really good mink," she pronounced. "Any openings in your line of business, Merri?"

In 1935 organized crime was still organized, under the aegis of Lucky Luciano. But Luciano obviously had more important things to do than have me killed. I gradually began to feel safe again. Luciano must have bought himself some other doctor. In 1936 Dewey succeeded in winning convictions for compulsory prostitution against Luciano and many of his henchmen.

Joey, however, remained part of my life. He came in with another proposition. "Doc," he said, "I'm going into the six-for-five business with some partners. If you want to put up some cash, I'll make you some quick money."

"What's the six-for-five business?"

"It's like this, Doc. We call it shylocking, too. You loan out five dollars, and at the end of the week you get back six. If the guy can't pay six then he pays one, and the five and another one get paid the week after. See? So at the end of a year, a guy could pay fifty-two bucks to use five, and he still owes you the first five. You get it?"

This small-loan business was conducted mainly among working people like cabdrivers and dock workers, and particularly those who played the horses. Sometimes the same people who took the racing bets loaned the money. They had a good thing going.

If a man didn't choose to make bets, he could be replaced at his job by a man who did. It was a trap from which there was no escape. Ordinary collateral was not accepted. The borrower's body was the collateral. Those who ran up debts they couldn't or wouldn't pay were visited by enforcers, who usually worked in pairs. The victims would be slugged back and forth between them and would be left with one, or preferably two, broken arms.

Joey went into the six-for-five business without me.

For some time two goons had been coming to my office. Their presence irritated me. They always came together but usually not as patients. They brought others as patients. They would sit in the waiting room and leave with the people they had brought. Often they brought girls, and I took it for granted that they were pimps. But they also brought in sick and elderly people from all over town, patients who were really in need of care. From their names I gathered that the patients were the relatives and dependents of mobsters. The hoods may have known that I didn't want them around, but they caused no trouble. I had no reason to tell them not to come, but I always felt uneasy when they arrived. They must have thought I was a good doctor.

We seldom spoke together, but one day one of the goons asked "to have words with the Doc." He took me aside and said, "Doc, your friend Joey is getting a bad name. He collects but he don't take care of his partners. Tell him."

It was almost a command. I decided that when Joey came in the next time I would tell him what I had heard. But I never had the chance.

Some days later the same two men escorted a new patient to see me. On the way out one said, "Your friend Joey is in Fordham Hospital. He had trouble with some bullets." That was all. I felt disturbed but said nothing.

About six weeks later, the same two came in again. I asked how Joey was.

"He's fine," said one. "The boys are going up to take him home." They looked at each other and laughed. I didn't like the sound of the laugh.

The next day Joey's body was found in an alley, riddled with bullets.

MRS. GELMAN

BELLE was looking out the window.

"It's fascinating," she said. "The whole world is just outside."

The whole world was. The street was busy with passersby and regulars: milkmen and grocery boys, the gas man collecting quarters from the meters, insurance agents on their rounds collecting the ten or twenty-five cents a week people paid for their burial policies. Then there were the newsboys—they must have been boys once—working both sides of the street. "Yuxtra. Yuxtra. Read all about it!" they shouted at the top of their lungs, waving their newspapers. Our neighbors hurried out to buy. They never learned. The only "yuxtra" was the price.

"Look, there go the Gelmans."

I couldn't help smiling. Belle looked stunning with her new pageboy bob.

"What about the Gelmans?" I asked.

"Just look," she said.

The Gelmans lived on the third floor in our ancient building. The structure had been built in the 1890s. It was one of the few neighborhood buildings that had an elevator. The elevator was small and decrepit, but it was a boon for aging people.

I looked down at the passing Gelmans. First I saw Mr. Gelman. He was the proprietor of a two-man cleaning and pressing establishment crammed into a twenty-foot store down the block. I was one of his customers. Mrs. Gelman walked six steps behind Mr. Gelman, unhurried and making no effort to catch up.

"What's so interesting about them?" I asked.

"Don't you see? They're still an Old World couple. She walks behind him like the women in a Polish or Russian *shtetl*."

A *shtetl* was a small, backward, and backwoods village whose Jewish population clung to habits of the Middle Ages.

Belle went on: "Mrs. Gelman is a lovely woman. She has the gentlest voice. I know her from the stores. The tradespeople around here cater to her more than they do to anybody else. They say that Mr. Gelman isn't mean, just grumpy. He complains when he doesn't get the service he expects."

"You are learning the neighborhood, aren't you?"

"Of course. It's like a picture book for children. Lots of things are always happening. Mrs. Gelman told me there are very few Jewish people in the area. Did you know?"

"Come to think of it, I didn't think of it. I have very few Jewish patients. Mainly I have Irish, German, French, lots of Italians, and some Orientals. There are even two Turkish families down the block who are my patients. But now that you mention it, you're right."

Belle smiled. "I'll tell you more about Mrs. Gelman. She told me at the meat market yesterday that she watches over Mr. Gelman as if he were a child. If that isn't the Old Country then I don't know my geography."

Some months later Mrs. Gelman rang my bell. "Mr. Gelman is sick," she said. (She always called him "Mr. Gelman.") "Could you maybe find the time to come upstairs to see him?"

"Of course," I said, "I'll find time now." I got my bag, walked to the front apartment, and told Belle that I was calling on Mr. Gelman.

"I hope it's nothing," she said.

"Most calls are usually nothing," I assured her.

The Gelman apartment was Old Country, indeed. All of the furniture was clean and polished. It had been cleaned and polished for years—for generations. Mr. Gelman lay in an old brass bed.

He was covered with a *daunenbett*, a lofty quilt filled with down. He didn't look good.

"I have pain here," he said, pointing to his lower abdomen. "It started this morning and gets worse."

I examined him. His abdomen was slightly distended, and the right lower quadrant was tense, almost rigid. I tried to lift my examining hand away as gently as possible but he jerked and let out an "Oy!"

In those days we had no antibiotics. I was fearful of an appendix that might rupture and cause peritonitis. I didn't believe that he had peritonitis then, because usually there is a short period of relief from pain after an infected appendix ruptures. His temperature was 100.5, and his pulse, at 96, was moderately rapid.

Mrs. Gelman had been standing by all during the examination. I told her that her husband's blood pressure and heart were good, that his chest was clear, but that I feared he might have appendicitis. For safety's sake it would be better to hospitalize him.

She shrugged. "You're the doctor. Whatever you say."

She indicated the phone in the kitchen. I made arrangements for the hospital to admit him and called an ambulance. Except for a few "oys," the patient had very little to say. I'd been told he never talked much anyhow.

"Can I go with him?" Mrs. Gelman asked.

"Of course," I said. "I'll be there shortly after they get him to bed. I'll arrange for a surgeon to see him."

I went downstairs to report to Belle. "I hope you're wrong," she said, with a toss of her head.

"You don't seem to have much confidence."

"Oh, I have confidence in your ability," she said. "But I think that Mr. Gelman can be a fooler."

I reexamined Mr. Gelman at the hospital. The right lower quadrant of his abdomen was still rigid. The laboratory report showed a white blood cell count of 14,000. A normal reading would have been between 4,000 and 10,000. The most common cause of a high white count is infection. But a high count could also be caused by the irritation of an organ or even by a good meal.

The surgeon, Dr. Alexander Kaye, came in to examine the

patient. I introduced him to a subdued Mrs. Gelman. When his examination was done he said, "We have an old expression about appendicitis: 'When it doubt, take it out.'" He walked to the elevator, leaving me with the prospect of immediate surgery ahead.

Mrs. Gelman pulled at my sleeve. Suddenly I realized how right Belle was. This was a remnant of an Old Country habit. She was an Old Country woman. Who else pulls sleeves?

Very quietly, trying not to hurt my feelings, Mrs. Gelman said, "Dr. Slocum, we had an old family doctor for years. He retired, so we come to you. Would you mind we should call him before we operate?"

I wanted to do all that I could to relieve her mind. "By all means. Give me his name and telephone number and I'll call him myself."

I got her former doctor on the phone. "I suppose you know that I don't practice anymore," he said. "You young fellows are more advanced than we were in my day. You should know what you're doing. Do you really want me?"

"Mrs. Gelman wants you, and if she wants you, then I want you," I told him. There was a perceptible pause.

"All right. I'll be there shortly."

The good doctor looked the part and was a thoughtful gentleman. He had a white beard and white hair—not silvery white but just plain white—and he was erect and a bit pudgy. He resembled everybody's grandfather. His manner was cordial and courtly. He put his arm about Mrs. Gelman and kissed her cheek.

He, too, examined the patient with me. Then he took me into a vacant room and closed the door.

"Doctor, I think it's wonderful the care you're giving this family. I can't stay any longer, but there's something I want to suggest.

"I've known these people for many years, and I know that Mr. Gelman suffers from periodic depression. There's never an event to trigger it. I believe he's simply one of those individuals who has a tendency to suffer depression. When he's depressed he functions poorly. One of the things that happens is that he withholds most of his urine. I've known him to do this a couple of times, and each time the result was severe abdominal pain. Why don't you try passing a catheter before you operate?"

He got up to go. "I have to meet my wife now, but give a thought to what I said. It's only a suggestion, but you can't lose anything by it." Then he left.

I sent for a catheter and passed it into Mr. Gelman with some difficulty. I recovered a large quantity of urine from him, and the patient immediately felt relief from his pain.

I sent the Gelmans home. By this time, Mr. Gelman was well enough to walk. He left the hospital six paces in front of Mrs. Gelman.

I called Belle to tell her what had happened. She sounded very smug. When I reached home, she was triumphant.

"I knew you were wrong, because I wanted you to be," she announced.

"Why should you want me to be wrong?"

"Sometimes it's better to be wrong," she laughed. "Besides, you ain't all that smart."

The Gelmans remained my patients for many years. "We like you. You don't make believe you're a professor," said Mrs. Gelman.

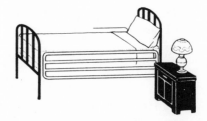

PATRICK SHAW

IT WAS an ordinary operation, although for a time we thought we were opening the abdomen to what might be a gangrenous gall bladder. I had told Paddy months before that the recurrent pain in his right upper abdomen was caused by stones in his gall bladder.

X-rays had disclosed the stones. The gall bladder was filled with them. There seemed to be dozens, of various sizes.

"It's just a vestigial organ," I explained to Paddy, "like your appendix. You don't need it. What's it there for? It's there to make money for surgeons!

"It's not the large stones that are disturbing you," I continued, "it's the small ones. Every now and then one slips into the canal leading out of the gall bladder and distends it. Then you have pain until the stone slides into a larger canal. When it can get through it no longer distends the tube and your pain stops. But one of these days a stone will lodge there and won't be able to get through. Then you'll really be sick. That's not the time to operate. The time to take that gall bladder out is now, when you're well."

I knew Paddy had respect for my judgment. I was the doctor for his whole family, three generations of them. Paddy gave the matter grave thought.

He wasn't really thinking. What he was doing was struggling with his belief, common among many of my Irish patients, that the hospital was a place you walked into but were carried out of. The hospital was the place you went to die. His decision was not to decide.

"I'll wait a little longer," he said.

A few nights later Paddy had a recurrence of pain. This time the pain didn't stop. At midnight his wife, in nightgown and bathrobe, was ringing my bell. I dressed and went to see him.

Like many of my patients, the Shaw family did not live on the street. You entered a tenement hallway from the street, walked straight back to a door that opened into a yard about twenty feet wide, and then into another house whose front door faced the yard. Paddy's rooms were one flight up. When people said they lived one flight up in the rear, they meant they lived in a building behind the building on the street.

There were a lot of relatives milling about in the rooms. Paddy and his wife used their living room as their bedroom. The children were in the next room back. Mrs. Shaw's parents lived in the rear bedroom next to the kitchen. The passage from living room to kitchen was through the two bedrooms. But the passage was not in the center of the rooms, as in a Louisiana "shotgun" house. The passage was along the side wall. Rooms like the Shaws' were called "railroad flats," but it was continental railroad carriages that they resembled.

Paddy was really ill. He had a fever of 103, ached all over, and could find no comfortable spot to lie on. The right upper quadrant of his abdomen was stiff as a board. I tried to be gentle, but he fended off my hand when I touched him. There was another sign I could have elicited—a sign known as rebound tenderness, which caused the patient pain when the examining hand was suddenly removed. This was a barbaric maneuver I seldom found necessary.

I went back to the kitchen to give my report to the anxious assemblage. Mrs. Shaw took me to the kitchen sink, where she had placed an immaculate towel and had opened a brand new cake of hand soap for me. Anyone would have loved these people.

There were a couple of open bottles on the table that had attracted the interest of Paddy's brother, his two nephews, and his father. They drew out a chair for me as they invited me to join them. I did, for one drink. I wanted to keep my head clear.

"What do you think, Doc?" Paddy's father asked. He poured a substantial amount of liquid with an almost steady hand. Two of his fingers were useless. He was receiving a pension from the Irish government for this wound suffered in the uprising of 1916. Like many others he had had to be smuggled out of Ireland under penalty of death. I had a dozen patients on pensions from the Irish Republic. They'd been wounded in the time of the Troubles.

"Hospital," I said, raising my glass. "If he doesn't go, he'll get peritonitis—if he hasn't got it already. Let's send him in, fix him up, and send him home."

I envisaged no difficulty from the operation itself. Paddy had the usual thin build of a young, hard-working Irishman. There was no fat to wade through, to become infected, or to retard healing. His muscles were deceptively scrawny, the type that when called on can deliver the blow of a pile driver.

In the colloquy that followed I remained silent. Paddy's sister-in-law and his nephews' wives had much to say. Despite their American upbringing, they were still Old Country people in their horror of hospitals. Finally Mrs. Shaw ended the argument.

"Joe, you run to the corner and flag down a cab. I'll dress Paddy. As soon as the cab comes, you men help him into it and get him to the hospital. I'll get dressed and I'll follow you."

I left them and returned to my office to make arrangements with the surgeon, the anesthetist, and the operating room. I told the hospital to expect Paddy.

The surgeon, the radiologist, and I went over the plates. The X-rays showed the gall bladder on the undersurface of the liver and the small, distended cystic duct emptying into the common duct. The surgeon had already been with me to examine the patient.

The surgeon was not one to keep his peace when he thought a patient had been mishandled. "Why did you keep him at home so long? Were you waiting for him to rot?"

I knew the man and loved him, and I was more amused than angry at his blast.

"Have you ever been in general practice?" I asked him. "You can't kidnap people. You just take care of the pathology, and afterward I'll explain it to you over the drink you're going to buy me."

The operating room was a lively place when the patient, already sedated, was brought in. The nurse at the table had all the essential instruments out and placed on trays to be most convenient for us. The circulating nurse and a probationary nurse—a student —were adjusting the lights to preclude any shadow on the surgical field. The orderly, after assisting in placing the patient on the table, moved back to a corner stool to await any command that might be given him.

"It must be great to be a surgeon," I said.

He ignored me. He was busy.

The surgeon was watching to make sure the entire abdomen was painted with a sterilizing solution. "Paint what you see," he stressed to the nurse. It was the surgeons' refrain. She went at her job with renewed vigor.

The surgeon was accustomed to having me as his assistant. "How many hands are you going to use tonight?" he asked, referring to my proclivity to handle instruments with either hand.

The operation took a little more than half an hour. When the gall bladder was exposed there was a small abscess where a stone had lodged in the wall of the duct and was burrowing its way through.

The cystic duct is a small duct leading from the gall bladder into a larger duct, the bile duct, which conveys bile from the liver to the intestine. The gall bladder and its cystic duct can be dispensed with without interfering with metabolism, but the bile duct must be maintained and open to allow bile from the liver to reach the intestine. Otherwise, trouble.

The small abscess had been just at the junction of the two ducts. When the surgeon was ready to tie off the cystic duct just below the abscess, I started to tie it for him. He struck my fingers with a hemostat.

"You keep out of there," he ordered. "That's one knot I intend to put in myself."

Oh, well. It was all for the good of the patient.

"He's a very, very lucky man," the surgeon said. "A few more hours—and a rupture and peritonitis. We caught him just in time."

Afterward, sitting over our drinks in a nearby after-hours club, I said, "This had to be an emergency operation. It took an emergency to bring him in. You thought we decided to operate? The family decided to operate! They managed to keep him out of surgery for months!"

I named the date that Paddy had first come to see me for severe abdominal pain. The surgeon shook his head in wonder. "He must have suffered."

"But anything was better than the hospital! And furthermore," I said, when I thought he could absorb the news, "They're poor. You're not going to be paid much for this job, Doctor. Neither am I."

For a time he was silent. He looked out of the window, where the first gray of the morning was beginning to lighten the sky. Then he said, "In that case, you pay for the drinks."

DRINK

Next door to my office was a dilapidated building, built before the turn of the century. It stood five stories high and presented to the street an unpolished but lovely granite facade. There were two apartments to each floor. A central lobby led to an elevator, which, when it ran, clicked and clacked at each landing as if warning the occupants of approaching guests.

Each apartment had two bay windows. The main rooms were large and bright. The living rooms and the dining rooms were separated by sliding doors, which could disappear into the walls to convert the two rooms into one. The apartments had maids' quarters and butlers' pantries.

Like many houses on the block, the building had been designed for wealthy people who were beginning to want "flats" instead of houses. These old apartments were still desirable because they were convenient to anyplace in the city via the Ninth Avenue Elevated Railroad. But the rich had long since moved to the East Side. The neighborhood had run down. People moved in because they liked big rooms at reasonable rentals. The tenants of my day had no pretense, but they had space, light, and comfort.

In this next-door building lived a dark-haired, dark-skinned, and dark-eyed young liquor dealer. He was eager and alert, and he was beginning to make a successful career out of wholesale distribution. After the repeal of Prohibition, the Mafia found more lucrative fields than the control of the liquor industry. The business was wide open. Felix had qualified easily for a license from the new state board.

His name was Nemour, Felix Nemour. I was uncertain about his origin but he was probably a Levantine. He told me, when I took his medical history, that he never drank. "It is against the principles of my people. Alcohol is forbidden." I never asked what his religion was.

Felix had married a blonde, shapely girl, one of the vast number of youngsters in the Thespian trade who never made it to the top. Xandra was an attractive woman who worked in one or another of the fancy Fifth Avenue dress shops. She told me proudly that she was "a perfect ten." I had to ask my wife to interpret. "*Size* ten," she said, exasperated at my ignorance.

When I first moved into the neighborhood the Nemours were finding it hard going, but Xandra wasn't worried about Felix's future or about hard times. She had confidence in her own ability to get jobs and to keep them. There would always be elegant dress shops, no matter the state of the economy. "The rich always have money," she said. She was right.

Soon Felix began to prosper, and over time Xandra developed a clientele of her own. They entertained a great deal, for business and pleasure. Xandra had decorated their apartment handsomely. It was fun to visit them.

"A lot of people who come to our parties come for the food and drink," Xandra told me. "It's good for my business at the store and it's good for Felix's business as well. I beautify the outer woman. He satisfies the inner man." She gave a sophisticated titter.

As I entered the office one morning Peggy was sitting at her desk. She turned to me with a saintly smile. She was entirely composed and serene, and I might have thought she was angelic if I hadn't seen the devil in her eyes.

"You're late," she said. "It would have been a good day to be early."

"What's the hurry?"

"The hurry is we have a madman in the office who can't or won't sit down. Where've you been?"

"I've been to Charlie's listening post and bootblack parlor. I got a shine and the latest on what's new in the neighborhood."

"I know. That's where you have your shoes shined so you can place your bets."

"Who told you Charlie's a bookie?"

"Charlie told me. He promised me he's not taking any more she-notes from you. He said you're always putting two-dollar bills on horses that pull milk wagons when they're not at the track."

Peggy got down to business: "You'd better take your friend Felix in first. He's wandering around the office like a caged lion. I can't get him to sit down. I thought he was your patient who sold liquor but didn't drink it."

"He doesn't drink it. It's against his religion or something."

"Well, maybe he's just changed religions. But take him first."

Felix came in. "I sat down on a glass, Doctor." He let down his trousers and underwear and leaned over my examining table. His buttocks were bleeding in many places. I spent a good half hour removing shards of glass.

"It was a champagne glass," he went on. "It was no fault of mine. When my guests have a little too much of what I sell they get careless. Well, this fellow stocks his store with my champagne. He said he was testing it. After he tested enough of it he left his glass on the seat of my chair. You know that upholstered chair I like so much? I didn't notice and I sat down on it. That's the whole story."

He left in good shape. I said to Peggy, "You may be damned smart, but I was right. He doesn't drink."

She was busy typing out reports, but she stopped for a moment and said, "There's a large bridge that connects Manhattan with Brooklyn. How'd you like to buy it?"

The end of the year 1937 came, and Felix and Xandra gave a bash to celebrate the fact that all was right with the world. At least, all was right with Felix and Xandra. The party was given in the oversized rooms of their old apartment. The space could accommodate any number of guests, particularly when the sliding doors between the living and dining rooms were pushed back.

It was a great party. Felix and Xandra were exemplary hosts. I didn't see Felix drink a thing. All evening he circulated among his guests, holding a tall glass filled with what he said was soda water. A pretty curl of lemon rind swam in the glass. Peggy wouldn't meet my eyes.

"Beautiful people, beautiful clothes," my wife Belle murmured. She looked beautiful herself, in a knockout dress she'd bought from Xandra at a knock-down price.

I got to the office a little late the next morning, wondering if Peggy would get there at all. She was there all right. And there again was that angelic, imperturbable smile: "Felix is waiting in your examining room."

Sure enough, Felix was there, his trousers and underwear down. His buttocks displayed multiple cuts and bits of gleaming glass.

"Don't tell me—"

"You're right, Doctor. Exactly the same thing. I sat down in the upholstered chair."

This visit lasted for more than an hour. Felix was very patient, although I noticed from his wincing that I was really causing him pain.

Through the examining room door I could hear the business of the office going on without me. Peggy answered the phone and the doorbell, and escorted patients into the waiting room. I heard her tell someone that the doctor was taking care of an emergency. That brought a murmur from Felix. Peggy did interrupt me once.

"Mrs. O'Halloran calling," she said, sticking her head in the doorway. "A bad chill."

The term "chill" has a specific meaning to the physician. I wanted to determine if Mrs. O'Halloran was really having one. I picked up the extension phone.

"Are you cold?" I asked her. "Are you shivering all over? Do your muscles shake? Are your teeth chattering?"

"I'm cold all over," she reported. "My muscles are trembling. But hold the phone a minute while I see about my teeth. They're in the bathroom in a glass."

I dealt with Mrs. O'Halloran's chill and went back to extracting glass. But Felix protested: "Doctor, would you mind waiting until you stop laughing?"

When I'd finished the job I dressed the wounds as best I could.

"You'd better go home and lie down on your face for a couple of days. The buttocks have poor circulation—there's no reason to encourage infection."

He agreed to that. "I must say," I commiserated, "that twice, for no reason, you have run into bad luck."

The corners of his mouth turned up.

"Bad luck? My dear Doctor, let's just call it the evils of drink."

He left. Peggy floated in, serene and expressionless. "Hey, Doc. You know that bridge I was telling you about—"

I threw a book at her. It was something by Freud, and heavy.

COLORED GIRL'S
DELIVERY

I LOOKED at the clock. It said 5:30—5:30 A.M. Sleep was impossible. My bones ached. I was sore all over.

My temper was short from fatigue, but I wouldn't let it show. I had no intention of oppressing my wife, Number One or Number Two Nurse, or my patients.

There were just too many night calls. I was determined to cut them down, but I saw no way to do it. I wondered if I shouldn't give up teaching. I didn't like emergency calls to interfere with my lectures. Could I, despite exhaustion, maintain the quality of my work? Had I done things right yesterday? Had I left anything essential undone?

Thinking I wouldn't be busy in practice, I had taken a teaching position offered to me by Dr. Schmahl, professor of medicine, whom I greatly admired. It was a nonpaying position. Physicians in practice weren't paid when they were on the teaching staff.

While I enjoyed the work, teaching had its disadvantages. One had to be in the lecture hall or at the bedside of a patient two or three times a week at an appointed time. That meant planning and organization. I kept completely clear of medical politics, and so the only evening meetings I attended were clinical meetings. Still, the timing was rough, and as I got busier it got rougher. Except for the hiatus of the Second World War, I held the job for twenty-five years.

That morning, a long hot shower followed by a cold one relieved my weariness. I dressed slowly, had coffee and a buttered bagel, read through the *New York Times*, and then, at about 7:30, went to my office.

Everything was in order there. Peggy sat pasting yesterday's laboratory reports into the charts. She gave me a quick glance but didn't deign to greet me.

"Either you're terribly devoted," I said, "or you're just plain dumb. What are you doing here this early?"

"I went to early Mass. I always go to early Mass on the way to work. Today I went earlier."

I knew from the sound of her voice that she was really disturbed about something. I felt it would be cruel to rag her, so I was silent. I indicated by my silence that when or if she wanted to, she could tell me all.

Shortly thereafter she came into my office and sat on my desk in her usual position—with her legs swinging.

"Dr. Slocum, I think I've committed a mortal sin."

"Before you go any further, Peggy, I must say that you're not the type. But tell me about it. I'll be glad to listen."

"Well, day before yesterday, after a party, I slept over at a friend's apartment on Riverside Drive. Yesterday morning I went to Mass at a church I'd passed the night before. It looked like a Roman Catholic church. There was a font of holy water inside the entrance. But during the service I began to wonder. No Latin! When I left I found out: it was an Anglican church. I feel very guilty. I don't know what to do."

For Peggy this was no small problem. The Roman Catholic Church did not take kindly to its parishioners attending the services of other faiths.

"I tell you what. I'm of the opinion that the Lord takes intent into consideration. You didn't intend to sin, if that's what you think you did. In fact, you intended exactly the opposite. The next time you go to confession tell the priest. I'm sure he'll agree with me."

"I'm afraid to go. I'm afraid of what he'll say."

"I can't argue a religious point with you, Peggy, because I can't reach you the way a priest would. If you want I'll call Father Roosens at the Belgian church and ask him."

I knew Monseigneur Roosens through my Belgian patients. I had often sat in a patient's home having a drink with him. At all hours, too.

"Maybe later," Peggy said. "Let me think. I almost always go to the Paulist Fathers. That's my church."

The doorbell and the phone rang at the same time. The day and its problems began. Mrs. Vicente's surgery was scheduled for later that morning.

Some problems are like Things in the dark that disappear when the lights go on. I didn't know whether the surgery scheduled for Mrs. Vicente would kill her or cure her. The cardiologist, the surgeon, and I agreed that her heart couldn't take much strain. We knew also that she couldn't live with the mass that X-rays clearly disclosed in her large bowel. Surgery was essential, no matter how bleak the outlook.

The anesthetist was doing all he could to be helpful. He suggested we use a rectal anesthetic called Avertin that had recently come to us from Germany. His experience with it had been good. Avertin was supposed to take some of the load off the heart. If necessary, other anesthetics could be used with it.

Like most medications, Avertin was here today and gone tomorrow. It has long since been forgotten. Most surgeons today have never even heard of it. I don't know why its use was discontinued, but there must have been good reasons. With Mrs. Vicente it worked better than we had hoped.

Mrs. Vicente was a sixty-seven-year-old woman with long, bushy gray hair, big brown eyes, and a sanguine disposition. Her complaint was loss of appetite and weight, and a recurrent diarrhea. I had diagnosed her disease as cancer of the colon.

The anesthetist gave Mrs. Vicente an enema of Avertin in her hospital room. When she came into surgery she was completely anesthetized.

The opened abdomen displayed the pathology. There was cancer all right, but it seemed to be isolated. No glands in the area were involved, and her liver was entirely free of metastases.

We excised the mass by cutting the intestine above and below it, and removed the entire involved area. We brought the severed ends of the bowel together, suturing the inner layers and then the outer, thus creating a continuous tube as functional as any bowel could be. The surgeon searched for any enlarged lymph glands and found absolutely none. Within an hour Mrs. Vicente, still sound asleep, was back in her room with a special nurse. In those days, nearly half a century ago, we had no recovery rooms.

The surgeon said to me, "Thank you for assisting. That woman will make a complete recovery, and from what you say about her family history she should live another twenty years." I had no doubts. That problem had solved itself.

At nine P.M. I was hoping the day was over. I wanted to relax, do some reading, and spend some time with my wife.

The bell rang. It was Jimmy Goodwin, the cop on the beat.

"Doc," he said, "there's some trouble down on Fifty-fourth Street. There's a girl in labor there with no one else at home. We had the ambulance for her, but she won't go to the hospital and the ambulance surgeon says he can't stay there and wait to deliver her. Maybe you can give a hand."

"Sure," I said. "Maybe I can persuade her to go in." I took my bag along just in case. Jimmy wished me good luck. "The door's open," he said.

The red-brick tenement was not prepossessing. Unlike most buildings of its kind, it had a two-foot lawn in front of it. An iron railing separated the yard from the street. The right front ground floor apartment was lighted. I knew the layout by heart.

What I wasn't prepared for was the immaculate room. Lying there on a carefully smoothed bed was a young black girl. A policeman was sitting by the bed. It was Leo Gates, the great giant of a man who had been a sparring partner of Jack Dempsey's.

"Glad you're here, Doc. I was going to stay until you came. I hoped I wouldn't have to deliver her." He heaved a huge sigh. "I sure am glad to see you." He pulled on his sweater and his greatcoat, patted the girl's hand, and left.

I turned to the young woman. Her face had become swollen and distorted by the travail of her recurrent labor pains.

"How old are you?"

She looked at me with great, troubled eyes. "Twenty-three."

"New in the neighborhood?"

"Yes, sir."

"Husband?"

"He's a seaman. I expected him back before today, but his ship's delayed."

"Why won't you go to the hospital?"

"I can't, Doctor. I'm afraid of hospitals. Besides, I have a three-year-old daughter. She's in the next apartment with the neighbors. She's asleep. I don't know them very well. The woman wanted to stay with me, but she's old and she has a bad heart."

Her pain was beginning again, and in her agony she grabbed my hand. The veins of her neck distended and she perspired copiously. When the pain subsided she got up from the bed.

"Look, Doctor. I'm all prepared." She showed me a pile of spotless sheets, cotton, gauze, and a stack of fresh newspapers. "I have water boiling in the kitchen. Yesterday I scrubbed the whole apartment with Lysol. I wanted to be ready to have my baby at home." She paused for a moment. "I can't pay you now, Doctor. I shall as soon as my husband comes home."

No question, the room was spotless. There might have been far more luxurious rooms, but none better kept or cleaner. It was quite a contrast to the day before, when I'd visited a private patient in an expensive hospital. A porter had come in while I was there— I wouldn't have believed it if I hadn't seen it—and began to mop the floor. He had no business interrupting my conversation with my patient or even coming in while I was present. I threw him out, but not before his dirty mop had left a splash of filth on the baseboard and the wall above it.

I had called the hospital administrative office to complain. The girl there said, "I'm sorry, but the union doesn't permit them to clean above the baseboard."

"But he put the dirt there in the first place!"

"We can't do anything about it. You'll have to take it up with the union."

I felt frustrated, but I decided to take my beating and not go further into the matter. That was one reason I looked with sympathy on this poor girl's wishes.

"All right," I said. "I'm licked. I'll stay, if you agree to go to the hospital if there are complications."

There was gratitude in her eyes. Another pain was beginning.

My nurse, Peggy, pushed into the room. "Mrs. Slocum called me and said there might be a long job here. She said Jimmy Goodwin told her. So I figured I might as well drop by."

"Drop by, hell," I said. "You're supposed to be in Washington Heights celebrating your mother's birthday. You're always look-ing for trouble. Aren't you afraid your boyfriend and your mother will kill each other?"

She gave me one of her malicious smiles. She knew how glad I was to see her.

She studied the room. "Everything's here that we need, and I brought the medical stuff." Then she sat by the bedside and talked to the girl.

"You see how men are. He wouldn't know how hard you worked to get this place in good order. He couldn't understand."

Three hours later we delivered a healthy girl. The exhausted young woman didn't even try to thank us. She knew that we knew what she thought.

Peggy went next door and carried back the sleeping three-year-old. "I'll stay the night. By tomorrow the mother can make other arrangements. She may be up herself."

"You know, Peggy, we keep the women in the hospital ten days."

"You don't have to," she answered. "Any healthy young mother needs twenty-four hours of rest after a normal delivery. That's what my mother says. On the farms in Slovakia, she told me, all the girls were back in the fields in two days. You doctors have a lot to learn."

She walked me to the door.

"Say, Peggy, how do you feel about what worried you so much this morning? I hope you know now that you did nothing wrong."

"I'm not sure."

"Well, I can tell you. Anything you did yesterday has been forgiven you tonight."

She closed the door gently in my face.

A MAN'S HOME

Belle and I felt exuberant. Our plans were all awry, for the good reason that we hadn't expected to live this well this soon. We now had two apartments. The one in the rear was our office; the one in the front was our home. A door cut into the wall between them was our private passage.

There we were, with a practice, a home, and each other. We even had an office nurse, so that Belle could move about freely. She could start a social life for us. I was busy. Enough money came in to keep us well-housed, well-clothed, and well-fed.

Then Belle got pregnant! All sorts of new conversation and interest entered our lives. My nurse, Peggy, was so excited, you would have thought she was Belle's younger sister. I was thrilled myself.

One morning when I was out on my hospital rounds, Belle called me. She was in active labor, but she hadn't been expected to deliver for another month and a half! I knew how rapid premature delivery could be. I had Peggy cancel everything and I hurried home. I telephoned Belle's obstetrician, loaded Belle into the car with her little suitcase, and drove to Policlinic Hospital. On the way Belle said, "If this is all there is to it, I could have a baby every week."

Belle was delivered easily within an hour of our arrival. The infant girl weighed only four pounds but was otherwise healthy. Or so we thought. She was a beautiful baby, a baby in miniature. We were anxious to see her gain strength and weight, and she did. Today the treatment of premature infants is a specialty of its own. Nurses and doctors train specifically for the task of saving the very premature and small neonates. They are housed in incubators, fed with eyedroppers, and their hearts, lungs, kidneys, and blood pressure are monitored constantly. Our daughter wasn't in that class. She was six weeks early and very small, but not considered dangerously premature.

The question of a name had not been settled. I was in favor of something dramatic and geographic, different, like Palmyra or Lusitania, Venezia or Fiorenza. Etta, my beautiful sister-in-law, entered the discussion. "How could you do such a thing to a helpless baby?" she demanded. We named the baby Susan Hope.

Our whole interest seemed to center about Susan. I have found this to be the usual thing. I used to wonder about such behavior in my patients. Now that we had our own baby I understood the fascination. There was much coming and going through our private door, as Peggy and I constantly popped into the front apartment to observe Susan and to play with her.

Then one day Belle said anxiously, "I don't like the baby's color." I took Susan outside to see her in full daylight. Belle was right. The baby's skin was almost lemon-yellow. I realized I had been seeing her indoors and by artificial light. In daylight it was obvious: Susan was dreadfully anemic.

We know now that Susan's anemia was probably related to the Rh factor. The Rh factor is a substance present in the red blood cells of most people. Their blood is called Rh positive. If Rh positive blood is mixed with blood which does not contain the Rh factor, called Rh negative blood, either or both groups of red blood cells have a tendency to be destroyed, causing anemia. Such a mixture could occur because of inadequate blood typing before a transfusion, or during pregnancy, if the parents' blood types differ. The name Rh was given to the factor because it was first discovered in the rhesus monkey. In 1936, no one knew about such things. All we knew was that our precious baby had severe anemia, the cause of which was unknown to us.

The pediatrician and the laboratory confirmed our fears. The pediatrician described to us how difficult it was to transfuse a child only a few weeks old. I knew better, and got rid of him. I would have gotten rid of anyone who said he couldn't help us. Belle and I were holding on with all we had in order to avoid panic.

In Vienna I had met Dr. George Ginandes from New York who wanted to observe transfusion of infants. He had come to study, but remained to teach. His own technique was better than any he could learn there, and he returned to New York. I called him. He was good enough to come at once and took our baby to the hospital. He searched for a suitable blood donor, and chose me.

This was fifty years ago, and what was sophisticated then seems rudimentary now. A needle was inserted into my vein. From it a sterile tube ran to a pump which could measure blood flow. From the other side of the pump a tube ran to Susan's arm. It was necessary to cut into the infant's arm at the elbow to find a large enough vein. Dr. Ginandes worked quickly and expertly.

Everything went well. With her anxious mother at her side, Susan slept the night through at the hospital. When she woke, her whole situation, as if by a miracle, had changed for the better. She was active, alert, and hungry, her skin was pink and glowing, and the laboratory reported an improved blood count. We went home.

From then on Susan grew; Lord, how she grew. I watched her with both love and a clinical eye. All I could find was a healthy, delightful, and delicious child.

One day I was at work in the office when Peggy announced, "There's someone in the consultation room you ought to see." That sounded mysterious: who could it be? I asked my patient to excuse me for a moment.

There in the consultation room stood Belle holding the baby. Susan must have been eight months old. She was wearing a white dress with a pink ribbon plaited through it, and a small pink bow was tied in her nearly-white hair. She smiled a big smile and held out her arms to me. She'd never looked so beautiful! When I took her I was lost, irretrievably and forever.

Belle was delighted: "It seems you have a daughter," she said.

Susan was born in late summer—on August 6, 1936, to be exact. In those days mothers and newborns were kept in the hospital ten days or more, and because Susan was premature she stayed even longer. By the time she came home summer was far advanced. There was a chill in the air and at night people kept their windows closed. The window of Susan's small bedroom looked onto an airshaft. Except for the occasional crash of a bottle set carelessly on a windowsill to cool—iceboxes were small—the airshaft was quiet through the night.

Only in daytime was the stillness of the airshaft disturbed. Then Mrs. Moran on the fourth floor might send down a bottle of milk, suspended in a wicker basket, to Mrs. Di Angelo who lived on the second, and people would converse across the void. No one minded the daytime activity, and Susan napped right through it. The voices were neighborly and the commerce-by-basket always amusing.

But when Susan was ten months old, with summer come again, people raised their windows and their voices, and noise of every sort resounded, reverberated, and ricocheted from the walls of the airshaft.

And then there was music.

When the last act ended and the final curtain fell in the Broadway theaters several blocks south, the participants would straggle home. Our building and our neighborhood were full of musicians. At work they played the same music over and over, night after night, and—if they were lucky—week after week: a long-running show was devoutly to be wished. After countless repeat performances the musicians began to question their creativity and maybe their sanity.

Nothing could soothe a musician more than music. In our neighborhood, at midnight or later, when most of the city had gone to bed, the clash of cymbals or blare of trumpets would signal that a jam session was about to begin. A jam session—or maybe even two: two jam sessions in two different apartments, both on our air shaft.

This was the heyday of jazz, and the building rang with fantastic improvisations on themes out of New Orleans. Saxophones wailed and trombones moaned. No doubt the players and playing were brilliant. But often we heard two improvisations at a time, from different windows and on different songs.

"This isn't music," Belle said. "It's cacophony." I agreed. We valued our friendly neighbors but we were tired. A doctor's workday starts early—and our dear baby wasn't sleeping.

At the age of one year, Susan was a poor sleeper. She was up every hour of the night, not calling out or crying, but babbling happily. It took a long time to settle her down again, and my wife had shadows under her eyes from worry and lack of sleep. We had come through one serious crisis with our baby. Were we headed for another?

Perhaps I knew too much: when I listened to our daughter's cooing I would lie in bed worrying, reviewing those diseases which irritate the brain and the nervous system and cause mental overactivity. The child was still somehow good-natured and alert, but she had only the minimum of sleep. Our pediatrician had no suggestions—but then he had no children, either.

Belle was exhausted. It was clear that we needed help. Together we thought of Gabrielle, Gabrielle Vandenborre, that nice young woman who had been a babies' nurse until her mother's illness. Would she come to us and help us take care of Susan? She would.

Gabrielle spent a single night on a bed next to Susan's crib. It was the night of a jam session. It was summer, and all the windows on the airshaft were open. "I cannot sleep in this room," she said. "How do you expect a child to do it? The airshaft has too much noise. *Pauvre petite!* When the beat of the music changes, she awakes. She has learned to awaken during the night, and she does it even when the music is over. This is her illness."

Of course, Gabrielle was right. We knew it in our hearts and we had known it all along, but we hadn't reconciled ourselves to the facts. We couldn't expect the musicians to stop playing so that we could have a peaceful night's sleep. But neither could we go on exposing our baby to intolerable conditions.

We arranged an experiment. Belle, Gabrielle, and Susan would go to Belle's mother's house to spend the weekend. The house in Sea Gate was quiet. Belle's mother would be delighted to have them, and there was plenty of room.

Our experiment worked. Belle called the next morning and her voice was joyous. "Susan slept through the night," she informed me, "and this morning she's bright and frisky. It's that awful noise. That settles it. Gabrielle and Susan will stay here, and you and I will look for another apartment."

We looked for an apartment on the upper West Side. My wife always tried to make things easier for me. The East Side was the more fashionable neighborhood, but living on the upper West Side would save me the crosstown drive to my office. Crosstown traffic was exasperating even then.

This was 1937 and the economy was still depressed. Vacant apartments in good sections were plentiful, the legacy of boom times in the twenties. Many buildings had been taken back from their owners by the banks. The banks were pressed too. They were often willing to sell properties for the mortgage plus one dollar, but there weren't many takers. The banks themselves ran the buildings. To salvage what they could they ran them well and kept them in excellent condition.

The view of the Hudson River along Manhattan's West Side had always intrigued me. It was beyond beauty. When I called on patients whose bedrooms overlooked the Hudson, my calls benefitted both patient and doctor. I particularly enjoyed the vista across the river to the Orange Mountains in the west and north to the George Washington Bridge. There was always busy river traffic—uncounted small craft and seagoing vessels. Except for the Fort Hamilton area in Brooklyn, overlooking the Narrows where the Hudson met the sea, I could think of no more stimulating a scene.

A nice gentleman showed us around two spacious apartments on a high floor of a well-kept building in the west Nineties. Both had breathtaking views of the Hudson. The broker mentioned a rent that was reasonable. Then he spoiled it all by saying that the president of the Pennsylvania Railroad lived on the same floor of the building and the president of the Diamond Match company lived on another.

I had had three years of private practice and was doing far better than I had expected. Because of the Depression and unemployment Belle and I had thought the practice would start much more slowly than it did. In fact, we had planned to write a book while we waited for the bell to ring. We were going to call it *What To Do Till the Patient Comes.* But we had no time for writing.

I had second thoughts. I said to my wife, "If corporation presidents can afford the rent, I can't." She told me that my second thoughts were always worse than my first; that I was going to make a mistake.

I made it. We moved into a lovely apartment in the same neighborhood on West End Avenue. We paid less rent but had no river view. Still, our apartment was high and light and spacious, and if you stood in the corner of the living room and pressed your nose to the pane you could see a wedge of the Hudson and a sample of its traffic.

But is it really a mistake, to do what makes you comfortable? Before Belle and I set out we calculated how much money we could afford to spend. Belle was the business person of our partnership, but I recall a pleasant joint session at my lamplit desk, with paper and pencils and an adding machine whose arm needed tugging every time an item was entered. I wish I could remember the figure we settled on, but as the saying goes, it was a figure we could live with. We should have asked for a hundred-year lease!

We set out looking at apartments with the sacred figure firmly in mind. Yet when I heard about those corporation presidents, my nerve failed me. I had seen much poverty. I took care of many people who had thought themselves on the way to riches but found themselves destitute. I was frightened by uncertainty. In fact, I was an economic coward. Our new rent was a good deal less than we could afford.

West End Avenue was beautiful and quiet. Some of its buildings were faced with pale limestone or golden brick. Ours was pink brick with a stone base, and the block north was lined on both sides with Dutch and English townhouses in the same crisp and cheerful combination. There was little traffic on the wide street and sunlight filtered through the leaves of the young plane trees to dapple the cleanswept sidewalks. We had traded rackety Hell's Kitchen for the restrained, respectable upper West Side. It was no wrench at all. Our apartment house was a small one, with only two apartments to a floor. We soon met all our neighbors. We liked our new apartment very much, and our daughter slept through the nights.

Our home was the medium for my wife's talents. Belle could do the most amazing things. She painted the ceiling of Susan and Gabrielle's room a light blue and spangled it with silver stars which delighted them by glittering in the dark. She knitted new throws in a gauge so regular and fine that they looked—ironically —made by machine. She crocheted new bedspreads and table mats of the finest linen. Handiwork was a sign of her pleasure in her house and household. She had created an establishment of serenity and charm. It was good to come home to.

Tucked away in a bureau drawer was a medal especially struck in Belle's honor by her school—the first time such a medal had been given. Homemaking was her expertise. Belle's hands were small—some of her antique bracelets had been made for children —and beautifully shaped. Those hands were always at work, and whatever she made approached perfection. Sometimes she was impish. When Gabrielle took Susan out in her carriage on winter mornings, Susan wore over her snowsuit an afghan with satin-bound slits for her head and arms. Susan's pet dog, Sheba, rode snuggly under the afghan at the foot of the carriage, with a slit for her own head and shoulders. The knitting neighbors were agog and the pattern for the afghan was much borrowed.

We joined a golf club in Westchester. The Hutchinson River Parkway was new and beautiful, and traffic was light. Susan, Gabrielle, and Sheba loved the club house and the putting green and the whole outdoors, and whenever I could escape from the city I played golf. Belle was a natural athlete. She'd been a champion long-distance swimmer at summer camp. Golf wasn't her favorite sport, but she often tramped the course with me. It was a wonderful clement time.

Having a daughter was fun. As Susan grew older—but still not old enough for school—she and I made up games together. This amused Belle and she sometimes joined in. But there was one game she wouldn't consider. That was the perilous game of rock-climbing, strictly for fathers and daughters. For this game we would go to Central Park, where glaciers had deposited boulders, some in clumps and some even five feet high. We would clamber over these glacial leftovers for a couple of hours. To a child Susan's size, these were big rocks indeed and Susan felt heroic climbing them. When we were exhausted and dirty enough we would wander home for a pleasant Sunday lunch.

One of our favorite places was the Museum of Natural History. Belle came along until she saw how we behaved. Then she was ashamed to be seen with us. First we would see what we wanted to see. Then we would play hide and seek among the monsters and other exhibits. When Susan was hiding she would always laugh. The guards, hearing strange sounds in their province, would march down the aisles of display cases. We would go on hiding, but hiding now also from the guards, who remembered us from the week before and slowly and cleverly chivied us in the direction of the lobby, and the grand exit. Just before they caught us, we would bolt for the great outdoors.

Nothing is perfect, of course, and Belle and I had our disagreements, especially about how to raise a child. Belle, mindful of our experience on Fifty-sixth Street, was firm against over-stimulation. I thought there was no such thing. My theory is that a child should be taught everything he or she is capable of understanding. It is never too early, but it's never too late, either.

"You're pushing the child too hard with your stories," Belle argued. "She can read all the advertisements in the streetcar, and yesterday I found her reading the *Ladies' Home Journal* to the children next door. You're pushing too much." When Susan was seven I bought her the *Books of Knowledge*. I'd been raised on them in Virginia and I'd found them fascinating. Belle almost told me to find another place to live.

When I tucked Susan into bed we'd do primitive algebra together, and years later on our car trips through the city we recited French and Latin declensions and conjugations. My uncles had attended school in Harrisburg, Pennsylvania, where they'd learned their Latin by rote. Fifty years later they could all still recite their lessons—and in the order learned, helped by the rhythm of the recitation. That was not the modern way, but I was in favor of anything which reinforced learning. The most important lesson I hoped to teach was that learning itself was fun.

And where was Gabrielle during all this time? Sometimes she took the child and dog to Riverside Park, chatting away in baby French. She went with us on our occasional trips to Virginia and she became a part of my family. She took care of household errands, so that Susan and Belle could have their times together. Her presence made it possible for us to go out in the evenings. She took over the household as much as Belle would let her, and turned out to be a good cook of European dishes. She was an alter ego, a second self, to my wife, and she made us all happy.

When I thought of the developments of the last four years I was overcome with wonder. Not very long ago I had been an intern, married and poor. Now I was an established teaching physician with patients, an office, and a nurse. I was a burgher whose household inventory included one wife, Belle, one daughter, Susan, one governess, Gabrielle, and a little black-and-white Boston bull, Sheba.

It did not escape my wife's notice that I was surrounded by females. Very kindly she explained to me, "A man's home is his harem."

DUNNIGAN'S
DAUGHTER

Peggy, my Number One Nurse, was straightening the office. She was her usual self, seemingly reserved but now and then flashing a brilliant smile.

"Where's Number Two?" I asked. "You know you're not supposed to do housekeeping."

"Number Two is out. I sent her on errands."

"Seems to me she spends more time out than in."

"Any more complaints before the day begins?"

"Why don't you go out and get some fresh air and let her do the work for a change?"

"She's got a boyfriend to have coffee with and I haven't. Anyway, it's not a whole lot of your business."

I wasn't going to argue with her. I was supposed to be boss, but Peggy had all routine matters well in hand, and I was satisfied with the way she ran things. She was devoted to her job. In fact, she was devoted to me.

"I didn't want to go out, because you're going to have a real day of it," she said. "The Dunnigan family is starting off with five physical examinations and boosters for the two young ones. From then on you're loaded."

I was fond of many of my people, and particularly fond of the Dunnigans. The family lived on City Island, part of New York

City but hardly urban. It is a peninsula at the northeasternmost part of the Bronx, nearly surrounded by the waters of Long Island Sound, and well-known and well-loved by fishermen.

Mr. Dunnigan was a bricklayer; his wife's family kept a tavern and were also charterers of sports-fishing boats. The women of the family made clam chowder in enormous vats, stirring the contents with a canoe paddle. When clams were out of season the vats held fish soup or corn chowder. The Dunnigan children helped, when they were not in school. Kathleen, the eldest daughter, was sixteen. It was a hard-working family.

I didn't like routine examinations. The patients were almost always too well to be spending money on doctors, and I seldom found anything to warrant treatment. However, I always took a thorough medical history and did a complete examination, ending with a urinalysis and whatever blood work might be indicated.

Still, there were advantages to such examinations. I had a chance to talk with interesting people and to inquire about their business. (How was I to know when I might want to choose some other line of work?) I was always pleased to watch the apprehension disappear when I told patients they were well. Most people, even healthy ones, fear what a doctor might tell them. To call any examination routine is a misnomer.

I often overheard my Number One Nurse lecturing the Number Two Nurse. Her message was: "Remember, the patients are usually frightened. Speak clearly. Don't singsong when you give instructions. You go through this many times a day but the patients don't. They're apprehensive. Don't use medical clichés, whatever the hell they are. Each patient is afraid, but he is an individual. Treat him like one."

Peggy was a smart nurse. That was why she was Number One.

When I was through with four Dunnigans, I asked after their daughter Kathleen.

"She didn't want to come in with us. She has a sprained ankle. Really, she's afraid of the doctor. She's out in the car with a book," Mrs. Dunnigan explained. "Maybe you could convince her to come in."

"A sprained ankle! That's a silly reason to stay in the car. Tell her I specialize in sprained ankles. Go help her in and let's get her examined."

Kathleen came limping in, supported by her father. She was a raving beauty. She had long, golden-red hair, large blue eyes, and a complexion straight from heaven or Ireland. Gregory the Great, before becoming Pope, once said of captured Western slaves that they were not Angles, but Angels. Kathleen looked like an angel.

Aside from her ankle the girl complained of fatigue. She had injured her ankle a few days before, playing basketball at school. Two weeks or so ago she had had "the flu."

Everything entered on her chart two years before had been normal. I began the examination, but moments later I stopped dead.

"I want to take your blood pressure again on both arms." I didn't believe what I'd found, but I found it again: 190 systolic over 130 diastolic. I could have accepted 120 over 80, but nothing higher in a child this age.

I examined Kathleen's eye grounds, the very back of her eyes, with my ophthalmoscope. I studied the retinas, the light-sensitive areas that receive the optical image, essential for vision. The veins of the retinas were distended and the arteries tortuous. There was a minute hemorrhage where a small artery had given way under pressure.

I knew that if there were red blood cells in the urine, then Kathleen was suffering from an inflammatory disease of the kidneys. We were able to do a complete urinalysis in the office. The red blood cells were present. The influenza virus might have inflamed her kidneys, just as it might have inflamed her throat. But hemorrhage in the retina usually occurs late in renal disease. Perhaps the influenza had accelerated an old, unsuspected disease.

The family had to be told; we couldn't ignore the situation. I left Kathleen in the examining room and had her parents brought into my consultation room. Because of the seriousness of the findings I couldn't hide anything in the hope of better news to report later on. I chose my words carefully.

I told the Dunnigans the result of the examination. "First we must have a complete X-ray study of the kidneys. Then, depending on what we find, we'll call a specialist."

Naturally the Dunnigans were stunned. I knew how they felt. I was stunned, too.

"Don't wait," I told them. "If you want another doctor's opinion get it now. But I want you to have the X-ray tomorrow. Talk it over on the way home and call me about your decision."

They left me with my day ruined. I could only imagine what their day was like.

Later the Dunnigans called and told me to go ahead with whatever had to be done. I had thought about little else since they'd left the office. I decided the best procedure would be to hospitalize Kathleen so that we could do what was necessary in the shortest possible time. They agreed, and the next morning Kathleen, the most beautiful and certainly one of the nicest patients I had ever had, was admitted to the hospital.

The X-ray specialist asked me to look at the girl's photographic plates with him. One kidney, the left, functioned well. The injected dye could be seen collecting in the kidney and staining the ureter, the tube leading from the kidney to the bladder. On the right side there was no sign of such activity.

The specialist studied the X-rays for a few minutes. "That right kidney is absolutely dead," he told me. He outlined the area with crayon. "Look. It's about one-tenth the size of the left. It must have been nonfunctional for years, possibly ever since birth." The dead kidney had never been detected because there had never been reason to X-ray the area.

We called in two brothers who were kidney specialists practicing together, and with them their associate, a man of wide knowledge and fine reputation. The five of us discussed all the possibilities, both of cause and treatment. Then we sent for Dr. Fishberg, a medical kidney specialist whose books on the subject were world famous.

There was no disagreement. The shrunken right kidney was probably interfering with the function of the other one. Experience had taught us all that often patients with kidney disease improved when a dead kidney was removed. The right kidney had to come out.

We sent for Kathleen's parents. Dr. Fishberg told them of our unanimous opinion. At the same time he said we could promise them nothing until we had seen what would result from the surgery.

The next morning we removed the small, contracted, and useless organ. The pathologist reported the kidney as being almost entirely a mass of scar tissue. Then we could do nothing but wait. Only time could tell us whether or not the dead right kidney had in some way interfered with the function of the left one.

At the end of ten days I sent Kathleen home from the hospital. She felt well and was anxious to get back to school. Her blood pressure had not changed. The specialists advised her to avoid all activity except her schoolwork and to rest as much as possible. No basketball for a while. Kathleen was disappointed.

The kidneys, one on each side of the body, are organs that excrete urine containing poisons and superfluous substances. As they filter material from the bloodstream, they resorb essential substances that might otherwise be lost. In addition, the kidneys manufacture hormones that help stabilize the blood pressure. The blood supply to the kidneys is profuse, transported by branches of the aorta, the largest blood vessel in the body. An artery goes to and feeds each kidney. Even a small obstruction of the blood supply can impair the function of the kidney.

The doctors agreed on the reason for the high blood pressure. We decided that the functioning organ had been under strain to do the work of two kidneys and that the viral influenza had been like a wrench thrown into the works. Frequent checks of Kathleen's temperature, which was higher than normal, indicated that the infectious process was still active.

I continued reexaminations from time to time. At last Kathleen seemed to be improving. Her fever disappeared, and I allowed her some social activity. Her blood pressure did not change.

One day, months after the operation, Mrs. Dunnigan called to tell me that Kathleen had been injured in an auto accident. She had fractured her lower jaw and lost several front teeth. The dentists were afraid to start repairs until I saw her. It was a long trip to the hospital, but of course I drove out.

Even bruised and battered, Kathleen was in high spirits. She wanted to look pretty, she said. When could she get new teeth? I could see no reason to withhold permission. The dentist had promised Kathleen that when he was through her teeth would be perfect. No scars would show.

The dentist was right. I couldn't tell the new teeth from the old, and Kathleen was as beautiful as ever. The trauma of the accident hadn't aggravated her kidney disease, but still her blood pressure remained elevated.

In those days we had no dialysis, no renal transplants, no antibiotics. We were short of the miracles that today prolong and save so many lives. But when you have practiced medicine for a few years you come to believe that nothing is impossible. I wanted to think that somehow nature would find a way to rectify the damage that had been done.

Then the sky fell in.

Kathleen suddenly began to lose weight. She had no interest in food and she was fatigued all the time. Going to school became too much of an exertion for her. She lost her sight in one eye because of hemorrhage into the retina. She took to her bed with severe headaches, nausea, and vomiting.

I visited at her home daily, trying to bring a little solace to Kathleen's family and to myself. The trip took hours out of my day. The way out was long; the way home seemed even longer. Back and forth I went, across the marshes separating the island from the mainland. The vigil we kept was useless to the girl. Kathleen's family had entrusted me with their faith and confidence. My efforts had come to nothing. I had failed them.

The end was horrid, as terminal renal failure is. Kathleen was restless, toxic, fearful. She tossed from side to side. Each day she was thinner and weaker. Her vitality ebbed. One day she lapsed into coma and could not be roused. Then the beautiful child died.

MRS. ESPINOZA

PEGGY, Number One Nurse, was always arranging and rearranging equipment in the office. She knew exactly where everything was and drilled each Number Two Nurse so that she could find immediately anything for which I asked. When no patients were present she was in constant bustle. But when we did have patients she was quiet, demure, and had an encouraging word for everyone.

"If you keep moving things from one drawer to another, how do you expect me to find what I want?"

"That's not your business. That's my business and Number Two's business."

Peggy would sit at her desk in a small office just outside my consultation room, nibble at her pencil, and think. That always disturbed me, because I couldn't tell what she was thinking. I teased her.

"You're not paid to think around here. I do the thinking."

"I don't get paid enough to think anyhow," she answered. "For the time being everything in this office is just where it ought to be. Shall we go to work?"

Among my patients that morning was Mrs. Maria Espinoza. She complained constantly of head noises, which she said had bothered her for years. I had sent her to ear specialists, a psychiatrist, and a neurologist, and the usual answer was that her disturbance was psychogenic. I didn't want to use the word *imaginary*, although some of the specialists did. In those days we didn't have advanced X-ray examinations, machines for scanning the brain, and other esoteric devices that could lead us to a diagnosis or away from it.

Mrs. Espinoza was badly disturbed when she came into my office that day. She clenched and unclenched her hands, talked a bit to herself, got up, stalked about the room, and sat down again. It took no genius to realize she suffered from overwhelming anxiety.

I decided to take her entire medical history again, expecting that that might quiet her or that I might even elicit something I had missed. She said she was willing, particularly as I promised her that when we were through I would give her some medicine to take away the noises in her head. At the moment I didn't have the slightest idea what I was going to give her.

I leaned over to get a history sheet from my desk drawer and when I straightened up there she was, poised over my desk, awaiting me with my sharp letter opener in her hand.

It was too far for me to reach her to try to wrest the letter opener from her hand, but not too far for her to go poking in the air in my direction. I yelled.

"Peggy!"

Number One was in my office in a flash. The sound of my voice told her not to waste time. She sized up the situation immediately, but by that time the woman had turned on her.

I knew my nurse was a bundle of taut wire, ready to spring. That was her nature, that was her build. But we had never had any such need, and anyway she was my nurse, not my bodyguard.

Peggy grappled with Mrs. Espinoza. When the patient raised her right arm to strike, Peggy caught her wrist and, holding her by the shoulder, dragged her right arm forcefully behind her back. The weapon clattered to the floor, and Mrs. Espinoza gave up. She subsided into a chair, helped vigorously by Peggy, and I walked around the desk to her.

Peggy stopped me. "Send one of the patients down to get her husband. They live in the next block and he works at night, so he should be home."

She knew her neighborhood.

I called a man from the waiting room. He was only too glad to do the doctor a favor, although he had no idea what it was about.

In a short time, Mr. Espinoza appeared. He had apparently dressed hurriedly, but he'd even put on a tie. One side of his shirt collar was under the tie. The other stood out like a paper napkin next to his ear.

I explained the situation to him and told him to take his wife in a cab to see Dr. Finesilver, an excellent neurologist and psychiatrist, twenty blocks due north.

As they left, Peggy put the letter opener into the top desk drawer, straightened the chair and desktop, and called in the next patient.

When the patient was out of earshot in the examining room, I asked, "Where did you learn that trick? It was really very neatly done."

"My boyfriend taught it to me, the boyfriend before the latest."

"What made him think you'd ever be in danger?"

She gave me one of her blank but serene stares. "I imagine," she said, "he was thinking of you."

Not more than a half hour after the Espinozas had left my office, the phone rang. "It's Doctor Finesilver, the psychiatrist," announced Peggy. "I believe he wants to talk to you about Mrs. Espinoza."

I picked up the phone. "Slocum!" someone roared at me through the receiver. "What the hell did you send that woman to me for?" I could hear him sucking in his breath from tension. "She's nuts!"

Altogether it had been a busy day. When we were through with office hours, I felt I had to get back at Peggy for the remark about the boyfriend before the latest, the one who had taught her self-defense.

"Peggy," I said, "I thought you told me everything was in its place so that we'd have no trouble finding it."

She was a little surprised.

"And what wasn't in its place?" she demanded.

"Well, for one thing, that letter opener shouldn't have been on top of the desk where patients could grab it and stab me."

This time she gave me a long, bland stare. "I'm not so sure," she said.

JOHNNY

My friend Johnny Small had been a prizefighter, and a good one. His reflexes were so fast that he could hit an opponent a half dozen times before the poor fellow got his hands up. The sportswriters predicted that Johnny was well on his way to being champion of the world in his weight class. He might have been, too, if the champion hadn't been even faster.

When I first met Johnny I wouldn't have given a nickel for his chances, not only to be champion but to be alive at all. He had a textbook case of pneumonia in which one or both lungs would fill with liquid exudate because of the presence of the pneumococcus, a virulent organism for which we had no specific remedy.

I didn't know Johnny when I was called to see him in his apartment on Fifty-sixth Street. His wife let me in. She was worried but tried not to show it. Mrs. Small had been a "pony" in Florenz Ziegfeld's Broadway shows. She wasn't a show girl—she was far too short for that; she stood just a bit below five feet in height—but she was a good dancer and had appeared in one show or another for six years.

Ziegfeld's ponies had to be good dancers. The "long-stemmed American Beauties," true show girls and a head taller, stood around looking gorgeous or trailed from one stage position to the next, balancing their fabulous headdresses. But the nimble little ponies danced.

Dianna Small was very pretty, with large, dark eyes, long, raven-black hair, and a charming smile that flashed on and off like the light of a turning beacon.

She led me into the bedroom, where I found a very sick man. Johnny himself was only about five foot four and was so thin that his ribs were visible. His chest heaved with the effort of breathing. It was obvious that he had pneumonia of the base of the right lung, because that area was rigid and resisted any movement. Every time he exhaled he made a noise that was described in the textbooks as an "expiratory grunt."

I listened to his chest and heard no breath sounds over the affected area; there were no breath sounds because the area was filled with fluid. Percussion with the fingers disclosed a distinct dullness. The diagnosis was obvious. The only question was, would Johnny live?

This type of pneumonia is rarely seen anymore. The majority of younger men and women in practice have probably never encountered it. It may be that antibiotics given for other purposes have destroyed the pneumococcus. Or perhaps antibiotics have rendered some pneumococci nonpathogenic. We are only beginning to learn about the appearance and disappearance of diseases.

The onset of the pneumonia had been typical. "I was waiting for the streetcar," Johnny told me, "when suddenly I got a severe chill. My whole body shook and my teeth chattered together. I've never felt so weak: I was lucky to get home. I was never so cold in my life. Dianna covered me with blankets and gave me a hot water bottle. But I'm still chilled."

I sent Johnny to the hospital. His case was so classic that other doctors asked if their students could examine him. He graciously assented.

The only treatment for pneumonia in those days was the best possible nursing care. (And this was the optimum treatment for many other common diseases such as typhoid and scarlet fever.) There was not much we could do with medicine. Oxygen, with cold sponges and aspirin to control the temperature—these were our standbys. We could only await the crisis.

The crisis in the pneumococcic pneumonia would occur from five to seven days after the onset of the disease. It was one of the most dramatic events in medical practice. The patient would become terribly ill, almost moribund. He might even seem comatose. Then there would be an hour or two of profuse perspiring, his temperature would drop to normal, and the patient, thoroughly exhausted, would fall into a profound sleep from which he would awaken hours later, drained of strength but with a feeling of well-being and comfort and the knowledge that he would get well.

If the crisis did not proceed in this fashion, it was just too damned bad. It could mean a prolonged period of illness, with more fluid accumulating in the chest and with spiking temperatures. In many cases the illness ended in death. People who got pneumonia were usually in the prime of life, between twenty and forty years of age, and the illness struck them in the midst of activity. One in four died.

Johnny made it, all right. He became a favorite in the hospital in the two weeks before we sent him home. All the denizens of Jacobs' Beach came to visit him, and so did dancers, musicians, playwrights, producers: the whole confraternity of theater and sports.

Stillman of Stillman's Gym came to call and so did the redoubtable Mike Jacobs himself. Another visitor was Ray Arcel, the trainer and fight promoter at the St. Nicholas Arena. (Years later, the mobster Frankie Carbo had Arcel's head beaten in by two thugs from Boston. Arcel survived. Carbo went to prison for a different crime.) Nat Fleischer, too, dropped by. He published *The Ring*, a magazine about prizefighting and related activities that is as much a bible for the fight racket as *Variety* is for the theater. They all came to see Johnny.

Jacobs' Beach was an ill-defined stretch of sidewalk on the south side of Forty-seventh Street between Broadway and Eighth Avenue, roughly in the middle of the block. It was so named because Mike Jacobs, promoter, boxing historian, and, by common consent, general supervisor of the fight game, had his office one flight up in an old building there. Fighters—both active and discarded—managers, handlers, trainers—many unemployed at the moment—and various assorted hangers-on eddied about on the sidewalk below Jacobs' office.

The street was filled with fight gossip, and many former champions of the world in one weight class or another would try to raise (but they would say "promote") a ten-dollar bill or so to see them through to the next fight. Mike Jacobs thought his charity was hidden. But there was so much of it that it was an open secret.

Johnny's introductions followed a formula: "Doc, I want you to shake hands with so-and-so, former light-heavyweight champion of the world," or, "Shake hands with so-and-so, former welterweight champion of the world." No one ever shook hands.

One day Johnny introduced me to Dino Arosa. "Doc, shake hands with Dino Arosa. You got a ten-dollar bill? Give it to him."

I had heard of Dino. He was a former prizefighter well-known in Lindy's restaurant and the other gathering places of sportsmen, gangsters, gamblers, and show people. They were all his friends.

I gave Dino a ten-dollar bill, as directed. I thought it was a loan from Johnny to Dino, and that Johnny would return it to me when he got well and carried a wallet again. But Dino peeled two tickets off a pack he had in his pocket and gave them to me.

After Dino had gone I asked, "What's the ten dollars for?"

"Read the ticket," Johnny said.

The tickets entitled me to attend a benefit performance at Madison Square Garden. They promised entertainment by big-name bands, big-time singers and comedians, and speeches by well-known political figures.

"This is good stuff," I said. "But what's the benefit for?"

Johnny smiled. "It's for Dino Arosa! Once a year he throws a benefit for himself at Madison Square Garden. He puts down the names of prominent people he knows. He never asks them and they never mind.

"He sells one thousand tickets—no more, no less—and that gives him five thousand dollars to live on. He's been doing it for years, and nobody minds. You're not supposed to show up. There isn't any party."

"But what about my ten dollars?"

"Oh, Dino will spend that for you," said Johnny with a smile. "You've done a good deed."

Johnny had been fighting professionally since he was eighteen years old. He was raised on the Lower East Side of New York, where you either defended yourself or you got yourself killed. He learned to defend himself.

Small and frail, Johnny seemed a good target in the ethnic warfare among the Irish, Italians, and Jews of his neighborhood. He was also a good target because his family was pious, and religious kids were not supposed to be good fighters.

Johnny soon discovered that he was far quicker than most of the boys he fought and that he hit harder. He had to fight his way to and from school almost every day. As time passed there was growing respect for his ability.

In those days there were a number of clubs devoted to prize-fighting. The clubs were good training grounds for aspiring young athletes. If they won consistently in small club fights, they could look forward to fights in larger clubs and even in Madison Square Garden. Most of these clubs no longer exist. They were replaced by radio and television. Young fighters today have little place to gain experience, so many are thrown into fights in which they are out of their depth. Because of this some are badly hurt.

When Johnny was eighteen, a friend took him to see a fight manager. The manager had heard of him and suggested that he enter one of the preliminary fights at his club. Johnny held back.

"If the other guy don't kill me," he told the manager, "my old man will. He thinks fighting is the lowest occupation in the world."

The manager said, "Take a try at it. One fight won't hurt anybody. If you lose you'll still end up with a couple of bucks in your pocket."

With no more training than his street fighting, Johnny went into the ring that night. Nobody was interested in the preliminary fight. They were all waiting to see two men who were contenders for a fight with a champion.

"I get into the ring with this guy," Johnny told me, years later, "and I see right away he wants to be a boxer. What did I know from boxing? I figured if I had him up an alley I'd kill him. So that's what I did."

The way he manhandled his poor opponent brought Johnny to the attention of the audience. He was booked the next week with a more experienced fighter; it would be a better paying fight. He hoped his father wouldn't hear about it.

Johnny knew only one way to fight: to tear into his opponent, give him no chance to defend himself, clobber him, and keep at him until he was finished. That's what he did with his second opponent. People began to notice Johnny. His father heard about it. Johnny told this story many times, with great glee.

The old man was very disturbed. He felt that his son had sinned. He wanted Johnny to quit, and at once. Johnny said, "Give me a break, Pop. I need the money. I'll quit after a few more fights."

The fight patrons were pleased with Johnny. He had a number of fights and won them all. Afterward he'd walk into his house and face his disapproving father.

"How did you do?" his father would ask without enthusiasm.

"I made a monkey out of him," Johnny answered.

After the next fight his father asked, "Did you make a monkey out of this one, too?"

"Yep, Pop. I made a monkey out of him."

Then Johnny's father became ill and was hospitalized. Johnny's conscience hurt, in addition to which he was very worried about the old man. He was scheduled for a fight that night, and he determined to finish his opponent off quickly so that he could visit at the hospital.

By this time he had become a hero in his neighborhood. He looked on this opponent as an easy one. Johnny would be fighting an old man nearing thirty, whose best years were behind him. "I was told he was an experienced boxer but had no punch," Johnny told me. "I killed boxers. That's what I intended to do to him."

When the starting bell rang Johnny came rushing out of his

corner. The older man walked out of his. "Don't hurt me, Johnny," he said. "I need the few bucks."

Johnny flailed at the man, hitting him hard on the chin. The older man staggered back to the ropes, his knees buckling. The crowd went wild, and Johnny hurried to finish the job. He rushed at his opponent, who threw his arms around Johnny, holding him and bearing down with his full weight.

Johnny struggled to break free, but the referee had to separate them. As fast as the clinch was broken the other fighter pinned Johnny's arms to his sides again and weighed him down. The round ended with jeers and boos from the crowd and with no more blows struck.

"I never fought a guy like this before," Johnny said. "I figured that if I hit him hard enough in the beginning of the second round, he would quit."

Again Johnny came out flailing. His arms were knocked upward and a glove caught his cheek, cutting it to the bone. His opponent caught all his blows on his glove and knocked Johnny back with an uppercut to the chin. Johnny's jaw shot open and his mouthpiece fell to the floor. He was dazed, but still he pursued the man. A glove grazed his forehead above his left eye. "I told you not to hurt me, Johnny," the older man said, backing away so that Johnny's blows hit the air. "I'll get you the next round," Johnny said. "There won't be no next round," was the answer.

Johnny rushed in again. A glove opened a gash above his right eye. Blood streamed down and Johnny could hardly see. His cheek was cut. A blow to the mouth split both his lips. He clawed the air. He was hit from all directions by blows he couldn't see. The referee stopped the fight.

Johnny spent a couple of hours at a nearby hospital for suturing and plastering. Two front teeth were out, his face was swollen, and his lips were so bulky he could hardly speak. He looked at himself in a mirror. What he saw made him afraid to visit his father at the hospital, but he was more afraid not to. He went.

His father watched him come into the room. Johnny didn't say anything. His father looked at him for a couple of minutes. "You didn't make a monkey out of this one," he said. "But now I know what a monkey looks like."

FAT LADIES

CATHERINE F. was a favorite in the neighborhood. She had an explosive laugh, and she laughed often. She weighed more than three hundred pounds. Rumor was that Catherine's housedresses were made for her by the Fuller Construction Company.

Catherine was the daughter-in-law of Mr. Flaherty, who was old and ill. He was comfortable at home with his son and Catherine, and received excellent care and true affection. Mr. Flaherty insisted on paying from his pension most of the household expenses. He cherished his independence and he had the satisfaction of knowing that his contribution was a real help.

It was a pleasure to make calls at their home. It was a place of courtesy and good cheer, and it was clean. Somehow, in spite of her weight, Catherine kept her rooms immaculately. On hands and knees, she would scrub every corner of the flat. "Roaches don't like us," she'd say. "And we don't like them."

Catherine brought her children to me only for routine vaccinations. She and they were too healthy to need anything else.

Every morning, housework done, Catherine would waddle down Ninth Avenue, rushing the growler. With one babe in arms, a small child clinging to her skirts, and a third strolling behind, she'd head down to her bar of preference, slinging a small tin bucket by its handle.

Ten cents to the barkeep, and he'd fill her bucket with beer until the suds came over the brim. Then Catherine would waddle home again with her babes and her bucket. Every few steps she would wait while the eldest, meandering, caught up with her. The youngster would lap a few suds from the bucket and stagger off again.

This was a daily ritual. The neighbors watched for it. Eventually the eldest went to school and had to forgo its treat. Its place was taken by the child next in line.

Catherine's children grew normally. It seems that those licks of beer added to their diet made them only more attractive.

Then delivery of beer became sophisticated. First there were bottles rattling in wooden racks, then there were cans, practical and hygienic. The growler was rushed no more. The very meaning of the words has been nearly forgotten, but not our good-natured Catherine F.

❋   ❋   ❋

We had another big lady in the neighborhood. It fell to my lot to take care of her.

Mrs. Hickley's six boys helped me up the stairs to their apartment. They got under my feet, dragged one another back a step or two to be the first to the top, bumped me accidentally, and were otherwise generally useful. They did carry my bag, each one fighting to get a hand on it and to share the glory. They seemed to vary in age from six to fourteen. I knew there was one grown girl, Evelyn, but I figured I would find her upstairs.

Evelyn was waiting, and as we came in she separated the children with slappings around, a bit of pushing, and threats to tell father. She finally gained my bag and victory, led me into her mother's room, and slammed the door.

"You certainly handle your brothers well," I said in appreciation of her efforts.

"They'd better listen," she declared.

I hadn't seen Mrs. Hickley for years. I knew her only from greetings exchanged on the street. I wasn't her doctor and I didn't know who was, but when I saw her I wished that he had come instead of me.

Mrs. Hickley almost filled a double bed herself. The flesh of her arms and body billowed out to the sides and rippled as she moved. She must have weighed four hundred pounds or more—more, surely, rather than less.

"My goodness. What happened to you?"

"I've been coughing for a week."

"I don't mean that. What happened to your weight? You were big, but not this big. You must have gained a couple of hundred pounds."

Mrs. Hickley sighed. "I guess I did. But right now I'm having trouble getting my breath. If I don't prop up on pillows I can't breathe."

I said no more about her weight except what was necessary to help her. I didn't want to hurt her feelings. But she didn't seem that sensitive.

To examine Mrs. Hickley I had to get both knees onto her bed. I pressed my stethoscope to her enormous chest. Her heart sounds were muffled, suppressed by the heavy intervening layers of fat. Her respirations were faint but frequent. Nothing could be determined from her abdomen: there was too much in the way. Vaginal and rectal examinations were impossible. It was her legs that told the story.

Her legs were massive. They were not only massive but distended, until it seemed the glistening flesh would burst. When I pressed one gently with my index finger I left an indentation an inch deep, which did not refill.

I wasn't surprised. Mrs. Hickley was suffering from heart failure. The pump was not strong enough, even when she was at rest, to force the fluid through her bloated body. I had known fat people who were freaks in the sideshows at Coney Island. They all died young. I wasn't going to permit Mrs. Hickley to do so. I had in mind six youngsters fighting for my bag. I could imagine what would happen to them if they had no mother.

"How do you manage the stairs?" I asked her.

"Oh, Mama doesn't go down the stairs," Evelyn answered for her. "In fact, she hardly ever gets out of bed. We use bed pans. I feed her in bed."

I took a quick glance at the girl. She was pretty. I thought how pitiful it was that she had become a prisoner of this situation.

"You make me a list of what and how much she eats and at what hours she eats it. I'm going to give her an injection that will take probably three quarts of water out of her. That's six pounds. I'm afraid you'll have to stand by overnight. Then I'll give her some digitalis that may help by strengthening the heart. It's helped millions of others, but their hearts were irregular and your mother's isn't. I'll give her a diet that has very little salt, and I'll prescribe a diuretic pill. We'll watch her melt away."

I saw Mrs. Hickley a week later. She was still lying in bed. Her legs were much softer on compression. The diuretic was doing its job.

"The diet you gave me is terrible. Who wants rice for his main dish?" she complained.

"It's not all that bad, and it works. That's what matters. I'd like to weigh you, but there's no scale I could send that goes high enough."

"I'll get weighed. You just help me get thinner. I know a scale that can weigh me."

This was a determined woman. She really ate only what I prescribed and took her medicine faithfully. In two weeks she was walking about the room. Her legs were still tremendous in girth but hardly swollen at all. At the end of two months she was able to help Evelyn set the table and do the dishes. I could see that Mrs. Hickley was losing a lot of weight: the flesh of her arms was beginning to sway back and forth.

She was still very short of breath and could walk only a few steps without resting. But she was trying; that was the important thing. On occasion, I added a few favorite foods to her diet and then removed them again. She was grateful for the changes but realized that they were temporary. She never complained when I took foods away.

It seemed to me that she was losing two or three pounds a week. Considering the situation I didn't want her to lose more than that.

I certainly didn't want any symptoms of starvation or vitamin deficiency. After the first few weeks I'd been able to obtain blood from her veins. When I first saw her that would have been impossible. I was willing to wait a year to get her into shape to climb the stairs. Once she went down she'd have to go up again.

Mr. Hickley became part of the picture. He wasn't as thin as his wife was fat, but he was tall, lean, wiry, and dour. A thatch of gray-brown hair hung down over his forehead. He peered through it. His mustachios drooped like a desperado's. He always came in when I was there, said very little, and didn't seem particularly interested in what we were doing. At least he never commented. Still, he paid for the process. The children seemed not too fond of him. I wondered if Mrs. Hickley had been previously married and if the children were hers and not his, but it wasn't really my business to ask.

About a year after my first visit, Mrs. Hickley appeared on the street. She was accompanied by Evelyn, who had acted so competently as her nurse and whose ministrations had been every bit as important as mine. Their neighbors were delighted and astonished. It did me no harm that Mrs. Hickley told them that I was the one who had made her lose weight and had cured her failing heart.

Her daughter brought her to my office. As she walked, the flesh of her arms swung back and forth like a hammock. I put Mrs. Hickley on my scale.

"I still can't weigh you. My scale only goes to three hundred pounds."

"I can tell you what I weigh, only don't mark it down," she said. "I don't want the nurse to see it. I know she won't talk, but still—I weigh three-twenty-two. Don't ask me where I weighed myself, but that is right."

I was curious but I didn't ask. "How much do you think you've lost?"

Her daughter answered, "My guess is one hundred fifty pounds. Is that too much?"

"Over a year that's about three pounds a week. Ordinarily that would be a little too fast, but a lot of it was water."

I knew that Mrs. Hickley had high blood pressure. I checked it that day and it was still high. After the mistreatment she'd inflicted upon herself, I didn't really expect to lower it. I took advantage of the situation to take Evelyn's pressure as well. I was startled to find it markedly elevated for a woman of twenty-four.

"I don't like to say this, but your blood pressure is high and you're very young," I told her. "It isn't often that we see a parent-child combination with such obvious high blood pressure. If you let me lower your pressure to normal I promise you'll be written up in a medical journal."

Evelyn's urine showed no red blood cells or infection. Blood tests indicated that her kidneys were not putting out as much waste product as they should have done. I placed the girl on a low-salt, rice diet like her mother's. I decided to give her no medicine until I saw what diet alone could accomplish.

Months went by. Now I could weigh Mrs. Hickley on my office scale. She was down to two hundred and eighty pounds and confessed she'd been weighing herself on the platform scale at the butcher's. I didn't expect to have a patient this obese again, but she'd taught me where to turn in case I did.

I was worried about Evelyn's blood pressure readings. I had found it necessary to give her medication and her pressure was somewhat lower but not nearly as low as I wanted. As for Mrs. Hickley, her pressure had come down and I felt that she would continue to do well.

Enter another complication: Vanity.

Mrs. Hickley didn't like the loose skin hanging from her arms. She knew the only answer was surgery, and was quite content to have an operation. I wasn't content. I was afraid of infection. Of course the plastic surgeons would hurry to operate, but I was afraid of them too.

I pointed out as many complications as I could think of and some that I made up. I explained that the blood supply to fat tissue is poor, and that infection was a probability because of the elongated lesions she would have on both arms. Mrs. Hickley was adamant. Finally she said, "If you won't arrange it for me, I'll find someone who will." There's little defense against that sort of attack.

I took her to the best surgeon I knew. After he examined her he told her that he would operate but that he didn't want any return engagements.

"Get below two hundred pounds, say one hundred-eighty pounds, and then come back to see me," he told her.

That mollified Mrs. Hickley, although she wasn't pleased to wait.

"You asked me a long time ago why I let myself get so fat," she said one day in a confessional mood. "I'll tell you now. Mr. Hickley is my second husband. He's insanely jealous. He made my life miserable. I decided I'd stop his jealousy by getting so ugly no other man would look at me. That's the story."

Mrs. Hickley had deliberately eaten her way to monstrosity! To me, her tale was incredible. But then I wondered: there were six young children. Could her husband have thought to keep her faithful by keeping her constantly pregnant?

"I've changed my mind," she added. "I'm still a woman and I'd like to look good. Even my husband wants me to look better now. I want to be able to wear a summer dress without having my flesh flap around."

"You know you're going to have long scars down both arms?"

"On the undersides. It's better than this." She held up her arms and the flesh hung loosely. I was forced to agree.

In another six months and minus another forty pounds, Mrs. Hickley insisted she was ready for surgery. Evelyn had kept her mother's morale at a high level. She'd even bought new dresses for what Mrs. Hickley called "my new body."

The surgery consisted of six-inch incisions down each arm, removal of adipose tissue and excess skin and suturing of the lesions as neatly as possible. The surgeon told me that he had already warned the Hickleys of the possibility of stitch abscesses, but Mrs. Hickley was firm in her decision to go ahead.

The next morning I saw Mrs. Hickley in her hospital bed, looking pleased with herself. "I'm glad it's over but I'm gladder we did it. Now I can look like a woman again."

The nurse removed the bandages from both arms, which were swathed from just below the shoulder to just below the elbow. The wounds looked clean and neat, but this was only the first postoperative day. I ordered warm soaks every three hours, to be applied to both arms through the bandages. I wanted the bandages to be left on, to minimize the risk of infection. I hoped for a perfect result.

As expected, by the fourth day a number of small stitch abscesses had developed on both arms. We watched these carefully. They were all superficial and disappeared a few days after the surgeon removed his multiple sutures. Despite our fears, healing was entirely satisfactory.

I was still very interested in the obvious family relationship displayed by the high blood pressure in mother and daughter. Would Evelyn improve on the medication and diet I'd prescribed?

One morning, about three o'clock, I was called to the apartment. What I feared had happened: Evelyn had had a stroke. She sensed something was happening to her, tried to get out of bed, and fell to the floor. Her left leg and arm were useless.

Slowly, over several months, Evelyn's arm regained some function although her fingers could not hold small objects like cutlery. Her speech was clear but she had some trouble thinking, so that she expressed herself slowly. I had her treated for a few weeks at a hospital in New York that specialized in rehabilitating function in such cases, but her left leg remained useless. She could not shift herself or transfer herself from bed to chair. She would spend the rest of her life being lifted into and out of a wheelchair.

One day I met Mrs. Hickley wheeling Evelyn in her chair, as she did every day when the weather was good. The family had moved to ground floor rooms to make things easier. The roles of the two women were now completely reversed. Evelyn was the patient and Mrs. Hickley the nurse.

"There's something I think you should know," Mrs. Hickley said, "because you did mention writing an article about a mother and daughter both with high blood pressure.

"I have six children, not seven. Evelyn isn't my daughter. She's my husband's daughter by a previous marriage. We just *feel* that we're mother and daughter."

So much for my career in medical research.

PEGGY'S
MARRIAGE

Something was going on that I could only vaguely sense. It was so indefinite I wasn't sure that it was there at all. Whatever it was, it affected both my office and my home. Peggy, my Number One Nurse, and Belle, my wife, were very good friends: but could the same situation be disturbing them both?

Peggy, outside of her work, suddenly had nothing to say to me. That was odd, because I'd always enjoyed our conversations and thought that she did, too. Time and time again Belle seemed on the point of saying something but then didn't. She, too, was un-usually quiet. There was an undercurrent of tension. I could feel it, but I couldn't bring myself to ask about it. How could I ask, "What's wrong around here," when I might be the only one who thought that something was? I didn't know what to say, or even if there were anything to say. And so it went for a few weeks.

The mystery was solved one evening. Belle had served me a good dinner of the steak-and-potatoes type, the sort of dinner I really liked. Then she struck.

"Trouble with you," blurted Belle, "you don't know anything about the people who help you every day. You're not interested in anything but medicine."

"Have I neglected you lately?" I asked, expecting anything. I didn't know which way the blow was coming, so I didn't know which way to duck.

"It isn't about me at all," Belle said. "It's your nurse, Peggy. When was the last time you saw her?"

"Today at the office. Anyhow I think it was Peggy. Both girls were there; one of them had to be Peggy."

"That's all you saw?" This with a trace of scorn.

"You'd better tell me about it."

"Did you know that she's very unhappy?"

"Why should she be? I recently gave her a raise. At least I think I did. She makes out the checks."

"Peggy's worried about getting married. She was here for lunch with me today and she's afraid she's going to marry Chris."

The word "afraid" set me back on my heels. Since when did girls get married out of fear? The only time I knew of when fear played a part in marriage was in a so-called "military wedding," in which the members of the wedding party included the bride's male relatives and their shotguns. Even then it wasn't so much the bride who was afraid, but her groom. Unless he'd fortified himself beforehand with strong drink.

"What do you mean, 'afraid'?" I asked Belle. "Anyway, she never said anything to me about getting married."

"She's grown up. She doesn't need your permission."

I thought about that. It was true. But this fear business was something else. "What is she afraid of? He seems attentive enough. He calls almost every evening to take her home and sometimes he takes her to lunch, too. I guess he's been around a while now, but she never acted as if she were serious about him, and she never said she was afraid."

"Listen to me," Belle ordered. "See what you can do to break up this courtship. It would be one hell of a marriage. Peggy likes Chris, but she doesn't want to marry him. She says he'll kill her if she doesn't. She's scared half to death. He's very jealous and he keeps her cornered. That's why you see him so often. You haven't seen any other young men around recently, have you?"

I tried to think back. "Yes, there was one, a musician fellow. He was very nice and polite and seemed to want to date her. He did, a couple of times. Then he quit coming. Don't ask me why or when."

"I don't have to ask you," Belle flared at me. "I know, and you should be ashamed for not knowing. He didn't come back because Chris beat him up. Twice. He went to the police and they told him to make a complaint and to swear out a paper of some sort to get Chris to court. He didn't do it because he didn't want to be beaten up again. Peggy liked him, too. And others. But she's afraid of Chris."

I felt ashamed that so much was going on I didn't know about. Peggy had been with me for years. She'd become a loyal nurse and a good friend, yet somehow I'd been paying less and less attention to her. Now I felt I should do something, anything necessary, to help her.

"What can I do?" I asked, stressing the pronoun.

"You can at least be sympathetic. And talk Chris into leaving her alone."

I could see this one coming from a long way off. I was now to be a surrogate uncle and to try to break up an unsuitable match. In fact, I hadn't spoken to Chris enough to decide whether to like or dislike him. When we did talk he always regaled me with the latest vaudeville stories he'd heard at the Palace Theatre. He seemed to spend a lot of his afternoons at the Palace, which was the flagship theater of one of the important vaudeville circuits. All the best entertainers appeared there.

Perhaps the Palace would give us a starting point. Besides, I'd rather face this male animal than face Belle in her wrath. Yet I knew she was right. I decided to have a talk with Peggy and Chris separately to see if they knew what they were getting into.

We had evening office hours three times a week—Mondays, Wednesdays, and Fridays, from six to eight. The idea was to accommodate some of our working patients. I was so interested in medical practice that I overlooked the obvious: my nurses had work to do when they got home. Peggy and her assistants never complained, but when Belle pointed out that I was taking terrible advantage, I cut back to one night a week. Then the patients complained.

At evening office hours the next night we were busy enough to forestall my talking to Peggy. When the last patient left I called her into the consultation room. Peggy and I always spent a few minutes talking over the events of the day; she'd gotten into the habit of sitting on my desk and swinging her legs as we chatted. She felt comfortable about it and so did I, because it meant that she was perfectly at home and found the office pleasant.

"What's this about you and this fellow Chris?"

"Mrs. Slocum been talking to you?"

"Don't be a Brooklyn girl: don't answer a question with a question. Tell me about it."

"Chris wants to marry me."

"Do you want to marry him?"

"I like him all right, but I don't want to marry him."

"You're young and pretty and you have lots of friends. Why don't you go out with other boys?"

"He'd kill me if I did." She looked me straight in the eye without blinking. I could see she meant it.

"I want to talk to him."

"All right," she agreed, sliding off the desk to her feet. "Just remember; if you try to interfere he may kill *you*." She left the room to change from her uniform.

Chris didn't call for her that night or the next. He had a job as a private detective at what he called a "stake-out." Peggy said he was with another man, a photographer, to gather some evidence in a divorce case.

In those days in New York, with its powerful Catholic Church, the only ground for divorce was adultery. When a couple wanted to divorce it usually fell to the husband to play the part of the miscreant. He would hire a hotel room and a girl for the occasion. He and the girl would go in, remove their clothes, and get into bed. Then, suddenly, the wife's witness and a photographer would break into the room (the door was always left unlocked) and with a few hasty pictures obtain the evidence. It was as easy as that to "prove" adultery and it was a common practice.

On the third night Chris arrived in high spirits. He had been well paid for his work and looked forward to a nice evening with

Peggy. I called him into my office and asked him to close the door and sit down. He told me the latest vaudeville jokes and then, when he saw I was serious, he became serious, too.

Chris was a red-faced, broad-shouldered Irishman with pleasant blue eyes and a lively manner. He stood about five foot ten inches and was in his early forties. He had told me about his family. He had been married, but his wife had walked out on him years before. She'd left their two boys with relatives. Chris saw the boys at rare intervals, perhaps once every three or four years. He'd been informed that his wife had died. It wasn't an auspicious history.

Not knowing anything better to do, I decided to plunge right in. Fast.

"I hear you want to marry Peggy."

"You hear right."

"What's this talk about your threatening to kill her if she doesn't marry you? That's one hell of a way to court a girl."

"Peggy knows I'm only fooling," he said, in all good humor. "I've been married before and I know what it takes to make a marriage. She'd be very happy."

"Do you really love the girl?"

"Sure I do," was his answer. It was irrefutable.

Where was I to go from there? "Look, Chris," I said. "This is important. Peggy must be fifteen years younger than you and she's much less experienced. Why don't you fight it out with a woman your own age?"

For a few seconds he looked at the floor, thinking. Then he said, "I know I've been pressing her hard, but she's the only girl I want to marry. I hurt her, but I'll make up for it. We like the same things: ball games, maybe a glass of beer with friends. And we have the same friends. About my threatening her, you can forget that. It won't happen again."

I had gone as far as I dared go in a matter that wasn't my business—a matter I didn't care to pursue.

"All I can say, Chris, is that Peggy is someone special and I'm not willing to see her hurt. Whatever she decides, I wish her happiness, because she deserves it."

Chris and I shook hands and he left with Peggy. A week later she told Belle that she and Chris were going to be married. We didn't express our misgivings. What can one really know about the feelings of another? We could only hope it would work.

The wedding was to take place at the church of the Paulist Fathers at Fifty-ninth Street and Ninth Avenue. This was a grim, foreboding building that seemed to have been designed by a dyspeptic architect. It was built of red stone in front and gray at the sides, and it imparted gloom to the immediate surroundings. But it was an ingredient of the neighborhood and it belonged. It had been there longer than I had, and people cherished it.

Peggy particularly liked it. It was the church at which she attended early Mass each morning on the way to the office. Peggy had been raised in Swissvale, an industrial town in western Pennsylvania, and she said the dullness of the church reminded her of the overcast skies and general lack of color of her hometown. But I knew she hated her hometown! One doesn't try to understand these things.

Both she and Chris seemed to enjoy what remained of their courtship. Belle invited them over for coffee one evening and Peggy asked, "Where should we go on our honeymoon?"

"Who told you you're getting time off for a honeymoon?" I asked.

"Mrs. Slocum told me," she said, sticking her nose into the air. "I don't expect to marry more than once."

Belle asked, "Where have you been that you liked most?"

Peggy thought for a moment. "I haven't been anywhere. I escaped right from Swissvale to study at the hospital here. As far as I know there are only two states, Pennsylvania and New York. I'd like to see something entirely different."

"What about you, Chris?"

"I've been to New Jersey, but not for long. As soon as I leave New York, I get nervous being amongst a bunch of foreigners. They don't seem to know how to talk. So I come back."

Belle thought for a moment. "If you want something entirely different that won't cost too much, why not go to Florida, to Miami Beach? It's out of season, but if you get a place right on the beach there's always enough breeze to keep you cool. Dr. Slocum and I will give you the train tickets as a wedding present. I think that would be much better than any other gift."

"Whoa," I shouted. "That's my money you're spending."

Belle looked at me, smiling sweetly. "Isn't it worth it to get rid of them for two weeks?"

Peggy's brother was to be the best man. Belle and I had met and liked him. Later he married a young woman who had all the qualities of which my wife approved. "She's a smart, decent, hard-working girl and a good wife and mother." Coming from Belle that was high praise.

The church could have been crowded had Peggy let it be known that she was getting married. She said she didn't want to acknowledge good wishes for days on end. The truth is, she was shy. Word did seep out anyway and there must have been more than a hundred people from the neighborhood. Peggy didn't wear a bridal costume, but dressed for travel. She and Chris were to leave immediately after the wedding to catch their train.

Belle and I were seated in a front pew. The priest was a man in his forties, businesslike and anxious to get on with what had to be done. Peggy and Chris stood before the altar facing him. They were on a dais a few feet from us. I whispered to Belle, "This is the first I've noticed that Peggy's slightly bowed in the legs." Belle pinched me.

The priest talked to them in a low voice, giving the usual advice but in his own way. We could barely make out what he was saying. It was about better or worse, sickness and poverty.

I nudged Belle. "He scares the hell out of me. I could give them the best advice of all. I would say unto them, 'Go now. Stand not upon the order of your going.'" Belle gave my arm another pinch. This one left its mark.

And so the wedding ended. We tossed rice as they came out of the church. We couldn't decorate a car, because they took the first available cab.

After they'd gone, I said to Belle, "Well?"

"I don't know yet," she answered. "We can only wait and see."

MRS. FIERRO

EVERYONE in the neighborhood knew about Mrs. Fierro. Most of the neighbors hadn't seen her for years. I was asked occasionally why I didn't try to do something for her. I could answer only that I had never been asked to take care of her, that I had never seen her myself, and that I wouldn't have known her if I'd fallen over her.

Mrs. Fierro had not been out of her rooms for a long time, for at least twelve or fourteen years. Her husband devoted his entire life to her. He did the marketing and the cooking and the housework in addition to attending to her needs.

Most people who had been acquaintances of the Fierros' had long since become discouraged from visiting.

"Poor fellow," the neighbors said. "He lifts her from the chair to the bed, from the bed to the chair, and does it all without complaining. But there's no use visiting, because he's constantly running to her side to see if she wants anything, and she's always too tired to have visitors."

Long before I opened my office Mrs. Fierro had used up all the other doctors in the neighborhood. She had gone through them one by one. She complained to her husband that this one wasn't interested in her "case," the other was too abrupt with her, and the third had told her to get up and get out of her house.

I don't know why she finally allowed me to visit. I was the newest and youngest doctor in the area, and she was sure that she herself knew her "case" better than any of the older men. I think her husband was persuaded to make one more try at having her treated. I can even now imagine his travail before she allowed him to call me.

Mrs. Fierro's illness began specifically on Ninth Avenue and Fifty-sixth Street when she was returning home with bags filled with vegetables. Ninth Avenue was then a two-way street. She was headed south to her home on Fifty-second Street (I tell the story this way because this is the way it was told to me) when she heard screams behind her.

A motorcycle skidded past. The rider seemed to have lost control, and it was he who was screaming, as Mrs. Fierro said, "like a frightened woman."

The motorcycle ran onto the sidewalk and the cyclist fell off. The machine smashed through a plate-glass window. Except for a few bruises the rider was unhurt. No one else was injured.

Mrs. Fierro calmly continued home, walked the two flights up to her rooms, placed the vegetables in her icebox, put on a nightgown and kimono, and got into bed. And there she stayed. Atrophy from inactivity seemed to be her only illness.

After I heard her story, with some supplements from her husband, I decided that the situation was a challenge that I'd like to meet. And so I undertook to treat her.

I found her heart and blood pressure normal. Her lungs seemed clear, and she had no abdominal masses. She must have weighed about eighty pounds, but she was a small-boned woman, not more than five feet tall, so that didn't bother me. Her arms and legs were freely movable, her skin was warm with no obvious lesions. Her tongue, lips, and gums showed no evidence of disease. She wore dentures, which I presumed she had put in for my benefit. Vanity is sometimes a great stimulus. I drew some blood to test at the office and asked that her urine be sent to me the following morning. I did not expect to find any pathology.

All the physical findings were negative. I diagnosed this as a psychiatric case. I concluded that Mrs. Fierro was suffering from hysteria and that she found satisfaction in her illness and had no intention of giving it up. But something about the case bothered me, something I couldn't put my finger on.

I wrote a prescription to impress upon Mrs. Fierro the fact that I knew what I was doing. The medicine was innocuous but, of course, I added something to give it a bad taste, thus increasing its potency. I suggested that I return three days later.

To my surprise, Mrs. Fierro agreed. She said how nice it was to have a doctor who really examined her and "took an interest." Those last words belong in their quotation marks. I left, but I went with the feeling of having missed something vital, something that I should have noticed.

The following morning Peggy told me that the urine specimen Mr. Fierro had brought in was normal.

"Poor man," she said. "You can't help but be sorry for him."

"You can say that again. With a cracked wife who really could take care of herself if he used a little suasion."

"I don't mean that. I mean the man is sick. He helps his wife when he can barely help himself. He stops every few steps to catch his breath. And his voice! Didn't you notice the hoarseness?"

I knew then what I had overlooked. Mr. Fierro had had nothing to do when I examined his wife, so he'd sat in a chair near the bed and volunteered an occasional comment. It was his voice that I had unconsciously noted. That was what had bothered me when I left the Fierros' apartment. I grabbed my bag and hurried back there.

I found Mrs. Fierro sitting in her chair. When I knocked I had to wait, probably while she put her dentures in. She greeted me with a smile and told me that my medicine had helped her. She felt stronger.

I was in no pleasant mood. "I want your husband to go to the hospital, now, today, for X-rays of the chest and to have a throat doctor take a look at him. I think he has some pressure on a large nerve that controls his voice." Mr. Fierro stood beside her chair, shifting from one foot to the other.

"You know, Doctor, because of my condition he can't go into a hospital."

[181]

I decided to lay it on the line. "Your husband may have cancer. From what little I know about him I think it's so. You will let him go to the hospital." Mrs. Fierro's smile became a grim line.

Mr. Fierro died within three months. His widow appeared at the funeral in deep black, supported on each side by a neighbor. It was her first trip out of her home in more than a decade. I was told that she stood the ordeal well. She gradually regained her strength and returned to all the usual activities of a woman her age.

The neighbors commented that, like many Italian women, Mrs. Fierro would probably wear mourning for a long time. I knew better. I knew she would wear it forever.

CAR TROUBLE

COLUMBUS 5-5780: that was our phone number. The ring would be answered by Peggy, by the Number Two Nurse, or by the cheery voice of an operator at our answering service. One way or another I got the message. When I was away from the office I was always calling in; from pay phones—my pockets sagged with nickels—or from people's bedside telephones.

Peggy called me at my home one morning to give me a list of house calls that had come in. There were four, all in the neighborhood within a few blocks of the office.

By then I had advanced in life to the ownership of a canary-yellow Studebaker convertible. I parked the beautiful machine in front of a tenement to make my first call. The patient lived in top floor rooms. The second call was also to top floor rooms, in a house in the same block. It sounds arduous, but it was easy: I did what any denizen of the neighborhood would have done. After I visited my first patient I simply climbed a ladder to the roof, went over a few parapets and down another ladder, and was soon knocking at my second patient's door. After I had taken care of that patient I used the stairs and made the two other calls on foot. Then I walked to the office.

In the middle of office hours that afternoon Peggy answered

the telephone and listened intently. She had one of those conversations it's easy to ignore: "Yes, yes. He's here now," she said. "No, but I'll ask him." When she hung up, there was a questioning look on her face. "Where's your car?" she challenged.

I was busy. She'd caught me with a chart in my hand and my foot on the threshold of the examining room. It was no time for nonsense. "Look outside," I commanded imperiously. "You'll see it in front of the office."

"Oh, yeah?" she drawled. When Peggy said "Oh, yeah?" things of awful significance could occur. Now she said it again: "Oh, yeah? If it's outside the office how come the Eighteenth Precinct called to inquire if it was stolen? The sergeant said it had been standing on Fifty-second Street for so many hours that they thought it had been stolen and abandoned. They took it in." She smiled sweetly. "There'll be a small fee for towing."

I've had all sorts of car trouble in my time.

❋   ❋   ❋

Sheba, our Boston terrier, was black with a swath of white across her face and chest. She came from a kennel in Queens. I had made a call near there one day. In my car, for company, were Susan, who was now one-and-a-half years old, and her nurse, Gabrielle Vandenborre.

Once Susan saw the little animal in the shop window I couldn't get her away—but I wasn't anxious to leave, either. Susan wanted to go inside the store and pet the puppy. I wanted to, too, but I wouldn't say so. I was supposed to be an adult. Gabrielle nodded, giving permission, and so we all went in. We came out carrying the puppy. It seemed to take to us, and we had become its captives.

Belle met us at the door. She was shocked at the sight of the little creature and then enthralled.

"What on earth are we going to do with it?" she asked.

Gabrielle, who had been raised in the Belgian countryside, said, "Don't worry about the dog. It is only another child in the house. I know how to care for her." And indeed she did. Our dog was named Sheba because Susan called her that: we never found out why.

The little animal liked to ride in the convertible. Often, when I knew I was to return directly home from a house call, I took Sheba with me for company. She'd hop eagerly into the car, and when we returned from our call she would stride out of it, as if she were proud of what she'd accomplished. She was an equal partner.

Gabrielle had warned me never to take Sheba with me unless someone else came along. But I knew better. One day I parked on Forty-seventh Street just west of Fifth Avenue, closed the car door without looking behind me, made my call, got back into the Studebaker, and started off again.

Suddenly I realized the seat next to me was empty. Sheba was gone! I tried not to panic, and drove back to Forty-seventh Street as fast as traffic would allow. There I found her. She was smart. She hadn't left the area, but was trotting back and forth, looking anxiously into the faces of the passersby.

I pulled to the curb and opened the door. Sheba immediately jumped aboard and licked my face as if she forgave me completely. If ever I saw gratitude in the look of man or beast that small animal showed it that day. She settled down at last, snuggling under my right arm. She seemed fine, but I felt ten years older.

I was ashamed to tell Gabrielle, but I finally owned up, to ease my conscience. But I'd been shaken up. Ask any dog lover.

❋   ❋   ❋

It had been a long, tiring day. When evening office hours were done I went home to dinner. Just as I was getting settled, sure enough, a house call came in. I invited my wife to come with me. We would return home immediately after the call.

The patient's home was near my office. I parked the convertible in front of a candy store on Tenth Avenue.

"I may go visiting," Belle said, pointing to the store. She knew the place and its owners well.

I took care of my patient, called my telephone answering service from a phone booth in the front of the candy store, got the message that I had yet another house call, jumped into the car, and was on my way. I had completely forgotten Belle.

An hour later, in all innocence, I arrived home. I parked the car, rode upward in my usual elevator trance, reviewing the day's diagnoses, unlocked the front door, and went in. Belle was sitting in a comfortable armchair in our living room, reading the latest Civil War novel recommended by her friends at the Mercantile Library. She looked up casually and greeted me.

Suddenly, it was as if someone had pulled the whole building out from under me. Belle shouldn't have been there at all! She should have been in my convertible on Tenth Avenue!

Belle didn't mention it, so I didn't mention it. It was not the sort of thing that was supposed to happen to husbands and wives.

When we got around to talking I heard the tale. Belle had been in the living quarters behind the candy store, chatting with the owner's wife. I had come in to use the telephone and she had made ready to leave. Then through their portieres she had seen me drive off. Belle was a sensible girl and had simply shrugged her shoulders at her husband's absent-mindedness, hailed a cab, and gone home. Nor did she ever upbraid me. But it seemed to me that for a long time after, if I turned my head to intercept her glance, there was something about her eyes, her mouth—could she have been laughing?

❖   ❖   ❖

The Case of the Business Card: that's how I think of it. It began when I was doing desk work at a hospital. I was, as always, behind schedule filling out charts. I regarded the job as a chore, a necessary evil, but more evil than necessary. I was working fast and hard when I was disturbed by a nearby conversation. It was a monologue, really, in which an insistent young pediatrician lectured a nurse about how good a doctor he was. The poor nurse was as polite as could be, but it was obvious that she wanted to get her work done. So did I. When she escaped, the young man turned his attention to me.

I finally was able with all courtesy to break away from him and to resume my work, but not before he had forced his card on me, hoping I might use it for future reference.

The United States had just entered the Second World War. Gas rationing was introduced in 1942. There were strict rules about when automobiles should and shouldn't be used. Yes, for medical purposes; no, for personal ones. The rules were meant to save gas and rubber. Special agents rode around on motorcycles, enforcing the new rules. Their sidecars often contained volunteer police.

After my stint of paperwork, I made a house call on Fifty-second Street. My patient's home was near Lindy's. It was lunchtime. I was hungry, and Lindy's was a good prospect. I had long ago become inured to the idiosyncracies of its waiters. In fact, I thought Lindy's waiters much-maligned. They never meant to be rude; they meant to be helpful and friendly. When they joined into diners' conversations it was a sign of genuine interest. "This Aunt Bea sounds like trouble," a waiter might say, or "Sign the contract already." They rejected orders of which they disapproved: "Take the pastrami. The corned beef is fatty today." Or, "Who in his right mind would order schav when there's borscht?" Lindy's cheesecake was the best in the world. Few could resist it. But an order for a slice would sometimes make a waiter suspicious. "Cheesecake? You sure you don't have diabetes? For diabetics it's no good."

How would it affect the war effort if I were to leave the car parked where it was, and take it back to Fifty-sixth Street after lunch instead of before lunch? I strolled to Lindy's.

When I came out I found a special volunteer police officer standing at my car. He had seen me plain, emerging from Lindy's restaurant. Neither my car's medical plates nor the fact that I was carrying a black doctor's bag availed me. He would listen to no explanation.

I summoned up hidden reserves of gall. "Officer," I said, "please don't hold me up. I have house calls to make." I handed him the young pediatrician's card, and drove away.

THE SECRET

Mrs. Ferguson was a small, wiry woman of Scotch-Irish descent. She had come to New York from Kentucky. She lived with her daughter, Agnes, on the third floor of a neglected red-brick tenement in the upper Forties just west of Ninth Avenue.

Mrs. Ferguson had never been a patient of mine, but now she brought her daughter to see me. Mrs. Ferguson peered at the nurse, she peered at the other patients, she peered at me. Was she nearsighted, or was she suspicious? I was glad she was present during the entire consultation and examination of her daughter. But I couldn't have kept her out.

Agnes complained of mild, fairly constant digestive distress with burning in the epigastric area and sour eructations. Her occupation seemed not to be the cause of her illness. She was a clerk in the office of the telephone company. There were perhaps a hundred women in the same office doing the same sort of work.

Agnes was a long, gaunt girl of twenty-seven. She had a disorderly mass of jet-black hair. Her eyes and mouth were large, and her complexion was sallow. She stood nearly six feet tall because of her very long torso and legs. Her arms were in proportion. I had her enclose her thumbs in her fists and found that the tips stuck out beyond the outer side of her hands. There was no question of the diagnosis.

I told Mrs. Ferguson, "Your daughter has a peculiar condition known as Marfan's syndrome. It's not a real disease but it will be with her for the rest of her life. It will probably do her no harm, and the only way to take care of it is to live as sensibly as possible and to treat symptoms if they arise."

Marfan's syndrome, characterized by weakness of the ligaments and muscles and poor functioning of the internal organs, can produce all sorts of symptoms. The real danger was in the heart and larger blood vessels, with the possibility of a rupture of the aorta or the valves of the heart.

Mrs. Ferguson wasn't happy with the diagnosis, for reasons of her own. "Is it anything the neighbors shouldn't know about?" she asked.

"Of course not," I said. "If the neighbors should ask, tell them. I'll write it down for you. It's a rare condition, but it has afflicted some of our best people."

"Who?" she asked. I could tell she was looking for a tidbit to gossip about.

"Well, maybe Abraham Lincoln, for one," I answered. She thought about that and dropped the subject.

I wasn't going to discuss the possibilities of the condition if I didn't have to. I didn't want to frighten the women with a list of problems that might never arise, and I doubted their ability to comprehend the situation.

In Virginia, both the Fergusons would have been described by the all-encompassing "not right in the head." Agnes seemed dull because she was just not interested in anything, and although her lack of interest was startling, she was smart enough to read, write, and calculate, and was perfectly well-fitted for the demands of her job. Mrs. Ferguson, on the other hand, seemed subnormal. She wrote poorly, never read anything, and could do no mathematics at all. I made it my business to find out these things.

I saw nothing more of the Fergusons until several months later, when Mrs. Ferguson came to my office door.

"My daughter's real sick," she told me. "She has a terrible pain in her belly that comes and goes. It began this morning and comes every fifteen or twenty minutes, and just when we're sure it's gone away it comes back again."

I promised to visit as soon as I had completed my morning office hours. I wasn't overly worried about the girl because her pain was abdominal. Had the mother said the pain was in her chest I should have been really disturbed and gone at once.

The wooden stairs of their building were splintered. There was an odor of rot in the hall, and light bulbs were missing.

"You stay out of the bedroom until I've examined your daughter," I told Mrs. Ferguson. "She's a big girl, and I want her to talk to me. She may not if you're there." Mrs. Ferguson reluctantly complied.

Agnes was lying in bed and was having one of her painful spasms. I uncovered her abdomen and saw a distinct mass to the right at the level of the umbilicus. I placed my open hand on it and felt what I was sure was a spastic uterus. When her pain had subsided I asked, "Didn't you tell your mother you're pregnant?"

"Dr. Slocum, you're insulting. I'm not pregnant. I'm not even married!"

"Hell, girl, you don't have to be married to be pregnant."

"It isn't so," she insisted. "I've never been with a man in my life. I don't even have any dates with men." She was vehement.

Agnes had my sympathy. First she was stricken by nature. Then she was stricken by man. I was determined that she not be stricken by the neighbors. Agnes would live among these people for the rest of her life. I wanted no gossip about her.

Agnes continued to upbraid me while I completed my examination. She could not be pregnant. No man had ever touched her! Her pains started again.

"All right," I told her. "Whatever you say. You're not between three and four months pregnant but nevertheless you *are* having a miscarriage. Tell your mother what you want to tell her and I'll tell her what I have to tell her, but I won't say you're pregnant."

I spoke to her mother, who was sitting in the kitchen, her hands folded across her abdomen.

"I want you to wrap some ice in a towel and put it on your daughter's belly. You have ice? All right, then. Place a pillow under her buttocks so that they're higher than her chest. Then give her an aspirin tablet every four hours. Is there any in the house? Good. We'll see what happens. You'll need me again tonight or tomorrow. She'll be all right soon."

Mrs. Ferguson was very pleased to know that her daughter was not dangerously ill.

As I walked down the stairs and out into the street I felt really depressed. I was surprised to find it still early and still light. I had stepped out into another world. I looked up at the Fergusons' windows. In those rooms, life of a sort hard to imagine was lived. Agnes and her mother were like grotesques in a Dickens novel. I was assailed by questions. What sort of man could Mr. Ferguson have been, and where and when did he go? What sort of woman had the mother been, when Agnes herself was conceived and born? What—if anything—did Agnes and her mother talk about? Leaving that atmosphere was like walking from the dark ages into the modern world.

About four o'clock that afternoon a neighbor's child spoke to Peggy at the door. Mrs. Ferguson wanted me right away. The messenger was a shrewd, bright-eyed girl who wanted to know all the news.

"What'd the doctor say Agnes has?" she asked. She was a bold one. Peggy had her answer ready.

"The doctor said that Agnes has belly pains from things she eats."

"What sorts of things?"

"All the things you like to eat best." Peggy shut the door and called me.

This time at the Fergusons' I found Agnes sitting in a battered chair at the kitchen table with a half-filled cup of coffee in her hand. Mrs. Ferguson's behavior was unusual and confirmed my belief that she could have been brighter. She clasped her hands and with a beatific smile said, "Dr. Slocum, it was a *baybee!*" She was not indignant or upset in any way.

Agnes gave me a quick, shallow smile but was really not very interested. She seemed to trust me and was satisfied.

An important thought disturbed me. "What did you do with it, Agnes?"

"I threw it down the toilet in the hall."

I grabbed a pot and some kitchen towels and ran to the toilet, hoping no one had tried to use the common facility. The chances were in my favor because it was still afternoon, although late. Working people wouldn't be home much before six. I didn't want Agnes's story making the rounds.

The small fetus was there, still attached to the placenta. It was too large to have been flushed down. I put it into the pot, covered it with the towels, flushed the toilet, and went back to the apartment. I told the women I would send for the fetus but that they would have to pay the man when he came. I instructed them to say nothing about the baby.

"If anyone asks, tell them Agnes had food poisoning."

Agnes didn't want me to leave until she had spoken to me in the bedroom.

"My office had a midnight sail on the Hudson River boat. One of the boys got at me behind the smokestack. Could that have done it?"

I nodded. "Yes, Agnes, it could."

"Oh my," she said.

Could anyone be so ignorant, so innocent, in this sophisticated city and in the twentieth century? I would have to think about it. Agnes had not been prepared for life. There were things she would have to know. I supposed I would be the one to tell her.

When the undertaker arrived at my office I was pleased to see that he had followed instructions. He had come on foot and brought a small wicker basket, the sort all the neighbors used on their errands. No hearse would pull up at the Fergusons' door. I had a signed Stillborn Certificate waiting. "I depend on your discretion," I told him. But he understood such situations. He nodded and left for the Fergusons'. Agnes's secret was safe.

MRS. MORRIS

MRS. MORRIS wore her hat jammed down on her head, its torn veil skirting her eyes. Once stark black, the hat had attained a greenish sheen that matched the iridescence of her ancient dress. Her dress hung at an odd angle, disclosing as she walked the cracked leather and worn heels of her high-button shoes.

An observer would think that Mrs. Morris was an old gentle-woman, still vigorous, who had outlived her money and her time but was determined to maintain her standards to the end.

On all counts the observer would have been wrong. Mrs. Morris was neither vigorous nor poor. She was wealthy, and she was ill. As to her being a gentlewoman, that was a matter of definition.

Mrs. Morris had been sent to me by one of a group of dowagers who had become my patients. They were pleasant people, all in their sixties or older, some of whom had known one another since their school days. Most were members by birth or marriage of long-established New York families. All, save Mrs. Morris, were beautifully groomed and dressed. They were meticulous about keeping their appointments, and they were blessed with general good health. All, that is, save Mrs. Morris. She really needed medical care, and of course she was the only one absent from the office for long periods of time.

Mrs. Morris had pernicious anemia. As any doctor would, I suspected this after her first examination. She complained of easy fatigue, breathlessness, and distress after eating. She said that she suffered pain, numbness, and tingling in her legs and feet. Yes, she had tried propping her feet on pillows, but the sensations continued. Her skin was lemon-yellow and almost pellucid. She disclosed a tongue that was beefy red in the center but tender and eroded at the tip and sides. Her laboratory findings showed severe anemia. I was concerned to hear that her diet was sparse and did not contain any beef liver to help her produce red blood cells.

"Mrs. Morris," I told her, "you're a sick woman but a lucky one."

"Can you do anything for me?"

"I certainly can. I can't actually cure you, but I can make you feel so much better that a cure will hardly matter. I can keep you practically well for the rest of your life."

"What do you want me to do?"

"First, add beef liver to your diet three times a week. I'll do the rest."

"What will you do?"

"I'll give you an injection of vitamin B_{12} daily for a week, once a week thereafter for a month, and then once a month for the rest of your life."

Mrs. Morris hesitated. "Liver costs so much. And the injections. I really can't afford the treatment."

I knew nothing then about her finances. Her acquaintances were well-to-do, but I saw the sheen of her once-black hat and the green luster of her aged clothing and my heart was touched. I was not in the habit of abandoning the poor.

"Let's do it this way. Come for your first set of injections and I won't charge you. You should feel better by the end of the week. Then come in weekly and later monthly. Perhaps you'll be able to pay for those visits."

Mrs. Morris paid something for her first visit, came in the rest of the week for her free injections, and then disappeared.

It was several weeks before a bedraggled, breathless, lemon-colored Mrs. Morris returned. "I couldn't afford the carfare," she explained.

As Diamond Jim Brady said, it's all right to be a sucker if you can afford it. I was truly sorry for her and undertook another week's treatment at no cost to her; I even gave her carfare. She took her treatments for the week and disappeared again. Some weeks later she telephoned. Her voice was almost inaudible.

"I wondered how you were," I told her. "I can't hear you. Will you speak louder?"

"I can't." Her voice quavered. "Will you please come to see me?"

I knew the street well. The address was between West End Avenue and Riverside Drive. I couldn't understand how she managed to live there. It was a street of brick and granite mansions. Its buildings had not yet suffered the degradation of being turned into apartments or rooms to let.

The address brought me to one of the mansions. The door was opened by an aged, white-haired black man, who told me that Mrs. Morris was in the library, one flight up to the left. "She spends all day there," he said. "I take her food up." He looked too frail to carry a tray.

There was a marble balustrade that curved from the first to the second floor. The stairway was at least six feet wide. I could see into a living room which had a white grand piano. On the mantel of its marble fireplace stood two vast vases. Queen Victoria, painted on one, simpered at Prince Albert, painted on the other. The walls of the living room and hall were silk brocade. I began to get the picture. The more I looked, the angrier I became.

The library with its white-and-gilt furniture followed the pattern of luxury I had seen below. Mrs. Morris was lying on a sofa that was upholstered in faded silk. She barely opened her eyes when I came in. Her skin was almost translucent. She was very weak.

I pulled a chair up near her. "Sick as you are," I said, "you'll have to get another doctor. You need a transfusion, and I'm not taking care of you anymore. You took advantage of me. You made a fool of me. Now call some other doctor and make a fool of him."

Her hand quivered upward. "I want you to take care of me. I'll repay you. Take me to the hospital if you want to. Do what has to be done. I'm just too sick."

"You'll have to pay in advance. I wouldn't trust you around the corner. And if you won't pay, I'll call a city ambulance and send you to Harlem Hospital, where they'll treat you in the ward."

"My son will be here soon. He'll take care of everything."

I was surprised. She'd never mentioned a son. He arrived a few minutes later. He was a replica of Abe Lincoln. He was tall, had long arms and legs, and walked with a slight stoop. A cowlick hid part of his forehead and his reddish-blond hair straggled over his collar. I judged him to be in his forties. He was wearing a long, black, moth-eaten coat. His black coat, just like his mother's favored dress, was turning green. They did their shopping in the same attic.

"Your mother needs a transfusion," I told him. "That means the hospital. It's expensive."

"Do what's necessary. Tell me what it costs and I'll write you a check."

Calculating rapidly, I gave him a good round sum to include the hospital, the blood, the ambulance, and my fee. "If it's more I'll tell you, and if there's any left over, she owes it to me."

He looked pained as he wrote the check. He seemed to take after his mother. "How can you part with it?" I asked.

"It's her money. I just keep the books."

A few days later at the hospital, Mrs. Morris, as expected, was a different woman. I was still angry with her, and disgusted.

"When can I go home?" she asked me.

"Now."

"Will you still take care of me?"

"Mrs. Morris, you're a miser, and if there's one type of person who's too much for me, it's a miser. I'll take care of you if you do what I say and pay in advance."

I knew I was being very bold, but I was angry, too. I could afford to be; I no longer had to worry about paying my office rent and the nurses' salaries, or about my family's room and board. Maybe, had I had these things still to think of, I might have patted Mrs. Morris's hand instead of telling her off. Necessity can make cowards of us all.

For months this woman listened to me, took her treatment, and functioned well. Then another disappearance, another emergency transfusion. I called her a miser again, but I collected in advance and brought Mrs. Morris through another crisis.

Considering what I knew of her behavior, I arranged thereafter to treat her at home. At least then I'd have some control. The old black servant would open the door for me, limp off to the rear of the house, and disappear. I never saw any other staff.

I was curious. "This old man. He seems too weak to work. Is he the only housekeeper?" I asked Mrs. Morris.

"He was my husband's valet for thirty years. He really is too old to work now. But I won't turn an old servant out. He sleeps next to the furnace, where it's warm in winter. He's well taken care of. I give him fifteen cents a day for his food. He's lucky to have a nice home," Mrs. Morris assured me.

Fifteen cents a day! Even then, in 1940, it was enough to starve on. "God, you're a miserable woman."

Like all the misers I've met, she took no offense at being called one.

One day she said to me, "Doctor, I'm going to prove you wrong. I'm going to show you that I'm not a miser."

By now she had the strength to come and go as she pleased. She asked me to follow her, and she headed for the stairs.

The basements of these old mansions were two steps down from the street. Large windows protected by handsome, curved grilles let plenty of light and air into the basement rooms: the kitchen and pantry, the servants' quarters, and, at the rear, the furnace room. There was supposed to be a cook in the kitchen, and food was to be sent up by dumbwaiter to the dining room above. A walkway alongside the house led to a service door. This door was the staff entrance and the delivery point for the butcher's boy and his confreres. Canvas sacks of coal were hauled down the walkway and delivered to the furnace room.

Mrs. Morris led me down her marble stairway to the ground floor, down a flight of service stairs to their terminus in the basement hall, and thence into the furnace room. In one corner was a cot, with its bedclothes neatly folded. I judged it was for the ancient family retainer.

I was more than curious.

Resplendent in a frayed silk dressing gown long ago made for a gentleman, Mrs. Morris picked up a piece of firewood and went to a side wall. She pushed away the cot. She struck the wall vigorously with the firewood until several bricks shifted. I made no effort to help her. I had no idea what she intended to do.

Mrs. Morris stacked the loose bricks on the floor, put her hand into the hole she'd made, and pulled out an old metal box. It was like an old-fashioned biscuit tin with a hinged lid. Its garish paint was peeling.

Mrs. Morris lifted out a diamond necklace. It must have contained twenty good-sized stones. "My husband gave me this for Queen Victoria's Jubilee. He was always an Anglophile." She lifted out a pearl necklace, a diamond bracelet, and large diamond pendant earrings. She mentioned the occasion for which her husband had given her each of them. There were still other jewels left in the box. She put back the jewels she had removed, closed the box, replaced it in the hole in the wall, and pounded the bricks into place with the firewood.

"You still think I'm a miser?"

I was stunned. What stunned me was not the display of jewels but the fact that even one small item could have been traded for a lifetime's supply of liver, vitamins, and doctors' bills. The old valet might have had a few square meals. More than ever, I was convinced Mrs. Morris was exceptionally stingy.

"You're a miser all right," I said, but once again my saying so didn't antagonize her. "One good thing. Your son will be a wealthy man someday, though I think he's a miser just like you."

"I had another child, but she married a man with no money at all. I disinherited her." Perhaps she noticed the look on my face. "I may leave her something, too," she added, trying to sound generous.

One day not long after this visit, Mrs. Morris called my office. "I need your help."

"You seemed all right when I left you last."

"I am all right. It's my husband."

This was staggering intelligence. I had assumed Mrs. Morris was a widow. I had never asked about a husband, and she had mentioned him only as the source of her jewels.

Once when I'd visited, I'd been disturbed by muffled thumps coming from a room adjacent to the library; a sound like wet laundry being hurled against the wall. Of course the very notion was ridiculous. When I inquired Mrs. Morris fended me off: the valet was mopping, she said.

This time the servant, more scrawny than ever, led me to the door of the room behind the library, where Mrs. Morris stood by with a key. She unlocked the door and let me in. There, lying on the floor, was a long bag of bones that had once been a man. Mr. Morris made an effort to rise, and the old black man and I ran to help. Once we had him on his feet, he sagged again to the floor. We finally dragged him to the bed. He didn't know we were there, nor did he know anything else. He was naked and had soiled himself. He was obviously starving, completely unaware of his surroundings.

The room was in disorder, the bed unmade and filthy. Chairs were overturned and rags and dishes scattered on the floor.

"This man isn't a case for me. He's starving and dying of thirst. How did you let him get like this?" I was appalled.

"He's only been here about a year," Mrs. Morris said. "He lost a lot of money in two business deals. He wasn't in his right mind. I kept him here to stop him going to the office. I thought we could treat him here. But he got worse and worse."

There was no time for my hundred questions. "I can imagine. But we have to get him to the hospital for emergency treatment now, today, this minute."

Mrs. Morris looked down at her husband and hesitated.

"Won't that cost a lot?"

I struggled to control myself. "It will."

"Can't we send him to Harlem?"

"You can if you want him in an overcrowded ward with a lot of poor people. They'll do their best for him."

"Maybe he ought to go there."

I called the Police Department for an emergency ambulance. I waited until Mr. Morris had been taken away. Mrs. Morris went along in the ambulance to give what information was required. Then I left.

A few hours later, Mrs. Morris called. She sounded well pleased. "As soon as they knew what sort of people we were, they put him into a small private room they keep for sick nurses."

"Did they say how he was doing?"

"Yes. They don't expect him to live more than a few days." There seemed to be no concern in her voice.

"Mrs. Morris," I said as calmly as I could, "I think it's time you got yourself a new doctor. I have suddenly become too expensive even for you." I hung up.

I never saw her again.

Strangely enough, there was more of her story to come. Some five years later, not long after I'd returned from overseas and left the Navy to return to private practice, a lawyer called me.

"Do you remember a Mrs. Morris?"

"I'm afraid I do."

"She died recently. I represent her son, who says he met you. Is it possible we might see you at your office? The sooner the better."

"Come right up. But tell him he pays for an office visit before I see him."

I had no idea what they wanted, but I soon found out. Mr. Morris was wearing the same black coat, now glazed green. The collar was turned up and his red-blond hair overlapped it. His suit was vintage 1910, with frayed cuffs. His long face was grooved from lips to chin. Abe Lincoln come again.

The lawyer took over.

"Did Mrs. Morris ever tell you she had jewelry?"

I decided not to volunteer anything. "Yes."

"Did she ever show you any?"

"I don't know why I should bother to help you."

"In the name of common humanity," said the lawyer.

I laughed out loud. I believed this man had all but conspired with his mother to starve his father to death. And for such a man, I was to do a good deed!

"Yes, I saw some jewelry. If we find it, will you take care of your sister?" I enjoyed the dig.

I could feel their excitement mounting.

"Do you know where she kept it?"

"Yes. In the furnace room in a box in the wall."

They both rose and leaned on my desk.

"Could you show us where?"

"Only if this man pays me in advance for my time." I wasn't going to be worked for a sucker again. To stress the point, I used an old New York expression: "It'll cost."

There was no question now about the tension. The lawyer paid. I was their man and they knew it. On the way to the house the lawyer was jovial. Mr. Morris remained in sober silence. Perhaps he was worried about the cab fare.

In the empty and shadowy furnace room I picked up a piece of firewood as Mrs. Morris had done. I didn't remember the exact spot and had to strike the wall in several places before I elicited a hollow sound. They watched me eagerly. The theatrics of the situation struck me.

Finally I found the area of loose bricks. I gave the lawyer the stick of wood.

"Hit here and I think you'll find it."

It took him several hard blows to loosen the bricks. He pulled out half a dozen and there was the old biscuit tin. Mr. Morris and the lawyer both grasped it eagerly to open it.

The box was empty.

HUMANITY

Not long ago, before medicine became a quasi-science, doctors of good conscience sometimes doubted their own value. They wondered if what they offered their patients justified their existence.

We had only three specific drugs: quinine, morphine, and digitalis. There were vast numbers of medications handed down to us through their pragmatic use in folk medicine. Many of these were later refined and sold to us by pharmaceutical manufacturers. Some, like the smallpox vaccine, had real value. Insulin was produced in the twenties. But it was not until 1937, with the introduction of the sulfa drugs, that doctors really knew that their function was invaluable.

My wife, with her knife-edged perception of values, had other ideas. Belle said, "There's one great factor you're forgetting, the most important factor of all. That little black bag you carry with you has more in it than medications and instruments. It contains the greatest medication of all. It contains hope."

I thought it over. She was right. I realized that no matter what the doctor thought, as long as he did no harm he had the potential to do good. When the physician could not remedy a situation medically he could sometimes turn to surgery. Much surgery that is routine today was then still new and experimental. Surgery was known as the failure of medicine.

When the sulfa drugs first came into use I was teaching as well as practicing. One of my interns asked me if I had followed the literature concerning the medicine. I said I had, but that I would wait a long time before using it. "It sounds too good to be true," I told him. "I've seen these miracle drugs come and go. I'm not too sure of any of them."

The intern gave me a sidelong glance. "I hope you're wrong," he said.

I'm glad I was.

One day I returned from a call after treating a child for tonsillitis. I felt confident that the sulfa drug I had ordered would kill the organisms and cure the patient. It was between office hours. I let myself into the office with my own key and found my nurse, Peggy, sitting at my desk.

"Howyu, Doc," I said.

Peggy was nibbling at the eraser of her pencil.

"Sit down," she said. "You talk to everyone else. Now I want you to talk to me."

"If it's about your salary, I refuse to reduce it."

"It isn't about my salary. Of course I want a raise, but I always want a raise. I want to talk to you about your patients."

Peggy always had ideas, and I was always willing to listen.

"The reason we work such long hours here is because you talk too much to your patients. Why don't you try talking less and getting them out a little faster?"

I thought that over for a moment. "I guess you're right, Peggy. I take too much of an interest in them and their families. I like to know all about everybody. When I see interesting people on the street I'd like to be able to approach them. I'd like to find out who they are, where they come from, what they do. I can do that in the office. I imagine I'm too garrulous."

"What's garrulous?" asked Peggy.

"I don't know," I said, "but I'll look it up."

The phone rang. Peggy answered it. "Wait a minute." She handed me the phone. "Somebody's in trouble."

It was a woman's voice. "Doc, this is Angie. Can you come right away? Something terrible's happened."

I asked for some particulars.

"I can't tell you. But come." She gave me an address in the low Sixties between Central Park West and Columbus Avenue.

Peggy handed me my bag. "What's the matter with Angie?"

"I haven't the slightest idea."

"Don't be long. We have lots of patients coming."

Peggy knew I liked Angie.

"I'll be back as soon as I can," I said with dignity.

"Bah," Peggy said, and closed the door behind me.

The address was that of an old, solid building. I climbed to the second floor. A number of people were milling about on the landing. I guessed they were neighbors, because they were talking together. As I came up they pointed to the right-hand door. I could hear raised voices and hurried footsteps. I knocked. The door opened enough to admit me, and a woman's arm beckoned me in.

The woman was Angie. She was, despite her youth, a madam. She took my hand in her moist one and pulled me into one of the bedrooms.

Angie was one of my favorites. She was a five-foot-five-inch slender brunette with carved features, blue eyes, and—well, what legs!

Now she was panicked. "Mygod, Doc, what are we going to do?"

One of her girls was lying naked on the bed. On top of her was a man, also naked, who weighed perhaps two hundred-fifty pounds. Compared to him, the girl he was lying on was tiny. She was squirming, pulling, pushing, grunting, trying to get out from under. A young girl in a kimono stood pulling at the man. But the two girls struggled without coordination so that each was constantly counteracting the other.

"At least I got her to stop shrieking," Angie said.

The man was ashen. I thought he might have fainted, but a good look proved that he was dead. He had probably been dead for more than a few minutes. His back was cold and clammy and his legs hung loosely, shifting as the girls tried to move his body.

"For heaven's sake," I said. "Use your heads. Come over this side and all together roll him over. Roll, don't pull. And do it from one side."

Angie, the kimonoed girl, and I were able to roll the fat man onto his side. The trapped victim crawled out and fled.

"Ohmygod, ohmygod, ohmygod," gasped Angie. "What'll I do now?"

I sat down on the bed next to the body to catch my breath. "Now," I said, "the matter is out of our hands. We call an ambulance. A policeman will come before the ambulance does. Then more police will come because the ambulance surgeon will pronounce the man 'dead on arrival.' The doctor on the ambulance won't take the body because it won't be his business to.

"After that, if the police see there was no foul play, they'll call the coroner. The coroner will call for the wagon from the morgue. They'll leave a policeman here until the morgue wagon arrives."

"How long will that take?"

"Hours."

"What about my clients?"

"They won't come in when they see the excitement." I picked up the phone, called the Police Department, and asked them to dispatch an ambulance. I told them we had a corpse on our hands.

Within a very few minutes a gray-haired sergeant came in, followed by another policeman. Then came the ambulance surgeon, pushing his way through the crowd gathered at the door.

"Nothing here for you, Doctor," said the sergeant. He sat down heavily and unbuttoned his coat, revealing a brown sweater underneath. The ambulance surgeon examined the naked man for signs of life. Finding none, he made out a slip, marked it "D.O.A.," gave a copy to the sergeant, and shouldered his way through the crowd. Very soon, puffing and panting from hurry, the policeman on the beat arrived. The sergeant saw him and said, "Send those people home."

With a little pushing and shoving the policeman cleared the area and came in and closed the door.

In the meantime the sergeant's driver had gone through the dead man's clothes. He handed some papers to the sergeant, who studied them closely and motioned me over to read them. The dead man was president of a bank in a small Connecticut town. He had apparently come to New York for relaxation. He had had a bit too much of it.

The sergeant said, "Now, you girls. Get this man dressed. Put all his clothes on. Put his hat and anything else he had beside him. Hurry to it."

The girl in the kimono looked questioningly at Angie, who said, "You heard the man. Let's get to work."

It was no easy job. The corpse was a dead weight, literally. It took them at least fifteen minutes. The underpants and trousers gave the most trouble.

"Now," said the sergeant, "the coroner will come and then the ambulance from the morgue. This is what you're going to say." He addressed himself to Angie.

"You heard a thud at your door and the sound of something heavy falling. You found this gentleman lying there. You never saw him before in your life. Your door opens inward. You pulled him in to try to help him but you were too late. You called the doctor and he called the ambulance. That's all you know and not a thing more. Someone in the crowd told you this man was here to investigate a loan. A loan on the building."

The sergeant sighed and heaved himself out of his chair. "I'll leave one of my men here," he told Angie. "Send the girls home, one at a time. You go now," he said, motioning to the girl in the wrap.

The girl scurried away. I looked out the window. A dozen curious people stood in front of the building. No one would pay attention to the exit of a single girl.

The sergeant and I left together. On our way out I said, "You did a really nice thing."

The sergeant shrugged. "The man probably has a widow and children. It was the right thing to do. I'm going to keep doing nice things. Somebody has to. It says in the Book of Job, 'Man is born to trouble as the sparks fly upward.' "

THE HONEYMOON
IS OVER

"IT WAS WONDERFUL," Peggy had told Belle and me in the office one day not long after her honeymoon with Chris. My wife had come by to pick her up for lunch. "In Florida everything grows all year round, and the colors of the plants are unbelievable. I don't know how you knew we'd love it so much, but we did. It was sometimes terribly hot, but our room faced the ocean, so we were cool and comfortable the whole time."

Belle said, "I hope you didn't spend your next year's salary on your room."

"Oh, it was luxury, all right. But we got it for very little. Chris used a due bill."

Belle gave her a sideways glance. "What on earth is a 'due bill'?"

"Well, it's this way," Peggy explained. "One of Chris's clients, a hotel manager Chris did some detective work for, couldn't pay him in cash. But when he heard we were going to Florida he said he could give Chris a note. It was good for two weeks' credit at half price at our hotel. That's what they call a due bill.

"It's a sort of barter, don't you see? No money changes hands. But a lot of places exchange due bills. It's the Depression. Lots of middle-class people live on paper. It was a luxury room, but first there was a discount for its being out of season, and then there was the due bill to cut the rest in half. That's how we stayed in a beautiful room in a beautiful hotel in a beautiful place. And your present of the train tickets helped, of course."

I had to leave for the hospital.

"I hope you ladies enjoy Chock Full O' Nuts," I said.

Belle and Peggy exchanged a glance.

"That's not the sort of lunch we're having," Belle replied. "We're going to the Parisien."

"Ah, I see: *that* sort of lunch! Not cream cheese on date-nut bread. Omelettes! Salade! A tarte! Well, bon appetit!"

I was envious. The Parisien was one of the prizes of the neighborhood. It had been among the better speakeasies, and it had survived the repeal of Prohibition because of its excellent chef and its faithful clientele.

The Hearst organization was across the street, and Hearst cartoonists had left their mark on the restaurant's walls. My favorite mural depicted the midnight unmasking at a masked ball. One elegant male creature was peeling off a wolf mask. Beneath it was the face of a wolf.

Belle and I talked it over that evening. Belle said that over lunch Peggy had told her happily about palm trees and rum drinks with coconut, and dining and dancing out-of-doors. "It does seem as if their marriage is working out," she said.

"It certainly does," I agreed. "Chris comes by to take her home at night, and when he's free he takes her out to lunch. Last week he even took *me* to lunch. He did order three martinis. I told him to save them for later in the day, but he said, 'I didn't ask you,' so I let it go at that."

All did go well, for many months. Then one day my Number Two Nurse said that Peggy had called to say she couldn't come in for a couple of days. She wasn't feeling well.

I telephoned to see if there was anything I could do.

"My mouth's swollen and I can't talk," Peggy told me in muffled tones. "I've been to the dentist. I'll be in as soon as I can. I hope Mrs. Slocum can help in the meantime."

"Stay home until you're well." She thanked me; we hung up.

Three days later, Peggy came in. Her jaw was swollen and she wore dark glasses. "Infected tooth," she said, pointing to her jaw with her thumb.

Belle was in the office at the time. "Let me tell you about your boss, Peggy. I used a taxi to get to work and I stopped off to buy sandwiches and coffee. When I told him I spent two dollars a day getting to work he said, 'Well you're certainly worth it.' I haven't figured that out yet."

"He'd do the same to me," Peggy answered. "Except he's afraid I'll quit." It was hard for her to smile.

Belle and I both knew there was no infected tooth. Chris was to blame.

"I don't mind if they quarrel," Belle said. "But I resent bitterly that he strikes her."

I determined to tell Chris off when I saw him. He must have had some shame—he stayed away from the office for months. Whenever he came for Peggy, they met at the corner.

There were other incidents, but few and far between, over the passing years. Or so we thought. Chris once again came to the office to meet his wife. Peggy and Chris seemed happy enough. They did have many things in common, as Chris had told me: friends and a love of baseball, among them.

Then, years later, early one morning, a doctor I knew called me. He was the chairman of the Obstetrics Department at Jewish Memorial Hospital in upper Manhattan.

"About your nurse, Peggy," he said. "She still work for you?" I told him that indeed she did.

"Well, I was passing the female surgical ward this morning and I'm sure I saw her there. Not working there, but in bed. She looked badly beaten. Maybe you'd better get up here."

I took the West Side Highway and was at Jewish Memorial Hospital within half an hour. There was Peggy. Her face was black-and-blue, both eyes were swollen shut, and both arms and shoulders were bruised.

"I can't take it anymore," she said. "What should I do? What should I do?"

I held her hand. I didn't want to examine her; she hurt in too many places.

"The resident told me you have no fractures of the facial bones or skull. Belle and I want you to come to our house until you're well. When you're with us, we'll talk."

I called Chris at home. "If I were you," I advised him, "I'd get into my office within the next hour or two. We have some talking to do."

He agreed to come. His voice sounded gruff and growly, but I suspected the tone was due more to being awakened from an alcoholic stupor than to anger.

He came to the office, contrite. I wasn't sure of my ground. I didn't know my rights and duties in a domestic relations situation, or even if I had any. Could I make a citizen's arrest? Should I talk to his parish priest? And, if I threatened to take any steps, would he smash my face in as he'd smashed Peggy's?

"If this ever happens again, Chris," I said, "I'm going to find some way to get you picked up for attempted murder."

"It won't happen again," he told me. "It's only when I drink I get mad at the world. I promise from now on I won't drink."

Peggy stayed at our apartment a long time. She must have had a minor cerebral hemorrhage that caused vertigo and weakness. We discussed her situation. Did she still love Chris? Yes. Had her attitude toward him changed? Yes. She was afraid of him now, but she also felt protective of him. Did she think a person could change his character? No. Leopards can't change their spots. Did she want to go on being married to him? No. But in addition to all the complications of human relations, there was the Roman Catholic Church, of which she was a devout member. How could Peggy possibly end a marriage made in the sight of God?

In due course Peggy returned to work. She had gone back to her own apartment against our advice, telling us simply, "Chris wants me there."

"You know damn well he'll get drunk again. Someday he'll kill you. I want you to go to the Powerhouse and talk to someone down there about an annulment or divorce," I insisted.

"That's what I intend to do," she said, "first chance I get."

"Go do it now. Number Two is here, and Mrs. Slocum will come down to help if we call her."

The Powerhouse was the laity's name for the administrative

center of the Roman Catholic Church in New York. Perhaps even the clergy called it that. Its offices were in one of the former Villard mansions, which now belonged to the Church. St. Patrick's Cathedral was just across Madison Avenue.

Peggy went. Hours later she came back, in tears. "Divorce is out of the question, and I have no grounds for annulment. And anyway they said it would cost too much to get one. The priest refused to speak to me about it any more."

I don't know if my talk had anything to do with it, but Chris began to show a better side. At Peggy's insistence, he came to me for examination. I discovered he had diabetes. If he kept drinking, I told him, he'd run the risk of complications. When he heard what the complications were it scared the hell out of him. Maybe that did it. He became subdued, not another person but a more peaceful one.

Belle and I looked on this respite as a truce, as the calm before the storm. We were not at ease about them. We would never be. But there was nothing we could do. And so the years passed.

HONEY

HONEY CALLED ME from her hospital bed in a small town in North Carolina. I hadn't seen or heard from her for a few months. On her last visit I had taken blood tests so that she could marry the man who was to be her fourth husband.

I knew the man was a rogue. The only question was how much of a rogue. The answer came from Honey, long-distance: "The car went over a cliff," she said. "He did it on purpose. He tried to kill me."

Honey's doctor in North Carolina filled me in. "She's a brave little woman. I wouldn't have given much for her chances. Funny thing: you know how it is, when you break the bad news to the husband—you wonder how they're going to take it? Well, I tell this fella about her fractured skull, the internal injuries, the broken hip, the coma. It's hard for him to stop reading the sports page. And then do you know what he does? He leaves town!"

Honey had no intention of dying. She surprised the hospital staff by emerging from a deep coma and making a steady, uneventful recovery. When bills were presented she signed checks to cover them. She was a good and cooperative patient, regained her health and mobility, and returned to New York.

Honey was a southern girl who had buried three husbands. She had no children. Her first husband was a builder who died after a pleasant marriage of twenty years. She inherited a goodly sum from him. Her second was a widower with no children. He was much older than she and died within five years of their marriage, leaving her a small fortune in investments. The third owned two small but exclusive apartment houses. Honey took the whole top floor of one building, chopped out the walls, rebuilt the place to her liking, decorated it, and lived there in moderate splendor.

Honey was one of a set of dowagers who had become my patients. They were all friends or acquaintances, and all of them were rich. On her first visit I told Honey that she was a healthy woman and that she could return in a year or so for a routine checkup. The others who were told the same thing were quite pleased. But not Honey. Honey had other things in mind.

She would come in every few days with some minor complaint, be treated, and leave. She was always gay and cheerful. She was a slender, nicely dressed woman. From the rear she could have been mistaken for a girl in her thirties. Nor did her face tell her true age, which I judged to be in the late sixties. Honey was a honey.

My nurse began to take a grudging dislike to the woman. "She comes in at all hours," Peggy said. "She comes in to weigh herself, and to inquire about your family and your age. One of these days she's going to proposition you. Get rid of her."

"I have no reason to get rid of her. She bothers you more than she bothers me."

But Peggy was right. The blow fell that Christmas Eve. Honey called, told my answering service that she had burned herself, and said please to tell me to come as soon as I could. I went.

It was about eight in the evening. I took the elevator to the top floor and rang. Honey opened the door. She was wearing a black lace negligee and had a gold band around her head. She simpered.

It was late and I was tired, and I wasn't in the mood for having Honey simper at me.

"I hear you burned yourself."

"I did. Come in and I'll show you."

She led me into her living room. In one corner was a table set for two, with candles flickering. Wine stood in a bucket, cooling.

"Where's the burn?"

"Here." She showed me a small red mark on her wrist. "I leaned against the radiator, and it hurt so much I thought it must be worse than it looked."

"It's nothing. I'm going. I have work to do," I told her.

"Why can't you stay? Your family's out of town and it's Christmas Eve and my help is off and we can have a nice dinner sent up from the restaurant downstairs. You've got to eat sometime."

"How did you know my family was out of town?"

"I heard your nurse say so."

"I'll fire her the next time I see her. Now look, Honey, I have to finish my work and then I have other plans. You'll have to get yourself another boy."

I walked toward the door. She trailed me. The door closed with what I thought was an unnecessary slam.

That should have been the end of Honey, but it wasn't.

Not far from my office was a busy restaurant. It was a grill of the sort that attracts a big lunchtime crowd from nearby offices. There was little evening trade. Then it was hushed, and couples instead of businessmen carried on discreet conversations in the wooden booths. The maître d' was a big, pompous man whom the businessmen liked. They recognized the type. He looked like cartoons depicting United States senators or moguls of modern capitalism.

In fact, he had been a cardsharp, an actor, a car salesman, and many other things, and until now he had managed to fail at them all. But he was a good-looking man, and his bulk and carriage were impressive. He dressed nattily, even to white piping on his vest. When it was cold he wore spats.

Honey had not been discouraged enough to stay away from my office. It was there that she and the maître d' met. They sat next to each other and talked. They left together. On their next visit they arrived together. They wanted blood tests so that they could be married. They would honeymoon on a private island off the coast of South Carolina. Honey confided to Peggy that the location was very romantic.

My nurse came in, purring. "I see you lost out," Peggy said. Malice flowed from her.

I didn't see Honey again until she returned to New York. Then she told me the whole story. "He did it on purpose," she said. "First we went to my hometown. I gave him access to my safe-deposit box. I had about forty thousand dollars in cash there, plus more in negotiable bonds.

"We were on our way south. Suddenly he jerked the car to the side of the road. There was a cliff. He opened his door and jumped out, and the car and I rolled on down. The car turned over a couple of times. The next thing I know I'm in the hospital and he's gone.

"I didn't tell anyone but my lawyer about its not being an accident. I felt like such a fool. I suppose they suspect at the hospital. Of course, he went right back and cleaned out my vault. My lawyer will see he never gets any more. I have plenty left. I'd just as soon forget about it."

That was the story of Honey and how it ended. Almost but not quite.

I had a call one day from a partner in one of New York's well-known law firms. Would I examine Honey and testify, if I thought it to be true, that she was of sound mind? Yes, I would. And so I found myself once more in Honey's penthouse apartment.

There were two lawyers there and a young man in the uniform of the United States Marine Corps. The boy, about twenty-two years old, looked by turns sheepish and arrogant.

One of the lawyers explained to me that Honey was making a gift of money to the boy. She wanted no question later about her mental status.

She and I were left alone while I asked the appropriate questions and got the expected answers. I told her that I wasn't interested in her purpose, only in her psychiatric state. She said to me, "I'm giving him twenty-five thousand dollars. Doctor, he's the only man I ever met who loves me for my soul alone."

One of the lawyers walked me to the door.

"If necessary, will you testify that she is sane?"

"Of course I shall," I answered. "She's capable of handling her affairs. After all, what's money compared to love? But just between the two of us, she's nuttier than a pecan pie."

MONAHAN

Mr. Monahan was ashamed of his face.

Joseph Aloysius ("Lewis to you") Monahan was a quiet man who worked on the back elevator in a large apartment house. His job consisted mainly of removing garbage from the service entrances on each floor to the basement. On garbage collection days he shifted the cans to the street.

Monahan was a slight, undersized man with a florid face and thinning red hair. He had raised a family of three sons and a daughter. He was well liked in the neighborhood. After work he would visit his favorite bar, order a beer, and sit in a quiet corner with it until it was time to go home. The other men greeted him but had long since accepted the fact that he would not join them.

Years before, Mr. Monahan had developed a small wen in the center of his forehead. A wen is a rounded mass of cheesy material encased in a capsule. It resembles an Italian cheese. Medically it is called a sebaceous cyst. These wens are of no significance except as they deform the features or become inflamed.

Slowly, very slowly, this wen became larger. Many times it was called to Mr. Monahan's attention, and he became more and more sensitive about it. Sometimes he would be asked why he had a golf ball in the middle of his forehead.

I met him when I was called by Mrs. Monahan to take care of their children. He would stand by, listening, but taking no part in the discussion. He was afraid I would mention his wen.

Peggy said to me, "You can be a cruel and hard-hearted man. You chase around to take care of every bum in the neighborhood, but you won't give consideration to a nice gentleman like Mr. Monahan."

"You won't get another raise if you talk like that."

She shrugged. "I don't expect another raise anyhow."

"What do you want me to do? You expect me to sandbag him and get him here? He's more afraid of doctors than he is of sebaceous cysts."

"You've got to do something for him. Mrs. Monahan says they don't go out anymore. If she wants to visit anyone she has to go alone. When friends come he goes into another room. She says he's so quiet around the house that she's afraid she'll step on him, the way she steps on her cat. You ought to be smart enough to get him in here. Look at all your diplomas." She pointed to the wall.

She shamed me. There was no way out. We had to concoct a plot. Peggy made the arrangements with Mrs. Monahan.

"She's bringing him over with their youngest child tomorrow night after work. She's going to tell him that you want to see them both about their youngster. We think he's anemic. That'll bring the old man."

"All right, Miss Know-it-all. You have everything prepared, and when he comes I'll try to talk him into the surgical room. Ten to one he'll refuse and walk out."

"A buck?"

"A buck. Ten if you win."

The Monahans—mother, father, and son—appeared at the appointed time, just as I was getting through my regular hours. To keep the show going, I took the boy first. I did nothing for him (he was in on the scheme) and then called in his mother and father. The three of them stood in the room in which I did minor surgery.

Peggy, the real miscreant in all this, kept her back to us while she arranged the instruments. She had a new blade in my surgical knife, small sharp scissors, a half dozen hemostats—scissor-shaped instruments that are really clamps to stop blood flow—sponges, suture material already attached to the needle, and a 10cc. syringe containing a solution of 1 percent novocaine.

Suddenly she said, still with her back to us, "Mr. Monahan, get on the table."

Mr. Monahan was too appalled not to obey.

"Lie down," Peggy ordered. "Your wife and son are going to stay right in this room to see what sort of a man you are."

With complete disbelief he did what he was told. He was being shanghaied.

As quickly as I could, I told him he would feel the prick of one needle and then only pressure. He didn't know how to stop me. After cleansing the area I anesthetized near the cyst. Then, where the novocaine made a bulge in the skin, I gave three more quick injections. By then Mr. Monahan had surrendered to his fate.

The rest was easy. The knife Peggy had given me couldn't have been better. When the novocaine took hold, I made one careful incision into the thin skin of the forehead and then into the underlying tissue to expose the capsule of the cyst. Peggy stood by, sponging. She could have done the minor procedure as well herself. She took a second to give Mr. Monahan a reassuring pat on the shoulder. We hadn't given him time even to remove his jacket.

With the blunt end of my scissors I broke a few adhesions, lengthened my incision to expose the whole capsule, and then removed it entirely. It came out intact, the size of a cherry. "You'll never see that again," I told him.

Five interrupted sutures that plastic surgeons use made the wound almost invisible. "Come in next week and I'll take the stitches out," I told Mr. Monahan.

Peggy sponged the wound with soap and water. "You can get up now," she urged.

Mr. Monahan sat up on the table and stepped to the floor. "Look into the mirror," Peggy said, giving him a hand mirror.

He looked. Slowly a great smile appeared on his face. I hadn't noticed before how broad his mouth was. "Well, that's that," he said with satisfaction, just as if he had arranged the whole proceeding. Mrs. Monahan was crying quietly. "You look wonderful. Twenty years younger," she told him.

Peggy applied a pressure bandage and sent them out.

"You owe me ten," she proclaimed.

"Peggy! Did you really believe I intended to pay if I lost?"

She took a long stretch to rid her muscles of tension.

"No," she said, "but I certainly expected to get paid if I won."

I gave her ten dollars.

A MAN OF
MILITARY MIEN

MR., OR—PERHAPS—MAJOR, Marshall McCullough stood six feet tall, had broad shoulders and a slim waist, and was one of the most respected men in the neighborhood.

The talk was that he had been a cadet at West Point. He had graduated too late for the First World War, but he had served in the Second. From the trim bristle on his upper lip to the long sweep of his legs, he was a military man.

To our knowledge, there was no Mrs. McCullough. Everyone had the impression that there once had been. We supposed she had died before he moved in among us. He did not look the type of man a woman would give up. He was elegant.

Toward Ninth Avenue were some houses that had been built at the same time as the Elevated, in the expectation that the new form of transportation would allow high rentals. Their construction was remembered only by a few elders. These houses were four storys high and had an apartment on each floor. The rooms were large and square—the living rooms must have been thirty-by-thirty—and the apartments had the most modern plumbing and kitchen facilities, vintage 1900.

In one of these houses, two flights up, Mr. McCullough had what he called his "digs." He and his ancient housekeeper must have rattled around in all that space.

Let's call him the Major—that would have pleased him. One day when I met the Major on the street he asked if he might speak to me about a pain in his legs and back. In my comings and goings I had become accustomed to being consulted on the street. By that time I had become a sort of neighborhood fixture. I liked the warmth and trust that this informality indicated. The Major was a gentleman, and I was pleased to be consulted by him.

He tapped the lower part of his back with the head of his cane and said, "It's all right when I'm walking and active, but in bed at night it begins to hurt and keeps me from sleeping. The pain goes down both my legs. I get up out of bed and walk around until it feels better."

I told the Major that such conditions were most often temporary. The pain could have been caused by strain or even by inflammation from a common cold that might have settled in his back. I suggested simple medication. He smiled, thanked me, and was on his way.

A week or so later he came to the office to see me. "I must owe you for a visit. What you told me helped a great deal. But you won't get rich giving away your knowledge for nothing."

I assured him that it had been my pleasure and that I was delighted to know him. He seemed a kind man, but reserved. There was no question that he was one of our neighborhood's distinguished citizens.

After that he would drop in to see me, making sure I wasn't busy, and we would spend a few minutes talking about the sad state of the world and what could be done to improve it. The Major was especially interested in my experiences in the Second World War, in which I played a very small but not ignoble part.

War—and particularly World War II—interested him.

"You haven't ever seen my place," he said. "When would it be convenient for you to drop up and spend a few minutes?"

We set a date, and a few days later I was in his large living room, perfectly astounded.

There were long tables set up in the room, arranged so that people could walk around and between them, with every part of all the tables accessible. The tables were decorated with papier-mâché terrain and hundreds of toy soldiers. There were tank groups, artillery groups, even supply groups: their trucks contained miniature kitchens!

Some of the tables served as sawhorses for large panes of blue plate glass. The blue glass panes, of course, represented water. On them rested warships of all sorts, including tankers and submarines.

Above the tables, hanging from horizontal wires suspended from the ceiling, were minute squadrons of aircraft—British, German, and American. The planes could be moved along the wires with a pool cue.

My God, I thought, can this grown man spend all his time playing with soldiers?

He not only could, he did.

The Major gazed at the tables with a critical eye and moved some of the pieces. "This is where I have my war games. Everything you see here is a replica of what we had in World War II." He explained to me that there were strict rules of procedure to be followed to make the games as authentic as possible. "Would you like to play?"

I wouldn't have missed it for the world. He was enthusiastic and went into great detail about the rules.

It was just too easy. After a few maneuvers I said, "Your flank is turned and you're not able to deliver any more ammunition. My ships not only prevent your men from escaping by sea, but they prevent supplies from reaching you. I see no way out for you."

The Major straightened up and struck one of the tables with his fist. A regiment wobbled. "Beginner's luck. Let's play another."

I wasn't able to spend the time then, but later we did play again, with the same result. When he lost the second time the Major was really angry. He reddened, struck the palm of one hand with the fist of the other, and paced back and forth. "You've played before," he said.

I escaped as soon as I could, sorry to have disturbed him so thoroughly.

A few days later I met him on the street. He was less than

[223]

cordial and limping badly. "Your medicine doesn't seem to be working anymore," he said. "I hope you won't be hurt if I go see Dr. Sprague."

I didn't mind in the least. Dr. Sprague had been a teacher of mine. He was charming and rich and more than eighty years old. His office was on the ground floor of a mansion he owned on Fifty-sixth Street west of Fifth Avenue. The doctor lived on the upper floors.

Some weeks later Peggy came into my consultation room, flurried and excited. "You couldn't guess who's here to see you!"

"I couldn't guess. Tell me."

"It's Dr. Sprague," she said.

I got up from my chair. "Show him in, for heaven's sake. And get that bottle from behind the books on cardiology and wash the glasses. Show him in. Show him in."

The gray-haired gentleman, stately and courteous, took the chair that I drew out for him.

"I'm simply delighted," I said. "I didn't know you still made house calls. And on doctors!"

"I was passing and I thought it would do you good to have a drink with an old man," Dr. Sprague told me.

"But what are you doing in this neighborhood?"

"You know that friend of yours, the one who plays with soldiers? Well, he came to me for treatment after he saw you. He said you helped him, but not enough.

"He told me about his war games and described how he'd set them up. In his 'digs,' he said!" The old man's eyes twinkled. "After a time I couldn't resist, and I found them fascinating. That housekeeper of his must spend all day dusting! I'm not ashamed to admit that I've been up there several times to play with him. I'm not that busy anymore."

Dr. Sprague went on, "After you failed to cure him, I used a very old remedy I know, and now he's completely well."

"What was it you did for him that I couldn't do?" I asked.

The old man pushed his empty glass a bit closer to the bottle. He smiled at me.

"I let him win," he said.

IMOGEN

It was one of those hilariously beautiful days that exist only in New York—and only in autumn and spring. Zephyrs crossed the Hudson; the air crackled with electric energy.

I wanted to shout, to leap, to throw my arms into the air. Anything could happen, even if it didn't. I could see eagerness and exhilaration in people's faces and a look of surprised delight. This wasn't just another day; it was a special day. Wonderful weather! New York weather! It never lasts. But when it happens it is glorious!

I hardly wanted to go indoors at all; particularly I didn't want to go to my office. I wanted to steal off someplace, anyplace, to taste the joy of being alive.

I went to the office.

Peggy was at her desk, nibbling as usual on the eraser of her pencil. She stared at me curiously. "I didn't want to come to work today either," she said, "but I was afraid you and Number Two would mess up my nice clean office. Your friend is waiting for you," she continued, "the one with the cold head."

I knew whom she meant. She meant Miss Geoffrey, the lady from Central Park West.

Miss Geoffrey lived not far from our neighborhood in an old

apartment building that had two wings. A long straight walk-way between the wings led to the entrance. Like most build-ings on the avenue, this one had been built as a luxury apartment house, but the large apartments had been converted to smaller ones. Originally the long entrance walkway had been covered with an awning the doorman could roll back in good weather. With rent control, the doorman disappeared. So did the awning. The landlord saw no reason for luxury when no one paid for it. When it rained people coming in or going out were drenched. I had been, many times. But no landlord could take away the mag-nificent view of Central Park.

Even on summer days Miss Geoffrey covered her head. She wore a large kerchief tied under her chin like a babushka and tucked into her collar to cover her neck. She wore it indoors and out. Once, when we met on the street, I'd asked why. She answered that when she didn't wear it pain ran like a flame along the nerves of her head.

"What did your doctor suggest?" I asked.

"I don't need a doctor," she said. "Not as long as I cover my head."

At first I wondered if her condition was imaginary, a neurosis. Later I learned how easily stimulated and terribly painful an acute, recurrent neuralgia could be. A neuralgia is pain with or without demonstrable pathology. Even a breeze can cause agony.

Miss Geoffrey had never married, nor had her younger sister, Imogen, whom she had raised after the death of their mother. Imogen was the one person Miss Geoffrey loved, and she loved her unselfishly and with her whole heart. She had no pets. She needed none.

Miss Geoffrey was thirty-eight years old and her sister, twenty-six. Neither one worked. Where they got the money to live on I never knew, nor was it my business to know.

"I didn't come to see you about myself," Miss Geoffrey said. "It's about my sister. You know Imogen." Poor Miss Geoffrey. I realized as we spoke that she was possibly one of the few persons in all the city that day who wasn't buoyed by the weather. She was wearing a woolen babushka.

Of course I knew Imogen, although I had seen her only a few times, and then for minor ailments. I waited for more information. Miss Geoffrey lowered herself heavily into the chair I offered her but sat forward at the edge of it. She was wearing a housedress and had a heavy shawl over her shoulders. She looked like a peasant woman, although she'd been born and raised in New York City.

"Did you know that Imogen had been in a mental institution?"

I admitted that I had known. I always wanted to know everything about a patient's medical history. But Imogen had been vague. I knew no particulars.

"She gets depressed and withdrawn. I do everything for her. I don't mind, but she really suffers."

"How long has this gone on?"

"Ever since she became a young woman. She gets these attacks every few years. That's why she's never married. You know," she said, as if to herself, "Imogen is very beautiful."

I remembered the young woman very well. She was indeed beautiful: tall, with large, green eyes and long, blonde hair. She was very vivacious.

"When she gets depressed she usually gets some sort of symptoms. Headache or loss of appetite or a sore throat. Now she's complaining of stomach pains that come and go. They don't last. But they come maybe every three or four days and double her up for a few minutes. Then they leave and she's herself again. This may be the beginning of a new depression, but I doubt it."

"Why do you doubt it?"

"She never acted this way before. She never had such pain."

"Did she ever mention suicide?"

"Never! But she's very unhappy when she gets these pains."

"It would be better if I could see her. Can you bring her in?"

"She's afraid to see a doctor for fear she'll be sent back to an institution. She doesn't believe she belongs there."

"Tell her for me," I said, "that I never consider a mental diagnosis until I've ruled out everything else. Tell her that as far as I'm concerned she's a young woman with a pain in the belly."

That was how I induced Imogen to come to see me.

Peggy said, "Your friend Miss Geoffrey is here with her sister. She is awfully pretty." She gave me a look that said all sorts of things and left the room with a flip of her skirt.

I examined Imogen with even more care than I usually devoted to people with such complaints. Peggy murmured in passing, "Take your time," but left the room before I could strike her.

The girl showed no tenderness in the abdomen, was intact internally, and had no symptoms. She was cheerful, alert, and cooperative. When she smiled even Peggy melted.

I examined Imogen's urine for kidney function and for diabetes and followed with a half dozen blood tests to rule out syphilis, anemia, and peculiarities of the blood cells. I checked for abnormalities of the serum. I found no pathology.

"Nothing shows up in my examinations," I told the anxious sisters. "I'm sending a specimen of blood to another laboratory, where they do more complex work. For the moment I want you to watch what you eat and to mark down everything. We'll see if the pain follows any particular food. If the pain recurs after the medicine I give you, we'll X-ray your stomach, intestines, gall bladder, and, if necessary, your kidneys and bladder. The only thing I'm certain of now is that your symptoms are not imaginary."

The two sisters left quite happy with my negative findings and minimal advice. At least they had shared their worries. I gave Imogen a medicine that would stop the production of excess hydrochloric acid in her stomach and would help if over-acidity were the cause of her pain.

Three weeks later the sisters were back in my office. Imogen was less happy than before. "The pain still comes back when I least expect it. Food doesn't seem to affect it one way or the other. When I don't have the pain I have a good appetite. But the pain still comes. I wish it would go away."

Her plaintive voice indicated that Imogen was really discouraged. I was becoming worried that she might develop a depression from the pain itself. I wanted complete X-ray studies, and I thought the best place to get them would be the hospital. That would not only save her from preparing at home for the studies, which meant laxatives and enemas, but would save her

many trips back and forth. More important still, I would have
Imogen where she could be seen by any specialist I wanted to call.

The sisters readily agreed, and for three days Imogen submitted
to all the essential X-ray studies we had at the time.

All the X-ray findings were normal: stomach, intestines, kidneys,
gall bladder. It was time to call for more help.

There was a brilliant medical man named Solomon with whom
I had worked before. He and the X-ray specialist and I went over
the plates together.

Dr. Solomon said, "X-rays can be deceptive. They may not show
minor lesions. These machines are still crude. Wait for a week
until the young woman has cleared out all the barium. Then
re-X-ray the stomach and intestines."

The X-ray specialist agreed. I sent the patient home and re-
admitted her a week later. Again we submitted Imogen to X-rays
of the upper and lower gastrointestinal tract. The findings showed
no pathology.

She was examined by a surgeon who said, "Everything I find is
perfectly all right. If she had tenderness or rigidity I would consider an exploratory operation, but when I examined her I could
press her abdominal wall all the way to the back and there wasn't
anything to indicate disease."

The responsibility was still mine. Dr. Solomon said, "Well,
we're stumped. But I've been stumped before. Wait a few weeks
and re-X-ray her."

"That's an awful lot of radiation," I said.

"Of course it is," he agreed, "but there's something going on
in this girl's abdomen that shouldn't be happening. Watch her as
long as you can. Above all, keep her out of the hands of the
psychiatrists. In view of her previous history they're bound to
make a psychiatric diagnosis. She may end up again in an
institution."

Both the Misses Geoffrey were becoming impatient; both were
now speaking of psychiatry. With no physical evidence of the
cause of Imogen's pain, they wondered if it might truly be in her
mind. Impatience had reversed their opinion about seeing a psychiatrist. They agreed to wait another month while we experi-

mented with medications. The pains seemed less frequent and less severe. I expected the next X-rays to be normal. They were. But the stubborn symptoms remained. I was taking a beating; still diagnosis eluded me. I hoped nature might cure Imogen Geoffrey. Then her pains returned with severity.

Finally Miss Geoffrey insisted I call a psychiatrist for an appointment for her sister. She wanted Dr. Foster Kennedy, a man with a tremendous following, a carriage trade, and a large number of wealthy South American patients. I knew the man. I'd heard him speak and had read articles he'd written. He was a good doctor. I arranged the appointment for Imogen and made plans to accompany her to the doctor's office.

Three X-ray studies had disclosed nothing. It was impossible to believe pathology was present. I had done everything I could think of to establish a diagnosis. I could do no more. Still, when the sisters insisted on Imogen's consulting a psychiatrist, I made the call with hesitation. I was disturbed, yet couldn't refuse them. I could do no more for them than I had done; I felt I hadn't done enough.

Dr. Kennedy reviewed Imogen's records, questioned her, and said finally, "There is a big psychic element here. I think electro-shock treatment will help."

Imogen had had this treatment before, in which the patient was sedated, strapped to the table, and literally shocked with electricity. This caused convulsions followed by a few minutes of unconsciousness. Then the patient slowly returned to consciousness with a period of silent recovery.

Imogen knew she would suffer temporary loss of memory of the immediate past, but she was willing to submit to the treatments to stop her recurrent abdominal pain. The doctor outlined a course of twenty treatments. I watched some of them. I felt responsible for the whole case, but I could no longer interfere.

After a dozen or so treatments Dr. Kennedy said to me, "We're getting nowhere. I'm going to send this girl to Hillside Hospital in Queens, where they're doing all sorts of experimental psychiatric work."

I remembered very well Dr. Solomon's admonition to keep

Imogen away from psychiatrists. There had to be a physical basis for her illness, but I had failed to find it.

Whenever I called Hillside Hospital to inquire, Imogen's doctors told me that she was quiet and had had few episodes of pain. They had found no more answers than I.

Months later I was awakened at three o'clock one morning by the telephone. The caller said, "This is the surgical resident at New York Hospital. You Dr. Slocum?"

I admitted that I was. I wondered why the doctor was calling me; I had no patients at New York Hospital.

"We just operated on one of your psychiatric patients, an Imogen Geoffrey. I think you and your psychiatric friends should know that she obstructed at Hillside and came in as an emergency case. Her psychiatric diagnosis is cancer of the colon, with metastases."

There was undoubtedly triumph in his voice, that one who knew so much was so much brighter than one who had practiced so long. I didn't bother to argue with him. I had seen it too often, the fresh young intern showing his scorn for the aging practitioner. I knew that in time his freshness would be abraded by unanswerable questions, wrong diagnoses, and self-doubts. I merely thanked him for his trouble and hung up the phone.

ROMEO

THE SMUG, satisfied look on Peggy's face made me edgy. What had I done this time to give her occasion for a snide remark?

"I see you've been at it again. Playing Cupid. Have you taken to marrying off old women?"

Several marriages had resulted from patients meeting in my office. But I wasn't prepared for Peggy's news: "It's Mrs. Andrews and that young clown, Romeo Birnberg."

"My God, woman, you can't tell me that those two have anything in common. There must be fifty years' difference in their ages."

She spread her feline claws with satisfaction. "They do have one thing in common."

"What's that?"

"Her money, of course."

"Go away," I said.

The couple came for their blood tests. These blood tests were originally and rightfully proposed to screen potential parents and to prevent them from transmitting syphilis to their newborns. A fetus in the womb could contract syphilis from its infected mother. Usually the husband had infected the wife. Newly married girls were then supposed to be more or less chaste. A premarital blood test was of limited value in a woman long past childbearing age. But the law was the law.

I told Peggy to send the couple in separately. Even though some would say it was none of my business, I hoped I could talk the young man out of this marriage. I always worked on the principle that to prevent unhappiness or to dispel it was as much a family doctor's business as prescribing pills.

Romeo came in first. His hair was slicked down like Rudolph Valentino's. He wore a tight-fitting, electric-blue suit with wide lapels. His patent-leather shoes were so pointed I wondered where he kept his toes.

He worked as an entertainer in a song, dance, and comedy act at a third-grade Hungarian café on the Lower East Side. I knew nothing of his talent, but I believed that stardom was beyond his reach.

Romeo had first come to have me treat his gonorrhea. While he was under care he came to my office accompanied by a doll: a tall, beautiful show girl who towered above him and floated in a trance of love. I treated her for gonorrhea too. She looked vacuous. She was probably even more stupid than she looked.

"Why did you give the poor girl the clap when you knew we hadn't finished treatment?" I had asked him.

"I don't know if I gave it to her! She probably gave it to me."

I pursued the subject no further.

As I was preparing to draw Romeo's blood for the premarital examination my curiosity overcame me.

"I suppose you know what you're letting yourself in for. This woman is old enough to be your grandmother. What happened to your doll?"

He was good-natured about it. "Look, Doc, I've got a steady job, but I don't earn that much. I couldn't afford the doll. I'm twenty-two years old, but I support my whole family.

"My father needs an operation. My elder sister's a fool: she married a drunk to reform him. He took off and left her pregnant and without a dime. She's going to have an abortion. My mother can't work, and I'd like to help my kid sister through high school. Then she can work, too. But meantime there's not a penny in the house. She *was* gorgeous, wasn't she?" he asked wistfully.

"Gorgeous." I could only agree.

"Now the Andrews woman: I didn't pick her up. She picked me up, right here in your office. She thinks she's a kitten. I told her my problems and she offered to help, but only if I marry her first. I said, 'Okay, let's do it.' And that's what we're going to do."

Mrs. Andrews was all foolish and flirtatious. Her face was made up like a mask. I was afraid to say anything that would cause her to laugh, for fear it would crack apart. She confided that her affianced's name was "not Romeo, you know. That's his stage name. His real name is Julius." She blushed beneath her cosmetic mask. I could tell from her glowing earlobes. She touched my arm, she rubbed my sleeve, she edged against me. She was hungry for somebody, anybody. And now here was fruition.

Her background was interesting. She had been raised abroad. Her father was a French diplomat, but her mother was American. She'd been born in this country at her mother's request. The family had stayed here for only a few months after she'd been born. All her childhood there had been a free flow of money. There was even more money when she married a successful man. He had died several years before I knew her.

Despite the glamour of her background and despite her worldly experience, Mrs. Andrews was no sophisticate. She was what is called "a fool for love." But she was smart enough to know what she wanted when she saw it. And she was smart enough to negotiate to get it.

And so Romeo and Mrs. Andrews were married. The honeymoon was delayed while the new Mrs. Birnberg performed her part of the bargain. She paid for the father's operation and the sister's unlawful abortion. She set up an account for the mother so that she would not be in need. I thought the bride was a good sport for doing what she'd promised without any guarantee for her own future.

Julius—Romeo—came to see me a few weeks later. He was pale and haggard. He said he felt sick all over. I found nothing wrong with him.

"My God!" he exploded. "That woman's a tigress. She's impossible. She can't get enough sexual activity. I tell you, Doc,

I'll kill myself if she doesn't kill me first. And when she has no makeup on she's awful to look at. I throw a towel over her face sometimes when I mount her."

He left in great consternation.

"Don't worry about him," said Peggy. "He'll take it as long as he can or for as long as her money lasts, which might be forever. And remember: that woman's waited years for this."

My nurse was often closer to real life than I was.

Romeo began to come to the office with regularity. He had all sorts of complaints, from loss of appetite to headache to blurring vision. Some of his complaints stemmed from general unhappiness. But some of his problems were caused by sexual overindulgence, which was forced on him. I told him not to come in so often: I couldn't alter the life he had chosen. He came in anyhow, because I seemed to be his only emotional outlet. He wanted to come, and he paid his bills.

"God!" he said in amazement. "She's blooming! She acts like a twenty-year-old. She makes me do what a kid would want me to do. But the way I look at it, she can't last forever, and when she goes I'll have a good setup."

Our relationship ended suddenly.

The last time I saw Romeo he came to my office wild-eyed. "God, Doc," he said, "I'm taking off! I'll find some way to get divorced! That bitch told me she was seventy-six years old. I just found out she's only sixty-six. She could live forever!"

MR. COOLEY

"IT'S NICE to have a real gentleman come into the office once in a while," said Peggy, as she hung up my overcoat and jacket that Monday morning and helped me into my long, white laboratory coat.

"Well, that's lovely of you to say. That's the pleasantest thing anyone has told me today," I said.

"Oh, I don't mean you," she pouted. "You're no gentleman. You're the boss."

"That is a comedown," I admitted, "but may I inquire as to whom you are referring? Who is your latest love?"

"Why Mr. Cooley, of course. You know you're supposed to see him early today. He's been waiting."

"You have his latest reports from the lab?"

"Yes."

"How are they?"

"Bad," she said. "Worse than expected. I hope you can help him. What do you think?"

Our own little laboratory was equipped for many routine tests, but the more complex examinations were sent out to better equipped and more experienced laboratories. Peggy and I had discussed setting up a more complete laboratory and hiring a trained technician, but we hadn't gotten around to it yet.

I studied the reports that Peggy handed me. I had tapped Mr. Cooley's spine at his most recent visit and had withdrawn fluid, which I'd sent for study. This procedure is done mainly at hospitals now. Tapping the spine in the office was frowned upon by some, although I never saw any harm come from it.

Mr. Cooley's test results were not good. They indicated that he was suffering from syphilis of the brain and nervous system. I had expected these findings, although I'd hoped I would be wrong. I already knew that the spirochete of syphilis had badly damaged the large valve that governed the action of his aorta, the mammoth artery that passes blood from the heart to most of the rest of the body. I knew also that he had an aneurysm of the aorta itself. The organism causing his disease had eaten into and thinned out the wall of the aorta, so that vessel had stretched as the heart pounded blood into it. When I palpated Mr. Cooley's chest I could distinctly feel the pulsations of his aorta just above the heart, where the vessel had enlarged to the size of an orange. It was more remarkable that he was alive than that he was soon to die.

Peggy showed Mr. Cooley into the examining room. He was a tall, friendly, and loquacious man, thin and very active, with a good word to say for everybody. He was the office and business manager for one of the largest law firms in the United States. He would be practically irreplaceable.

This day he was particularly garrulous.

"You know, Doctor, a thought struck me last night. I was lying in bed thinking of nothing when suddenly the phrase 'three score years and ten' entered my mind. I'm not all that good at plain mathematics—I go in for the complicated kind—but I figured that if I was going to live seventy years and had already lived fifty-five of them, that left me only fifteen years to go. That means I'd better start living it up while I still have time."

Fifteen years! I wouldn't have given him a nickel for the year after next. I was sure he would be dead before the next twelve months were out. I only wished I could have done better for him.

Mr. Cooley had contracted syphilis as a boy in college. That would have been some thirty-five years before. In those days the disease was rampant. He had been subjected to the old treatment:

mercury salve rubbed into the body, and injections of bismuth and arsenic. About one-sixth of untreated cases died of the effects of syphilis. God only knows how many treated cases were killed by the treatment.

In Mr. Cooley's case the treatment was the best that could then be given, but the disease progressed, and the damage to his heart and blood vessels was obvious. That the disease was now present also in the nervous system was only an added insult. He would be dead long before he suffered symptoms from that area.

Mr. Cooley had no immediate family. His closest friend was a woman of his own age who looked much younger than her fifty-plus years. She was a consultant astrologer (there are specialists even in that field) who had originally brought him to me. At her own request she had done a study of my prospects and had decided that I was going to be king or president or something.

I hadn't informed either Mr. Cooley or his friend about his condition, since I couldn't see what good it would do. The usual Wasserman test showed that the astrologer was not afflicted with the disease. That was no surprise to me, because the longer syphilis has been present in a person the less likely he is to transmit it to others.

Peggy was attracted to Mr. Cooley, as was everyone who came into contact with him.

After he'd left she asked me, "Can't you help him at all?"

"No," I told her. "Men smarter than I have tried to help him in the past, and their treatment was not effective. From them I received a pile of human wreckage. I'll keep him coming at intervals because he may develop unpleasant symptoms and I might be able to treat his symptoms."

"If you can't help him don't you think you ought to send him to a specialist?"

"If I thought they could help him I would. But his condition is irreversible. I'm not going to expose him to a specialist who might tell him the truth and make him miserable. He thinks he's going to live fifteen more years. I think he won't live two. Why bother him?"

Sometime later Mr. Cooley came to the office bubbling over

with enthusiasm. "I decided to do something I've wanted to do for years. I always wanted a home on the south shore of Long Island where the swimming is good and the beaches are sandy. I finally found a place on Fire Island off Bay Shore. I expect to move in before summer."

I wished him good luck and told him to be sure to invite me out to see the place as soon as he was organized. He said his astrologer friend was moving in with him. It would be a regular home.

I hoped he would have the whole summer to enjoy himself. I didn't expect him to last long, but I wanted to be wrong. We said a cordial goodbye.

The rest is unbelievable.

At the entrance to the Hearst Building, at the eastern end of my block, a stairway led down to the Eighth Avenue subway. Below the street was a broad walkway, wide as Eighth Avenue itself, leading to the subway gates.

One day, after a visit to my office, Mr. Cooley walked toward those gates. Another patient of mine, Johnny Gunther, was backing down a different stairway to the subway. He had a bag of money in one hand and a pistol in the other. He was a young fellow about twenty-six years old, who had a number of minor criminal offenses on his record. He was wearing a red and gray lumber jacket and a cap with its brim pulled down over his face.

Police officers came dashing down the Hearst Building stairs. When Johnny saw them he turned with his gun extended and fired. He missed the officers. The bullet ricocheted off the concrete wall and struck a civilian, who fell dead. It was Mr. Cooley.

STREET BALL

THE GAME HAS NO NAME, but millions of Americans play it. It is baseball played in the street, with manhole covers as pitcher's mound, home plate, and second base, and any two distinguishing objects on opposite sidewalks as first and third bases.

The ball is soft, and the bat can be any piece of elongated wood. The game is enlivened by hazards, usually automobiles, both parked and in motion. Particular praise goes to the fielder who can catch a fly ball as it bounces off the windshield of a moving car. His teammates applaud him. His opponents curse their luck. Never mind what the driver says.

It was an especially good game that I watched on One-hundred-seventh Street just east of Central Park on a hot and humid summer afternoon. I was supposed to be making a call in the middle of the block, on the south side of the street. The north side was a fenced and empty lot, probably awaiting a developer who could find a way to make a building pay. The area was filling with Puerto Ricans; other ethnic groups were moving out. It was questionable that any structure could be put there with the expectation of profit.

The reason the game was so interesting was that the players were all young men in their teens and twenties, and they had the agility of trained athletes. Most were dressed in jeans and T-shirts. They must just have come from work. They were very noisy, shouting and yelling encouragement at every good play and razzing the victim of every bad one.

I was in no hurry to make my call. It wasn't urgent, and to make it I had to enter a hot, smelly building, climb three flights of urine-stained, malodorous stairs, and visit an apartment filled with innumerable dirty children and a constant flow of Spanish-speaking adults. To say nothing of two roosters.

The roosters were the household pets. They were always under-foot, or perched on furniture or on people, including visitors like myself. I could have done without them. They were not house-broken.

The greatest challenge was the cockroaches. These not only walked in lines, seeking out food particles, but, if the pickings were good, sometimes marched two or three abreast. Where there are no food particles, cockroaches do not breed. But when the food is ample, they breed, well . . . like cockroaches.

An interesting thing about this variety of livestock: like flies, cockroaches can walk upside down. It was common to find them on the ceiling, heading for who knows what. Every now and then one would lose its footing and fall with a plop to the floor or a table or anything else immediately beneath. The cockroach would right itself, not at all disconcerted, but there would not be a pleasant welcome at the receiving end.

There were times when Peggy wouldn't let me come into the office until I'd given my overcoat or jacket to her assistant to take to the rear yard for an old-fashioned beating out. She knew where I'd made my calls, and she would yell, "Don't you come into my nice clean office till we've beat the hell out of them bugs."

The call I was making now was in one of Peggy's least-favorite houses, and I watched the young men playing ball and tried to postpone the inevitable.

The landlord hadn't bothered to replace the stolen or broken light bulbs. I lugged my bag and myself up three flights of dark stairs and pounded on the door of the apartment where Mrs. Ordonez was queen.

Mrs. Ordonez had diabetes. I'd managed to control it. Her orders were to take thirty units of crystalline insulin daily. This medication was injected by her husband, a tall, lanky man with fierce but handsomely trimmed mustachios. He was not Puerto Rican, as his wife was. He was a Spaniard from north of Madrid, and proud of it. Because of his origin and Castilian speech, he considered Puerto Ricans provincial. He was an unofficial leader and general boss of his neighborhood.

I had instructed Mr. Ordonez to inject insulin into a different part of his wife's limbs each day, using arms and legs for alternate sites. He had been a good nurse, and we had had no troubles until now. Today I had been informed that Mrs. Ordonez had developed a sore on the bottom of her foot. Fearing a serious complication, I decided to call on her at home. The door was opened only after someone inside determined who I was.

In the apartment I found the usual chaos: adults, children, roosters, and roaches. There was much shouting, pushing, and pulling before we could clear the room in which Mrs. Ordonez was lying. Finally the room emptied, except for a man who was using a phone mounted on the wall, a man who spoke rapidly in Americanismos Spanish. I knew some Spanish but could hardly understand a word he was saying. Yelling and gesticulating, Mr. Ordonez propelled him out.

Mrs. Ordonez had an ulcer on the lower surface of her left foot, just posterior to the toes. It exposed the muscle and was about a half inch in diameter. She had struck her foot three days before, and the wound had gotten worse instead of better. When she'd phoned my office I had asked her to have a specimen of urine for me. Testing this at the bedside I found she was spilling sugar.

Diabetes is a result of insult to the pancreas. A diminished supply of blood prevents the pancreas from proper functioning, and halts its ordinary production and distribution of insulin. There are other factors that prevent insulin from being manufactured, absorbed, and used as it should be, but to me it always seemed that arteriosclerosis—hardening of the arteries—might be a basic cause of adult diabetes.

Although this lesion was of traumatic origin, an ulcer on the lower extremities of a diabetic is often evidence that the general blood supply to all parts of the body is diminished. The difficulty is that healing depends on a rich supply of blood, and so healing is slow and sometimes absent.

I cleaned the wound, poured some sulfa powder into it, and dressed it. I advised Mrs. Ordonez to increase her insulin to forty units daily and to stay in bed, with her leg lifted on pillows. I wrote out two prescriptions. One was for penicillin tablets, to be taken every four hours "when awake." (I deplore the practice of disturbing patients' rest to medicate them. Rest aids healing.) The other prescription was for sulfa powder. I explained to Mr. and Mrs. Ordonez how to wash and dress the wound. I would be back in two days, I told them. Privately, I made plans to hospitalize Mrs. Ordonez should healing not progress. I began to reassemble my bag, keeping an eye out for roaches.

Suddenly there was a crash of glass and a splintering of wood. Amid screams and shouts I heard voices ordering everyone to face the wall and keep his hands above his head. I ran to the door to look into the hall. Mr. Ordonez almost knocked me down as he rushed to the wall telephone. He bawled to Mrs. Ordonez that he was calling his poly and his lawyer. A "poly," I knew, was a local political leader.

Three young men burst into the room. Others were obviously in the apartment. Children were screaming and some of the adults were expostulating, but they all stood against the walls while they were being frisked. I was told to wait where I was while the apartment was searched. Drawers were emptied, furniture was overturned, mattresses were thrown to the floor.

It dawned upon me. These were the young men who'd been playing street ball! They'd been staking out the apartment. Now, on their T-shirts, they wore the badges of the New York Police Department.

With broad gestures, Mr. Ordonez continued explaining something to someone at the other end of the phone. A man older than the other policemen, but also in T-shirt and jeans, came over to me with a smile and offered his hand. "Sorry we had to break in like this, Doctor, but we're after narcotics. Before you leave, let me ask you something. Does this woman need hypodermic syringes?"

"Yes, she does," I said. "She has diabetes and takes injections of insulin."

"One more question," he said with a grin. "Does she need a hundred dozen?"

I couldn't help laughing. "That is a lot, isn't it?"

I waved him goodbye and left.

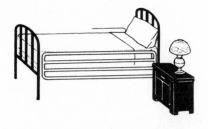

SURPRISES

A GROUP OF PHYSICIANS stood around the autopsy table in the Flower Fifth Avenue Hospital morgue. It was one of our regular pathological conferences known as Grand Rounds. This autopsy would be the end of the morning's study.

Grand Rounds are attended by a hospital's staff physicians, by its interns and medical students, and by practicing physicians connected with the institution. The session is conducted by the head of the relevant service.

Every good hospital has its Grand Rounds. Most doctors try to fit Grand Rounds into their schedules. Throughout the years of my practice I attended as many as I could. One never tires of learning. At these meetings physicians discuss their patients' illnesses. Most patients readily consent to be talked about. Finding themselves the focus of the concentrated attention of a whole group of physicians is a high point of many patients' lives.

When patients died, their doctors made an effort to obtain permission from their relatives to perform an autopsy. This was the practice in all the best hospitals. In fact, hospitals were once rated for their teaching ability by, among other things, the percent of autopsies obtained. It is at the autopsy table that the doctor learns his medicine. There he sees evidence, truly in the flesh, for the diagnosis he made or should have made. There he is able to correlate symptoms and their causes. Fewer and fewer autopsies are being performed. Perhaps pathologists no longer have the time to do them. The effect on medical education is noticeable and regrettable.

The pathologist's shirtsleeves were rolled up. He wore a thick leather apron and heavy rubber gloves. The sheet-covered corpse lay before him on the large slate table.

"Gentlemen," he said, "you've all heard the resident read the medical history of this poor man. You have heard the report of laboratory findings. You have seen the X-rays. Before we go further I ask you to give your diagnoses in this case."

Each of us gave his opinion. All settled on one diagnosis. All, that is, except an elderly doctor who had traveled in from the extreme eastern tip of Long Island. His diagnosis evoked skeptical smiles. It was outlandish. The pathologist shot him a quizzical look and proceeded with his work.

The findings astonished us all. The old doctor was exactly right! We congratulated him, but we insisted on knowing how he'd arrived at his conclusion.

"Gentlemen," he said, smiling modestly, "I've been making that diagnosis for many years. This is the first time I've been right."

The practice of medicine is full of surprises.

❖   ❖   ❖

I had admitted a merchant seaman with recurrent chills, fever, and weakness into the Medical Arts Center Hospital at Fifty-seventh Street and Sixth Avenue. I was not the first doctor he'd seen for this condition. I hoped to be the last. I was always mindful of the old saw that the last doctor is the lucky doctor.

Seamen with certain chronic diseases could sometimes be treated as outpatients. Since they traveled to all parts of the world and back again, there had to be a method of coordinating their treatment. This was made possible by a small book that they could present to whatever doctor they visited, anywhere.

Each doctor entered into the book his name and address, the

date and result of the examination, his diagnosis, and the prescribed treatment. Since there was no more critical audience than a worldwide group of doctors, one had to know his business. It did complicate matters a bit that the little book had entries in several languages. Most of the entries were in English, French, and German, and the prescriptions were all in that odd international language I think of as Medical Latin. Fortunately, New York is a polyglot city. Sometimes I could find a translator in my own waiting room!

My patient had served a long time on ships that called at ports on the west coast of Africa. All the doctors who had seen him in those exotic towns agreed that he had malaria. I agreed with them, but none of us had been able to find the *plasmodium*, the causative organism, in his blood.

A much older physician once told me that if malaria was suspected but was not demonstrated, an injection of adrenaline might squeeze out blood that was sequestered in the spleen; blood that might harbor the organism and make the diagnosis definitive. I gave the sailor an injection of adrenaline and asked to be called when his temperature spiked. The high temperature would be a sign that the organisms had broken out of the blood cells and had entered the bloodstream. Then I would have my chance to examine the blood under the microscope for the *plasmodium*.

The idea worked. On a blustery midnight I was called from my bed. The seaman's temperature was 103.5° F. I set out at once for the hospital. In the laboratory I found that the technician on night duty had prepared the slides and stained them for me. Sure enough, the organisms were there. No doubt about the diagnosis: malaria.

I ordered the medication then in use, quinine sulfate, five grains every four hours for four doses and then twice a day for ten days after the patient had been discharged. I instructed the nurse to reduce the sailor's fever with five grains of aspirin every four hours when needed, and to fan and sponge him until his fever had subsided.

We cannot cure malaria, but the symptoms in most cases can be suppressed. Patients will have relapses from time to time over a span of four to six years. Finally, the relapses stop. In a way, malaria "cures" itself.

A bout of malaria confers immunity on the patient, but unfortunately that immunity is very short-lived. The sailor had already had the disease several times. I advised him that when he recovered it would be best to avoid the west coast of Africa. He seemed to be vulnerable to the mosquitoes from that area. A peculiarity of the disease is that one might be sensitive to an infected mosquito in one part of the world yet be immune in another malarial zone.

I was surprised when the adrenaline did its work of coaxing the organism into view, and proud of the old doctor's sound advice. I only wished he could have been there himself to see the *plasmodium* under the microscope.

❀ ❀ ❀

I had a surprise of another sort when I was working at Medical Arts Center Hospital late on another evening. My answering service called me to tell me that a man in an apartment only two doors from the hospital had struck his head and was bleeding. The man lived in a converted mansion on West Fifty-seventh Street. I was told that I could reach the injured man's top-floor apartment by elevator. In theory that was true, but the elevator was out of commission. I labored up three flights of marble stairs. New York houses usually had sixteen steps to a story. This one had twenty. My bag was heavy. I was tired.

There was blood on the top step and blood on the door handle. The door was open. I was greeted by a distraught woman with terror in her eyes and a bloodstained towel in her hand.

"My husband was going out to get the early morning paper at the newsstand. He slipped and struck his head on the top step. Thank God you came quickly." Her husband was lying on a couch in a room with large skylights. It was both living room and studio. He was dazed but conscious, and still wore his bloody overcoat.

The wound was a six-inch laceration of the scalp that cut deep down to the covering of the cranium. It bled profusely. Using tight pressure, I stemmed the flow of blood with a towel. I didn't

[248]

want to release the pressure, so I told the wife to go to the hospital two doors away and to ask for heavy suture material and a suture set. I hadn't come prepared for such a catastrophe. The set would contain everything I needed: needles, hemostats, sterile pads, sulfa powder, and scissors. I continued to apply pressure for the time it took her to fetch the kit. Then I washed the wound with soap and water and was gratified to see that the bleeding had stopped.

The wound was so long that it took half an hour or more to apply the sutures. A local anesthetic would have been useless. I gave the patient a quarter grain of morphine to combat shock and pain.

I closed the wound to my satisfaction, but I was concerned that the man might have sustained a concussion or worse. I recommended hospitalization. "I'm not sure that you don't have a fractured skull, and you may need a transfusion." The patient adamantly refused to be hospitalized. Why had he fallen? Had he had vertigo? No. He had slipped on the marble steps, he said. "That damned elevator is always out of service."

I gave his wife my home telephone number. "I'm afraid you'll have to stay awake and watch him while he sleeps. If his breathing is abnormal or if he vomits or has any sort of shuddering or convulsion, call me right away. If that happens he must be hospitalized."

I was at home and in bed not more than an hour when she called. Her husband had vomited and was unconscious. I immediately sent an ambulance for him and set out myself to meet the patient at Flower Fifth Avenue Hospital, a hospital that had a fine Radiology Department. I ordered X-rays of the skull and, to consult with me, I called in Dr. Tarlov, an excellent diagnostician and neurosurgeon.

It was nearly dawn by this time. Dr. Tarlov, the radiologist, and I examined the X-rays. The radiologist pointed to an obvious shadow in the left posterior part of the brain. "The patient must have ruptured a vessel there. It's probably bleeding and increasing pressure within the skull. With the history of trauma and the size of the involvement, I'd go in immediately."

Of course we agreed on that. We scrubbed for surgery and

within an hour the neurosurgeon was making a burr hole in the skull where the lesion seemed apparent.

We X-rayed the patient on the table to determine that the instrument had reached the lesion. Then Dr. Tarlov withdrew the burr. Much to our surprise, no blood followed. Had there been an internal hemorrhage, there should have been a flow of blood. Something was very wrong.

For a few moments Dr. Tarlov was silent. Then he said, "I'm afraid we have to think about this patient in an entirely different way."

"I'll prepare him," I said. I sawed through the skull until I was able to lift out the plate of bone. Dr. Tarlov took over.

He went through the meninges—the delicate covering of the brain—and exposed the brain itself. "There's the problem," he said. There indeed was the problem: a tumor the size of a lemon, irregular in shape. It was growing out of the brain tissue and was inextricably a part of it. There was no use going further. The tumor was inoperable.

I took care of this unfortunate man until he died. On quiet days these many years later, I think of him. I still wonder whether his fall on the stairs was caused by the ravages of the tumor or whether the fall was an accident, a pure coincidence, that led to the diagnosis of his fatal illness.

MARTINO

CHIN-HIGH on corner lampposts every few blocks throughout the city of New York were green metal boxes. These held telephones by which policemen on the beat communicated with their precinct station houses. Above these boxes were green lights that could be switched on by the desk sergeants to signal officers to call in.

The cops called in at regular intervals to report that all was well or that it wasn't. The call was usually routine. The policeman unlocked the box, picked up the phone, and then waited until the desk sergeant or his assistant answered the ring.

I had just reached the street from an early house call when the cop on the beat hailed me. He pointed to the green light above his head.

"Hey, Doc, the Sergeant called to say your nurse needs you. She called the station house and asked him to find you. There's someone bleeding at your office. I'll call in and say you're on the way."

Morning office hours had not yet started when I let myself in. Peggy thumbed me into one of the treatment rooms. Anthony Martino, about twenty-two years old, short, muscular, and swarthy, was lying on the table. He had a large gash on his head.

"What happened, Tony?"

"I was coming home from work, and when I was going into the house they dropped a flower pot on my head."

"Who are 'they?'"

"Them Porto Ricans that are filling up the building. We been living on the ground floor for five years. First one Porto Rican moved in. Then more Porto Ricans came. Now they want our apartment, and when we said we wouldn't move they started to show us we had to.

"They know what time I come home from work, so this morning when my shift ended they were waiting on the roof. They dropped the flower pot. It was empty, thank God, but the edge got me. My mother told me to come over here, fast."

Peggy had put pads over the wound and had compressed them with a tight bandage. It was a good pressure bandage and it had stopped the bleeding. Then she'd shaved the whole area and cleaned the wound with soap and water and an iodine preparation. She'd sprinkled sulfa powder into the wound to prevent infection. Much of my work had been done for me.

The wound was four inches long, and deep. Ten cc. of novocaine in a syringe was neatly set out on a tray, along with needles and a needle holder and number oo thread, a couple of hemostats, and a scissors.

"Tony, there's no use trying to anesthetize such a large area by injection. I'm going to spray it with novocaine instead. That may make this procedure painless, although I can't promise. I'll have to put in about twelve sutures. Is that all right with you?"

"You're the Doc."

As I worked on Tony's wound I thought of how New York hadn't always welcomed its immigrants with open arms. "Irish need not apply," said the old advertisements. "No theatricals, no dogs, no Jews," read the signs once propped in boarding house windows. Nor had New York's immigrants always peaceably settled in. Wave after wave of people had displaced one another, vying for work and living space.

The end of the Second World War brought a horde of Puerto Ricans to New York. They were American citizens who could come and go at will. They crowded into neighborhoods on the

West Side, in the lower Bronx, and on the upper East Side of Manhattan, which became known as Spanish Harlem.

Congressman Vito Marcantonio met plane-loads of Puerto Ricans at the airport. The story was that Marcantonio took the travelers by bus first to register for home relief and then to register to vote. It was said to be his method of assuring reelection.

The new arrivals by their sheer numbers compressed the ethnic groups who had preceded them, and competed in the quest for a decent way of life.

Tony took the operation with only an occasional flinch and without comment. The wound was jagged but closed smoothly. Before applying the bandage I gave him a mirror so that he could see what I'd done. He looked at his tonsured head: "Geest, I look like a Benedictine monk."

Before he left Tony said, "Doc, the next time something's dropped on me it may be heavier than an empty flower pot. But I'm going to fool the bastards."

"What are you going to do?" I asked.

"I'm going to move."

OFFICE HELP

THROUGHOUT MY CAREER I asked only to be allowed to practice medicine. I believed—I do believe—that nothing should come between the physician and his patient. I suppose I thought about medicine the way President Garfield thought about education, that education was Mark Hopkins at one end of a bench and a student at the other. All the rest—the medical associations and their hierarchies, the office administration and the paperwork— did not interest me and did not matter.

I was spoiled, I know. Peggy spoiled me. We had a remarkable working relationship. Our teamwork was as silent and efficient as that of a surgeon and an operating room nurse. Whatever object I needed for examination or treatment appeared magically in my hand. But it was more than efficiency that made Peggy a great nurse. She had sympathy for people in their trouble. Like my wife, she was endowed with common sense. And she was fun.

My wife spoiled me, too. Whatever her schedule, Belle was always ready when we called on her. She made it possible for Peggy to take time off. When there were too many letters to type or too many folders to file or simply too many bottles to wash, she was there: typing, filing, sterilizing. Like Peggy, my wife was a quiet worker—deft, neat, and fast. She had a calm way about her, and her presence in the office was serene and soothing.

Over the years, under Peggy's direction, a procession of girls worked for us. Many were registered nurses; all had what seemed to be good references. These young women would work for a doctor or a hospital, tire of the routine, and want a change. Some left jobs to marry and then discovered they didn't want to be housewives. Even in Depression years they usually found employment. Skilled help was always in demand.

Whenever we were faced with hiring a new Number Two Nurse, I left the interviewing to Peggy. She ran the office. She in turn always tried to arrange the interview at my wife's convenience. "Mrs. Slocum can tell more about a person's character in ten minutes than I could ever tell," she said.

I intervened once in the hiring process. Once, but never again.

"Look, Peggy," I said that time, "let's try to get some paperwork off your shoulders. Let's call a secretarial school and see if we can't get help that's clerical instead of medical."

Peggy thought about that proposition. Then she said, "It doesn't sound right, but if you say so we can try."

The school we called said they had a new graduate who exactly fit our bill, assuming of course that we wouldn't mind that the girl was black.

That antagonized me. "You send her over," I ordered. "I want a worker, not a color. If she can do the work, the job is hers."

The girl appeared, good-looking, neatly dressed, and brimming over with gratitude and happiness. Her name was Myra.

We didn't question Myra's skills: she had just graduated from the commercial school "with honors." (This was an oversight that my wife later mentioned casually a number of times—she wasn't at that interview.) Myra told us she could type rapidly, keep books, and send bills. She had been taught medical nomenclature. That sounded good enough. She would be a lively person to have around.

"I never dreamed when I quit high school that I'd take this training and walk into such a fine job," she said. She was one of the happiest twenty-year-olds I had the pleasure of knowing. We began a new week with our new employee. Among other things, we put her in charge of the files.

Wednesday evening, after Myra had gone, Peggy came to me in a state of utter frustration. "I was looking for Mrs. Samuel's chart, to put in her test results. I couldn't find it. I checked the appointment book, to look through Monday's people. I thought we might have slipped Samuel's whole chart into someone else's folder. Not one of them's in the right place." She sighed.

"I found them all, finally: at the front of the upper left drawer. Maybe Myra's filing chronologically, not alphabetically! But where are the Tuesday files, and where are today's?"

Peggy and I went to work. We were in a mess. It would take hours to search the files.

"How were the letters you dictated Monday?"

It suddenly occurred to me: "I haven't seen hide nor hair of them since."

We looked at one another. "You did see her take them down?"

"In those pigeon tracks: shorthand. She took them down, all right. They just never came back."

I thought a good deal about Myra that night. I was angrier with the school than with the girl. I knew Myra never meant to deceive. The school, I felt, had deceived her (and how many others?), collecting its fees and then failing to teach what it promised.

When Myra appeared the next morning I spoke to her as gently as I could. "Would you put these in order?" I asked, handing her Monday's folders: Samuel, Clark, Dubin, Heller, White . . .

She shot me a terrified glance and shuffled the folders at random.

"Child," I said, "I have to let you go. I want you to find a school where they'll teach you to read and write. Give me your father's phone number."

The girl left, sobbing. Peggy and I were as disturbed as she.

Myra's father was the minister of a church in Brooklyn. I called him, told him what a lovely daughter he had, and explained why I had to let her go. Suddenly, without intending to, I burst out: "That poor child barely knows the alphabet!"

There was silence on the phone. I was aghast at what I'd said. Then I heard the minister's sorrowful voice: "Doctor, I'm grateful to you for calling. I know exactly what you mean," and he hung up the phone.

*　　　*　　　*

All my problems with office help paled compared with the problems of the psychoanalyst whose wife worked in his office. She handled both the practice and the man. She may have been a sweet girl when he married her, but she'd turned into a dreadnought of a woman.

The doctor himself was tall and finely built, a mustachioed man with a low, soft voice. He had a gentle smile and a gift for attracting the ladies. At social gatherings he was surrounded by females anxious to tell him their troubles. Intimate disclosures, he would caution, should be made only in his office. I think he was embarrassed to be thus mobbed at the homes of friends. His wife never minded. She was beyond embarrassment.

There was a nurse in his office, too, who kept the appointment book. What else she did, except to try to avoid his wife, Lord only knows. She was getting on in years, and we were all sorry for her. She was too old to take another job.

One night when we were socializing, the phone rang. The call was for the psychoanalyst. His wife rose before he could. "I'll take it," she announced. And she did. I enjoyed watching my wife's eyebrows rise.

"Such an interesting patient," she confided to the company at large when she returned. "A man in his forties. His family wants him married. They found a nice girl for him, near his own age. Everyone came to the wedding but the groom."

We all waited for the analyst to stop his wife from violating this confidence, but he said nothing. It was an intriguing story. "The bride-to-be insisted he have psychiatric care. My husband treated him. Another ceremony was arranged. The groom didn't show up for that one. He agreed to come to our office again. He just called about his next appointment." Very earnestly she said, "We must find out what this man wants."

[257]

One of the doctors had taken as much as he could take. "By God, woman," he roared, "don't you know what he wants? He wants out!"

It didn't faze her.

It happened that a woman friend had asked Belle to make an appointment for her with the psychoanalyst and to come with her to their first meeting. She was a very nervous woman. My wife duly called his nurse, and the appointment was made. Now the analyst's wife turned to Belle and said, "I hear you're coming to our office."

My wife gave her a cold stare. "I made an appointment with his nurse to see your husband," she said icily. "You have no business knowing that. And if you do know, you have no business saying so. The appointment is canceled as of this minute. As for you," she continued in the same frigid voice, "you can jump in the lake. I'd love some more coffee," she told our hostess sweetly.

That fazed the psychoanalyst's wife. The hostess poured. The assembled guests shifted in their seats. One or two coughed discreetly. A hand or two was raised to hide a smile. There was applause, but it was silent.

✿   ✿   ✿

Peggy told me she was tired of paperwork. The number of patients increased arithmetically, she said, but the paperwork increased geometrically. At the time there was no Number Two nurse to help out. "I want to go back to assisting you and let a second girl take care of the forms," Peggy told me. A young woman wanted the job, a trainee from another doctor's office. She suited Peggy, and Peggy wanted me to see her. "I don't know if Mrs. Slocum will approve," she said. "She's beautiful."

I saw her and she was indeed beautiful. She had good shoulders and the build of a Viking, long golden-brown hair, and the skin of a ripening peach. But it was her eyes that caught your attention. For some reason nature has endowed women with larger eye sockets than men's. This girl's eyes were a rich, warm brown, large enough to nail any young man to the wall.

Peggy said, "I interviewed her. She can type, she can take dictation. She can read and write. She has lots of good ideas about the files, and she can do ordinary laboratory work. I think we ought to give her a try."

Belle dropped in to interview the girl. "She seems all right," she told Peggy. "But there's something—something I just can't put my finger on. Hire her. But keep an eye on her."

"Take her," I said, "but keep her away from me."

Marjorie was a real find. She arrived at the office in the mornings before Peggy got there, straightened up the files of the previous day, ordered the cleaning woman about until that poor soul really began to work, and generally made herself indispensable. After office hours she checked over her work and never left until everything was in order. She was as neat and hardworking as a person could be.

Once I came to the office early and found Marjorie wearing coveralls and washing the windows, both inside and out. She wasn't in the least abashed to be found doing such work. "I didn't know you did windows," I said. "I do everything," she answered.

One day, after hours, Peggy came in and sat on my desk. "Let's chat," she said. "What do you think of Marjorie?"

"What can I think of her? If she satisfies you she certainly satisfies me."

"That isn't what I mean. Why do you think she hangs around here after hours?"

"I think I fascinate her."

"Don't kid yourself," Peggy said. "I think this girl has real problems. Personal, I mean. *She* fascinates *me*."

"What gives you that idea?"

"Well, she does love to work, but I think she hangs around because she has no dates and nothing else to do."

"And why do you think that? A girl with her looks can date almost any man she wants."

"That's the trouble." Peggy reflectively scratched her nose. "Something must have happened to make her miserable."

"I thought she was pleased with everything."

"A lot you know," said Peggy. "I found her wiping away tears.

[259]

I think she works hard to forget something." Peggy seemed determined to envision Marjorie as a tragic heroine.

Some days later Peggy came into my sanctum again. "I told you so."

"You told me what?"

"I told you there was something wrong with Marjorie. She finally confided in me. She was married once."

"I'm not surprised. So what?"

"She comes from Wisconsin. Her husband was a stunt pilot at county fairs. He was killed a few months after they were married. That was three years ago. Now she's in love with a naval officer, and he just left for eighteen months' sea duty. I knew there was a story to account for her being here at all hours."

"Well, I'm pleased," I said. "You solved that mystery to your satisfaction. I know you'll help her all you can."

"That's the trouble with men. No feelings."

Peggy couldn't get the girl off her mind. One day Marjorie didn't come in. Peggy told me she had called her.

"Nothing serious, I hope."

"It may not be serious to you, but it is to Marjorie. She showed me a letter yesterday. I guess it's all right to tell you. Her naval officer wrote to her and said that he'd been thinking about it a long time but he finally decided that he wasn't in a position to get married. He said he was all broken up. He hoped she wouldn't be, but when he came home it would be better if they didn't see each other. Of course she's broken up."

Marjorie showed up the next day as bright and pert as you please. She didn't bring up the matter of her letter. Peggy, who treated her as if she were a younger sister, asked no questions.

I received a telephone call about Marjorie: did I employ her? The caller identified himself as a collector from a department store. Marjorie had been charging things to her account. He wanted to urge her to begin to pay it off.

I called Marjorie in and told her what the collector had said. She wasn't at all chagrined, but she was very angry.

"There's a girl in the apartment next to mine who asked if she could use my charge account. I didn't see any reason why not, and so I let her. Now she's using my name and buying things and not paying for them. A man delivered some shoes to my apartment. My neighbor came in to get them. I told her to stop charging things. She said she would. I'll talk to her again tonight."

The next day Peggy reported that Marjorie was very disturbed. Her neighbor had left town for a month. Nothing could be settled until the girl returned. In the meantime we received a call from a different store about an unpaid account. All they wanted to know was whether we employed Marjorie. I said yes, we did.

One day Marjorie didn't come to work. Peggy dialed the number she had used before. It was disconnected. Consternation showed on Peggy's face. I was disconcerted myself. Had Marjorie flown the coop?

"This very afternoon I'm going to see Marjorie and find out what's going on," Peggy announced.

When Peggy returned she was flustered. "We've been had," she said. "She did live at that address but she left, lock, stock, and barrel, and with furniture that didn't belong to her and a couple of months' rent owing. She told everyone a different story. Her neighbors didn't know she owed rent or that she decamped with the landlord's furniture. I found out later, from the janitor. I feel ashamed. She fooled me."

"Well," I told her, "we didn't lose anything but face, and no one has to know that but us."

That wasn't the end of Marjorie. Bills came in, directed to our office, and following the bills came people to collect them. Of course we could give them no satisfaction. Marjorie had used her job to establish credit. By now, I told the collectors, she was probably working for someone else under another name and using that name and that job to establish new credit.

"What do you call people like that?" Peggy asked me pensively.

"We call them pathological liars. They aren't necessarily bad people. They can't quit lying any more than they can quit breathing."

"Interesting," Peggy said. "She didn't fool your wife." We thought about that for a time.

Peggy mused, "I wonder if anything she said was true. I

wonder if she was ever married at all. I wonder if there was a navy man. I know I saw his letter. At least I thought it was his letter. I'm glad I didn't have any money to lend her when she asked me."

A silence descended.

Peggy's eyes opened wide: "Don't tell me!" She clapped her hand to her mouth. "I don't want to know how much you lent her! 'We didn't lose anything but face!' Now who's a pathological liar?"

Exit laughing.

MARY MAHONEY

MARY MAHONEY didn't fit into the textbooks. I had never seen anything like her sickness—if you could call her condition a sickness. For no apparent reason the young woman would separate from reality for three or four days at a time, and exist in another life. The other life was called Television.

My first contact with Mary was through her husband, Brian. "I'm calling from the candy store on the Avenue," he said, meaning Tenth Avenue. "I'd like you to come see my wife." No, he had no telephone. "We use the phone in the candy store. They take our messages." Brian gave me the phone number of the candy store and his own address. I went that afternoon.

I wasn't surprised that the Mahoneys had no telephone. In those days few people in the neighborhood had. But nearly every home had a television set. It was considered a reasonable object to own, a source of entertainment for the whole family. Most people had an arrangement with the owner of a convenient store to receive telephone messages for them. It was an effective system for keeping neighborhood communications in working order. The storekeeper got a nickel for taking each call and an extra dime if he had to relay a message. The phone company also presented him an agreed amount from the change in the phone box. After school, small boys earned pocket money by delivering messages.

Up three flights of stairs, in the Mahoneys' rooms, Mary was lying on a sofa, her head and shoulders propped on cushions. She was watching a western on television. She gave no sign that she knew Brian and I were there. Bullets were flying, Indians and cowboys were chasing one another, and, in the distance, the U.S. Cavalry was raising the dust. Mary continued to watch, her attention riveted.

The television set was the crowning glory of the room. Half a dozen movie magazines were scattered on the floor. Brian scooped them up and set them neatly on a table. "There's nothing Mary doesn't know about the stars," he told me.

"She's been like this before, you said?"

"Sure. It started a couple years ago. It happens every few months."

"How long has it been this time?"

"Three, four days, maybe."

"Has she been drinking or taking any drugs?"

"Ask the neighbors, Doc. She never touches a thing."

I knew he spoke the truth. There was no odor in the room save a mustiness that could easily have been dispelled by opening the windows. But Brian was too smart to open any windows with Mary in this condition.

Mary had paid no attention whatever to our conversation. She went on watching television. The Indians had surrounded the cowboys, and the room was full of shouts and gunfire.

"I'll look her over." I pulled up a chair and started a routine examination. Mary made no move except to shift her head so that I didn't block the screen.

"What is her age?"

"Twenty-nine."

"How many children?"

"Three. They come home from school and stay with the neighbors. When I'm home I help them with their homework. Her sister and Mrs. Malvani next door make sure they're fed. The children can take good care of themselves."

I continued my examination. Mary didn't resist but went right on watching television. To her I was simply an obstacle. Her gaze was steady and her expression was alert.

"Physically, there's nothing wrong with her. She keeps herself clean and tidy. As long as you can take care of her here I think this is the best you can do."

"We can take care of her," Brian said. "She goes to the bathroom when she has to. She eats what we put in front of her. When I'm not here I leave the door unlocked. The neighbors always look in. Everybody looks after her and the children."

"Well, medicine is useless," I told him. "She doesn't need any. She's quiet. She's not unhappy or in pain. She doesn't cry, does she?"

"No, never. She just sort of sinks into herself."

"What does she do when you turn off that machine?"

"I never do turn it off; I just turn it low. That way she falls asleep sometimes."

I was prepared to go. Not once did Mary acknowledge our presence or turn her eyes from the television screen. The cavalry arrived, and the Indians galloped off.

"What does she do when the children come in?"

"She lets them crawl all over her, but it's like she doesn't know they're there."

"I tell you, Brian, some doctors are giving shock treatment with insulin and sometimes, lately, with electricity, but she can be hurt that way. If we just wait, she'll come out of it. But I do want a tracing of her brain waves and some laboratory work. I'll take her to see a specialist, too."

"Anything you say, Doc."

"I'll drop in Saturday and see how things are going."

"That's good. No ships Saturday."

"You a longshoreman?"

"Yup, a dockwalloper. But Saturday, there's no shape-up."

I said goodbye to Brian and to Mary, who paid no attention at all.

❧   ❧   ❧

On Saturday morning I knocked and then opened the door. Mary stood there with a bandanna tied about her hair and a broom in her hand. I was amazed at the transformation. The zombie had disappeared and an alert, purposeful woman had taken her place. It was like magic, and I was delighted.

Mary shook hands with me. "Brian said that you were coming. This place sure needed a scrubbing. I did the floors and windows this morning. I've been at it since six. I sent the kids to Florence Malvani's, next door. Brian went for some groceries. He'll be back any minute. Stay for a cup of tea with us. You'll find a towel and soap at the kitchen sink. I'll wash up, too."

Brian came in laden with fruit and groceries.

Mary said, "You didn't tell me when the Doc was coming."

Brian grinned at me: his wife was well enough to complain. "I didn't know," he said.

"You will stay for a cup of tea, won't you, Doctor?"

"Mary," I said, "nothing would please me better."

Over the teacups I asked, "Do you remember anything about your spells?"

"Of course I do. I see people come and go, but they don't matter. They don't fit in into what I'm thinking."

"How do you feel when a spell is coming on?"

"I don't feel any different at all, not when I get the spells and not when I'm having them. When I come out of them it's just as if I'd never had a spell, except I feel rested and full of energy."

"Will you do things to try to stop the spells, like being examined and seeing a specialist?"

"Sure. If I have to stop them. Everybody says I have to. Other people are more disturbed by my spells than I am."

So with Mary's permission I arranged for blood and urine tests at a laboratory and sent her to a neurologist, who made an encephalographic study. The encephalogram indicated that her brain waves were within normal limits.

Then I had Mary examined by Dr. Rosenhecht, a psychiatrist. He was a wise old gentleman who had seen every sort of mental illness.

"I've had a couple of patients who had similar symptoms," he advised me. "One was a fraud and the other suffered from hysteria.

This young woman is neither a fake nor a hysteric. She has no pain and she's reasonably happy at all other times. She seems to have a trance-like syndrome that actually renews her energy. I wish we could bottle it and sell it. If I were you I wouldn't keep pushing for a diagnosis and I certainly wouldn't treat her. What would you treat her for?" He shook his head in wonder. "You won't find a case like hers in all of medical literature."

Throughout the many examinations Mary was splendid. She was willing to do what we asked of her, and she managed to meet all her appointments and still take good care of her home and family.

Later I discussed Mary's case with Dr. Evan Evans. He was the head of one of the medical services at Roosevelt Hospital, a famous institution in midtown Manhattan. He had a tremendous practice in his ground floor office at Sixtieth Street and Park Avenue. His was mainly a carriage trade.

Dr. Evans was tall and lean and wore a stiffly starched, detachable high collar and a thin bow tie. His equipment was basic: a stethoscope, a sphygmomanometer, and a percussion hammer and safety pin to test reflexes. In his consultation room he had a bookcase on which two decoys stood. They were meant to have been bookends, but the ducks had long since turned to survey the room, and the books lay flat on the shelf. Why did those ducks fascinate me?

I stressed the fact that all our findings in Mary's case had been negative. "I agree with Dr. Rosenhecht," Dr. Evans said. "There are a lot of psychiatric questions we haven't answered."

His conversation took a philosophic turn. "In the more than fifty years that I've practiced medicine, the practice has changed completely, but the patients are exactly the same." He motioned me to come to his window, which overlooked Park Avenue, and he pointed to a cab stand with a row of four taxis. "How much we still don't know! Take an all-too-common illness: when I started to practice we'd diagnose a case as having a split personality. Later we'd say that the same patient had dementia praecox. Now we say that the patient's schizophrenic. Any of those cabdrivers out there would say that the patient is cracked. We still don't know any more about that disease than they do.

"Now, about this young woman, I agree with the psychiatrist

entirely. What would you treat her for? Watch her, and only treat her if need be."

The delightful little Mrs. Mahoney did improve. Her attacks became less frequent and shorter in duration. I expected them to disappear. I believed that I had done a good job by doing nothing; by not medicating or forcing any treatment. I was quite pleased with myself in the case of Mary Mahoney. I felt as satisfied as a stretching cat.

MRS. SCAGLIONE

ONE MORNING I had an appointment with my neighbor, Mrs. Corso. She arrived with her mother, and when I called Mrs. Corso into my office, her mother, Mrs. Scaglione, came too. I was delighted to see that Mrs. Corso had completely recovered from her minor illness. After I had examined and discharged her she said, "I want you to look at Mama too."

Mama sat there completely resigned. "There's no use looking at me," she said. "I'm going to die."

I studied her quickly to see what was going on. All I could see was a placid, good-looking woman of southern Italian extraction. She had fine olive skin, an oval face, and dark eyes so lovely that in her youth they must have sent many a young man reeling. Was she obsessed with the thought that she had an incurable disease? Had she been contemplating suicide? Was she heartsick about some trouble in the family?

"What do you mean you're going to die?"

"I'm old. Old people die," she said with a gentle smile. "I guess I'll soon be in Woodlawn Cemetery in Brookalyn."

She spoke English with a lilting Neapolitan accent. I was charmed to hear her say "Brookalyn" instead of "Brooklyn." Neapolitans and Sicilians pronounced it that way.

"You'd better go inside and get ready for an examination," I said to her. "Then I'll tell you when you're going to die."

She went reluctantly, led by my Number Two Nurse.

I asked her daughter, "What's going on here? What does she complain of?"

"Nothing in particular. She always complains. She's been dying for years."

I was thorough in my examination. I found nothing unusual except a deep concavity in her right lower rib area, where I noted a large, well-healed scar of many years' standing.

"You had an abscess of the lung?"

"Yes, when I was young—in my twenties. In Bellevue they had tubes into my lung for a long time."

"How old are you now?"

"Forty-six."

"Did they say you had tuberculosis?"

"No, they said lung abscess. But that was a long time ago. My daughter here was nine years old."

"This is a clean scar. You were lucky. The abscess could have drained for months."

"That's aright."

"Have you had any trouble with it since?"

"No trouble."

I called her daughter in. "There's nothing the matter with your lovely mother except that she's a depressed person. Many people are born depressed and go through life that way. They can be rich or poor, but they always see the darker side of everything."

I turned to Mrs. Scaglione.

"Mama," I said. "Twenty-five years from now you are going to be careless and be hit by a ten-ton truck. Nothing else will ever kill you. Your health is much too good."

Two years later Mrs. Scaglione developed pneumonia. I sent her to the hospital. When I examined her there, she said, "See, I told you I am going to die."

"Mama, remember what I told you: the only thing that can kill you is a ten-ton truck." She smiled at that.

The recovery was uncomplicated. I knew there was not a great deal of money in the family, so I arranged to have everything done as reasonably as possible. I worried about my patients' finances. I was brought up with the belief that a doctor treated the whole man. I didn't want the necessary medical costs to be a burden for a long time afterward.

I saw Mrs. Scaglione and the Corso family many times after that for one complaint or another. In fact, when I was near the Corsos' and had the time, I enjoyed dropping in for a chat, a glass of wine, and a good Italian sandwich.

There came a day when mother and daughter appeared without an appointment, at the end of office hours, "only to talk." I was always glad to see them.

"You tell him, Mama," the daughter said. They were smiling and entirely pleased with themselves.

Mrs. Scaglione said, "Dr. Slocum, we want to thank you for all you've done for me and my family."

"What's the occasion?" I asked.

"Well, finally, today, I am going to die."

"What brings this up?"

"You don't remember, but you told me once that in twenty-five years I would be hit by a truck and be killed. Today is twenty-five years from that day. So my time is up."

My nurse saw them out. "Look both ways before you cross the street," Peggy said. They left, laughing.

For the first time, I noticed that the young girl I had worked with for so many years no longer had blonde hair, but hair of a lovely silver-gray. She came and sat on my desk, her legs dangling.

"Twenty-five years!" We sat for a moment in silence.

Peggy studied my face. "They say that an old friend is the truest mirror." She sighed. She wasn't one for speeches. "Oh, well." She slid off my desk and headed for her own.

"I'll just see," she said, "what's scheduled for tomorrow."